Access 2000 Essentials Course

Brian Favro

Marketing Director: David Gauny

Production Management, Design and
   Publishing Consultation: The Cowans

Copy Editing: Laura Lionello

Composition: The Cowans

Index: Bayside Indexing Service

Proofreading: Laura Lionello

Manufacturing Coordinator: The Cowans

Printer and Binder: Courier, Kendallville

ISBN 1-887281-76-2

Manufactured in the United States of America.

10 9 8 7 6 5 4 3 2 1

LABYRINTH
PUBLICATIONS®

3314 Morningside Drive, El Sobrante, California 94803

(800) 522-9746 www.labyrinth-pub.com

Contents

Access 2000 Core Level MOUS Exam Objectives Map

Standardized Coding Number	Skill Sets / Activities	Concept Page References	Exercise Page References
AC2000.1	**Planning and designing databases**		
AC2000.1.1	Determine appropriate data inputs for your database	5	Not Required
AC2000.1.2	Determine appropriate data outputs for your database	5	Not Required
AC2000.1.3	Create table structure	7, 8	9-12
AC2000.1.4	Establish table relationships	92, 93	93-95
AC2000.2	**Working with Access**		
AC2000.2.1	Use the Office Assistant	40	Not Required
AC2000.2.2	Select an object using the Objects Bar	14	14
AC2000.2.3	Print database objects (tables, forms, reports, queries)	23, 24, 46, 47	26, 46, 50
AC2000.2.4	Navigate through records in a table, query, or form	20, 43	20-22, 43, 44
AC2000.2.5	Create a database (using a Wizard or in Design View)	5	6
AC2000.3	**Building and modifying tables**		
AC2000.3.1	Create tables by using the Table Wizard	26	27-28
AC2000.3.2	Set primary keys	12	13
AC2000.3.3	Modify field properties	8	9-12
AC2000.3.4	Use multiple data types	8	9-12
AC2000.3.5	Modify tables using Design View	17	18-19
AC2000.3.6	Use the Lookup Wizard	220, 221	221-223
AC2000.3.7	Use the input mask wizard	217	218-219
AC2000.4	**Building and modifying forms**		
AC2000.4.1	Create a form with the Form Wizard	96	96-97
AC2000.4.2	Use the Control Toolbox to add controls	143, 145, 148	145-147, 149
AC2000.4.3	Modify Format Properties (font, style, font size, color) of controls	145, 194	146, 194-195
AC2000.4.4	Use form sections (headers, footers, detail)	138, 145	138, 145-147
AC2000.4.5	Use a Calculated Control on a form	187-190	190-193
AC2000.5	**Viewing and organizing information**		
AC2000.5.1	Use the Office Clipboard	22	Not Required
AC2000.5.2	Switch between object Views	17	18-19
AC2000.5.3	Enter records using a datasheet	14	15-16
AC2000.5.4	Enter records using a form	43	43-44
AC2000.5.5	Delete records from a table	19	21
AC2000.5.6	Find a record	19	21
AC2000.5.7	Sort records	220	220

(Continued on the next page)

Access 2000 Core Level MOUS Exam Objectives Map (continued)

Quick Reference Index

Visual Conventions

This book uses many visual and typographic cues to guide you through the lessons. This page provides examples and describes the function of each.

Typographic Cue	What It Indicates
A **B** **C**	These characters indicate the order in which tasks should be performed in a Hands-On exercise.
`Type this text`	Anything you should type at the keyboard is printed in this typeface.
TIP!	This is an important tip which usually contains shortcuts or reminders.
Note!	This contains information that will help you understand a concept or a feature.
Warning!	Read and consider each warning before continuing with the lesson.
Command→Command	Indicates multiple selections to be made from a menu bar. For example: **File→Save** means you should click the **File** command in the menu bar, then click the **Save** command from the drop-down menu.
From the Keyboard **From the Keyboard** `CTRL`+S to Save	These margin notes indicate shortcut keys for executing a task described in the text. For example, `CTRL`+S to save your work in an application program.

Special Section	Purpose
Quick Reference	These sections contain generic procedures you can use to accomplish a task at any time. *Note: As you work through a lesson, you should not perform instructions in Quick Reference sections unless you are told to do so in a Hands-On exercise instruction.*
Hands-On Exercise	This section contains specific instructions for the exercise you are working on. You should always work through the Hands-On exercises. These exercises will guide you step-by-step through the topics. You will be told exactly what to do, which keys to press, and other steps to try out a new skill or feature.
Concepts Review	This section contains questions that help you gauge your mastery of the concepts covered in the lesson.
Skill Builders	This section contains additional exercises that provide opportunities for review.
Assessment	This section contains a test on the material covered in the lesson.

Creating Tables and Entering Data

In this lesson, you will begin developing a database for the Pinnacle Pet Care clinic. You will set up two Access tables and enter data in them. All data in an Access database is stored in tables. You will learn how to change the structure of tables and edit records within a database. You will also learn how to widen table columns, change the margins and page orientation, and print the contents of tables. The Pinnacle Pet Care database will continue to be developed in later lessons.

In This Lesson

Case Study

Al Smith is a veterinarian and owner of the Pinnacle Pet Care clinic. Al recently contracted with Penny Johnson—a freelance programmer and Microsoft Access database developer—to develop an order entry system using Access 2000. Al wants to improve customer service by giving the office staff instant access to customer account information. Al chose Access as the database tool because of the customization capabilities of Access and its integration with other Office applications. Al hopes Access and the other Office applications will make Pinnacle Pet Care's customer service as excellent as the care provided to pets.

You can use forms to enter data into tables and to display records.

Customers

Customer ID	1
FirstName	Mark
LastName	Roth
Address	760 Maple Avenue
City	Fremont
State	CA
Zip	94538-
Phone	(510) 234-9090
Last Visit	7/7/99
Current Balance	$235.00

GoTo New Pets Form

Record: 1 of 4

In Access, all data is stored in tables.

Customer ID	FirstName	LastName	Address	City	State	Zip	Phone	Last Visit	Current Balance
1	Mark	Roth	760 Maple Avenue	Fremont	CA	94538-	(510) 234-9090	7/7/99	$235.00
2	Tony	Simpson	312 York Lane	Richmond	CA	94804-	(510) 238-2233	9/7/99	$185.00
3	Jason	Jones	2233 Crystal Street	San Mateo	CA	94403-	(415) 312-2312	7/15/99	$48.00
4	Jacob	Samuels	2300 North Pratt Str	Atlanta	GA	30309-	(404) 367-8002	10/8/99	$250.50

You can create reports using data from your tables.

FirstName	LastName	Phone	Current Balance
Mark	Roth	(510) 234-9090	$235.00
Tony	Simpson	(510) 238-2233	$185.00
Jason	Jones	(415) 312-2312	$48.00
Jacob	Samuels	(404) 367-8002	$250.50

What Is Microsoft Access?

Microsoft Access is a relational database management system that lets you store, organize, and manage information. Access is a powerful and flexible program that can handle virtually any data management task. For example, you can use Access to keep a simple contact list, or you can develop a full-featured order entry and database management system. Access gives anyone with a personal computer the ability to organize and manage data in a sophisticated manner.

Access is an integral part of the Office 2000 suite of software tools. Access plays a pivotal role in Office 2000 because it is the data storage and management tool. You can share Access data with Word, Excel, PowerPoint, and Outlook. For example, you can merge a Word form letter with an Access database to produce a mass mailing. You can also export Access data to Excel, and then use the calculating and charting capabilities of Excel to analyze the data.

Starting Access

The method you use to start Access depends upon whether you intend to create a new database or use an existing database. If you intend to create a new database, then use one of the following methods to start Access. Once the Access program has started, you can begin working in the new workbook that appears.

- Click the **Start** button and choose Microsoft Access from the Programs menu.
- Click the Microsoft Access button on the Quick Launch toolbar (located near the Taskbar).
- Click the **Start** button, choose New Office Document, choose the General tab, and double-click the Blank Database icon.

Once Access is started, you can create a new database by choosing the Blank Access database radio button and clicking OK. Access will prompt you to save the new database and give it a name

Use one of the following methods if you intend to open an existing Access database. Once the Access program has started, the desired database will open in a window.

- Navigate to the desired database using Windows Explorer or My Computer and double-click the database.
- Click the **Start** button and point to Documents. You can choose the desired database from the Documents list. The Documents list displays the most recently used Office documents.

Hands-On 1.1 Start Access

1. Start your computer, and the Windows desktop will appear.
2. Click the **Start** button, and choose **Programs.**
3. Choose Microsoft Access from the Programs menu.
   Access will start, and the Access window will appear. If this is the first time Access has been started on your computer, the Office Assistant will appear at the lower right corner of the screen. Choose Start Using Microsoft Access *from the Assistant's message box if that option is available.*

Creating a New Database

You can create a new Access database from scratch, or you can use Access's Database Wizard to help you build a database. The dialog box that appears when Access is started gives you both choices.

This option allows you to create a new database.

This option launches the Database Wizard.

You can open a recently used database with this list.

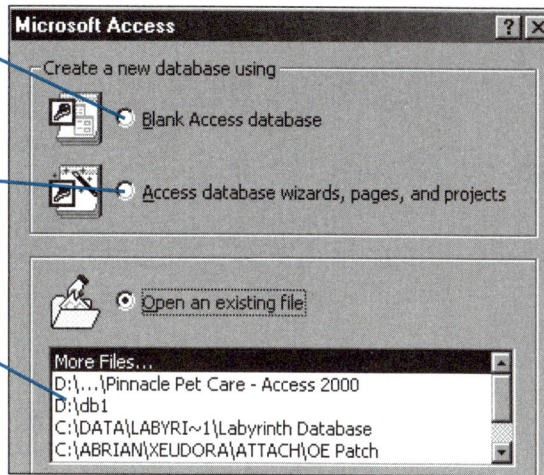

The Database Wizard

The Database Wizard lets you choose one of Access's built-in database templates as the basis for your new database. The Database Wizard takes you step-by-step through a series of screens that let you customize a built-in template to suit your needs. The resulting database is often sufficient to meet the needs of individuals and some small businesses and organizations. A database created with the wizard can also be used as a foundation from which a more sophisticated database can be developed.

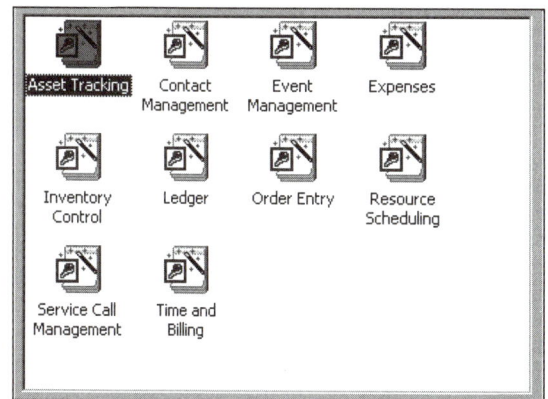

Built-in database templates.

Design View

You can also start with a blank database and add objects to your database as needed. An Access database is composed of various objects, including tables, queries, forms, and reports. Each object type can be created from scratch using a Design view for the particular type of object. Access also provides Wizards to help you set up individual objects. You will use both of these techniques as you develop the Pinnacle Pet Care database throughout this course.

Determining Data Inputs and Outputs

The first step in designing any database system is to determine the necessary data inputs and data outputs. Examples of data inputs include the name, address, telephone number, and email address of customers or contacts. Once the required data inputs are determined, the database can be designed to accommodate the inputs and store the required data. Likewise, the required data outputs must be determined before reports and other objects can be designed.

The Microsoft Access dialog box should still be displayed in the Access window from the previous exercise.

1. Click the **Blank Access database** radio button, and click **OK.**

2. Follow these steps to save the new database to your exercise diskette.
   Your instructor will provide you with a diskette or have you save your database somewhere on the hard disk of your computer system.

Ⓐ *Click here, and choose the disk drive with your exercise diskette. It is most likely the 3½ Floppy [A:].*

Ⓑ *Notice that Access proposes a name such as db1 in the **File name** box.*

Ⓒ *Type the name **Pinnacle Pet Care**, and it will replace the proposed name. (If you switched disk drives, then you may need to click in the **File name** box, delete the name in the box with the (DELETE) or (BACKSPACE) keys, and then type the new name.*

Ⓓ *Click the **Create** button.*

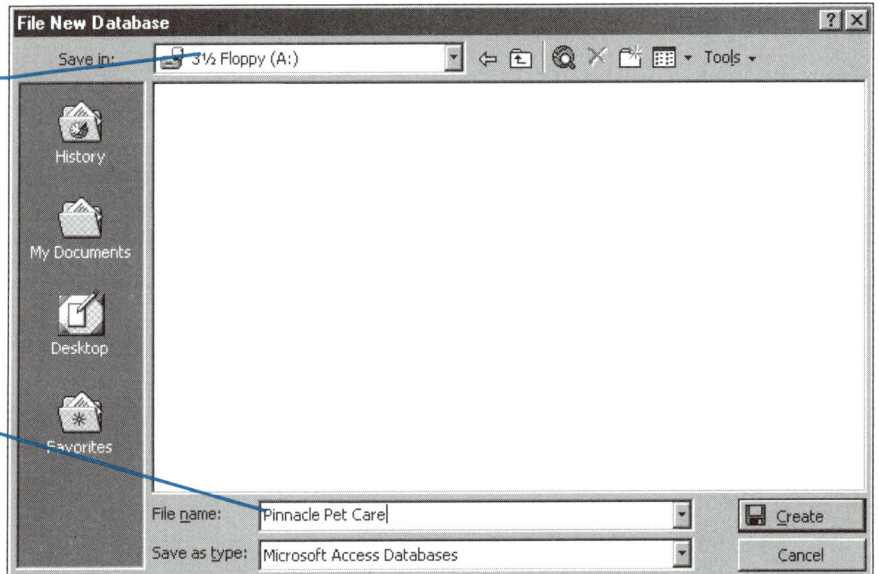

3. Follow these steps to explore the Access database window.

Ⓐ *Notice the various object buttons displayed on the **Objects** bar. An Access database is composed of objects. You can create new objects in Design view or with Wizards by choosing one of the Create options displayed in the window. Objects you create are also displayed in the database window.*

Ⓑ *Try clicking the various object buttons.*

Ⓒ *Click the **Tables** button when you have finished.*

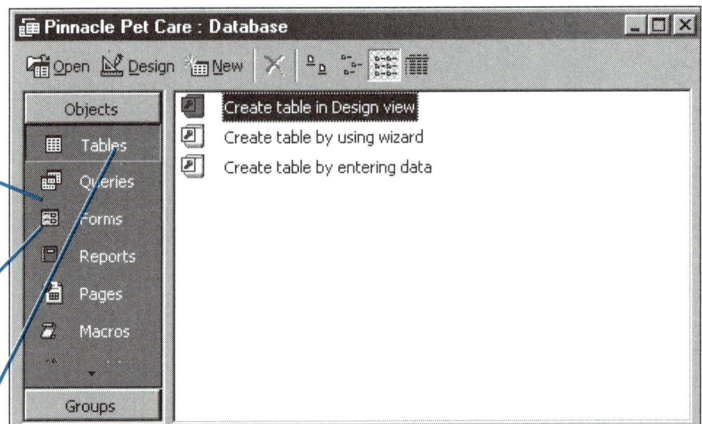

Access Tables

In Access, data is stored in tables. Tables organize data so that it can easily be output at a later time. A simple database may have one or two tables, while a sophisticated database may have dozens or even hundreds of tables. A separate table is used for each type of related data. For example, your Pinnacle Pet Care database will initially have a table for customers and a table for pets.

Records

Tables are composed of rows, and each row is known as a record. For example, your Pinnacle Pet Care database will have a Customer table that stores all of the customer information. Each row of the Customer table will contain data for one customer.

Fields

Each record is divided into fields. A record can have many fields. For example, the Customers table will have fields for the Customer ID, name, address, telephone number, etc. In Access, each column in a table is a field. Take a few moments to study the following illustration which shows the first two tables that you will create in the Pinnacle Pet Care database.

*The **Customers** table contains one record for each customer. All data for a customer is stored in one row of the **Customers** table.*

The records are composed of fields.

Customer ID	FirstName	LastName	Address	City	State	Zip	Phone	Last Visit	Current Balance
1	Mark	Roth	760 Maple Avenue	Fremont	CA	94538-	(510) 234-9090	7/7/99	$235.00
2	Tony	Simpson	312 York Lane	Richmond	CA	94804-	(510) 238-2233	9/7/99	$185.00
3	Jason	Jones	2233 Crystal Street	San Mateo	CA	94403-	(415) 312-2312	7/15/99	$48.00
4	Jacob	Samuels	2300 North Pratt Str	Atlanta	GA	30309-	(404) 367-8002	10/8/99	$250.50

Pet ID	Pet Name	Pet Type	Breed	Sex	Color	Date of Birth	Last Visit	Expenditures	Number of Visits	Customer ID
CT02	Max	Cat	Unknown	Male	White	1/7/86	9/7/99	$1,450.55	20	2
CT16	Stripes	Cat	Tortoise shell	Male	Black and brown	10/8/90	7/15/99	$450.00	9	3
CT92	Tony	Cat	Unknown	Male	Brown with black stripes	4/3/97	7/7/99	$145.00	6	1
DG12	Wolfy	Dog	German Shepherd	Male	Brown	6/6/91	7/15/99	$450.00	7	3
DG13	Dillon	Dog	Mutt	Male	Black	10/5/94	7/7/99	$150.55	3	1
DG24	Ben	Dog	Terrier	Male	Black	6/1/92	10/8/99	$480.00	3	4
DG25	Spike	Dog	Chow	Male	Brown	4/3/84	10/8/99	$890.00	12	4
RB23	Bugs	Rabbit	Jack	Unknown	Brown	6/7/95	9/7/99	$600.50	4	2

*Notice that the Customer ID field appears in both the **Customers** and **Pets** tables. Eventually, this field will be used to establish a relationship between the two tables. Establishing relationships between tables is what gives Access and other relational database systems their power and flexibility.*

Table Structure

In Access, you can set up tables in Design view or with the Table Wizard. In Design view, you specify the field names, the data type of each field, and any other parameters as needed. Design view lets you precisely determine the characteristics of each field. The Table Wizard automates the process of creating a table by letting you choose from a set of predefined fields. The Table Wizard lacks the flexibility of Design view; however, it is often useful for beginning Access users. Besides, you can always switch to Design view to modify a table that has been set up with the Table Wizard. Access gives you complete control in setting up and modifying tables and other Access objects.

Field Names

Each field in an Access table is identified by a unique name. The name can be up to 64 characters in length and can contain letters, numbers, spaces, and most punctuation marks. Field names cannot contain periods, exclamation marks, or square brackets [ ]. Some examples of field names from the Pinnacle Pet Care Customers table are Firstname, Lastname, Address, City, State, and Zip.

Data Types

Each field is assigned a data type that determines the type of data the field may contain. Common data types are text, number, currency, and date.

- **Text**—Text fields can contain any type of characters. The default size of text fields is 50 characters; however, you can increase or decrease the size as desired.

- **Number**—Number fields can only contain numbers. Number fields can be used in calculations. You should use the Text data type if a field will contain a combination of text and numbers.

- **Currency**—Currency fields can be used in calculations. Access formats the numbers in a currency field with dollar signs, commas, decimal points, and digits following the decimal point.

- **Date**—Date fields contain dates. Dates can also be used in calculations. For example, you could subtract two dates to determine the number of days between the dates.

Field Properties

Each data type has several field properties that can be used to customize the field. For example, you can change the Field Size property for text fields to increase or decrease the maximum number of characters allowed in the field. The field properties can be modified for each field in a table when the table is displayed in Design view.

Quick Reference

SETTING UP TABLES IN DESIGN VIEW

- Click the Tables button on the Objects bar in the Access Database window.

- Double-click the **Create table in Design view** option.

- Type a field name in the Field Name column of the table that appears.

- Choose a Data Type for the new field and type a description if desired.

- If necessary, modify the field properties at the bottom of the dialog box.

- Repeat the previous three steps for all desired fields.

- Close the table and give it a name when you have finished.

In this exercise, you will begin setting up the Pets table for the Pinnacle Pet Care database.

Define Text Fields

1. Follow these steps to display a new table in Design view.

Ⓐ *Make sure the **Tables** button is chosen on the **Objects** bar.*

Pinnacle Pet Care : Database

Open Design New ✕ □□ □□ □□ ▦

Objects   Create table in Design view
⊞ Tables   Create table by using wizard
⊞ Queries   Create table by entering data

Ⓑ *Double-click the* Create table in Design view *option.*

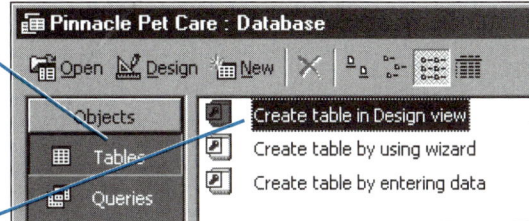

2. If necessary, maximize 🔲 both the Access program window and the table design window within the Access window.

3. Follow these steps to define a text field.

Ⓐ *Type **Pet ID** as the field name.*

File Edit View Insert Tools Window Help

▦ ▾ 🖫 🖨 🖺 ✓ ✂ 🗐 🖺 🗹 ↶ ? 🖋 ⅀ ⅀ 🖼 🖾

Field Name	Data Type	Description
▶ Pet ID	Text	Primary key for Pet table

Ⓑ *Tap the* **TAB** *key to move to the **Data Type** box. Notice the Data Type is set to Text. This is the correct setting because the Pet ID will be composed of letters and numbers. The Text data type is used if the field contains text or a combination of text and numbers.*

Field Properties

General Lookup

Field Size   6
Format
Input Mask
Caption

Ⓒ *Tap the* **TAB** *key to move to the **Description** box and type the description shown here. You will learn about primary keys later in this lesson.*

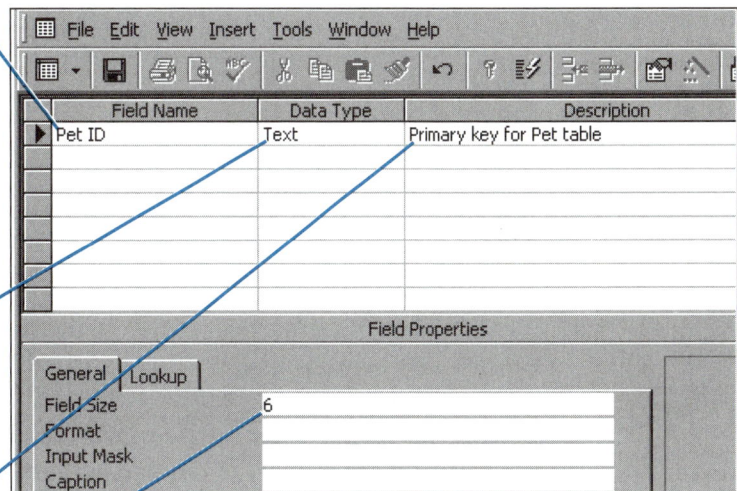

Ⓓ *Click in the **Field Size** box, and change the size from 50 to 6. It is OK to reduce the size of the* Pet ID *field, because the ID for each pet will contain a maximum of six characters. The **Field Properties** section of the dialog box reflects the properties of the current field (*Pet ID*). You will learn more about these properties as you progress through this course.*

You have just defined a field in your database. You will enter data into this field and other fields later in this lesson. You will use a data entry mode known as Datasheet view to enter the data. Currently, you are working in Design view, which allows you to define a table. The Text field type that you chose for the Pet ID field will allow you to enter any type of data in the field. However, the Pet ID for each pet will be restricted to six characters.

(Continued on the next page)

4. Follow these steps to define another text field.

Ⓐ *Click in the next **Field Name** box, and type* **Pet Name**. *The* Pet Name *field will contain the names of the pets.*

Ⓑ *Tap the* (TAB) *key, and* Text *will appear as the default **Data Type.** Leave the Data Type set to Text, and do not enter a description for this field. Descriptions are optional and are only used when necessary.*

Ⓒ *Click in the **Field Size** box, and change the size to 30 as shown here.*

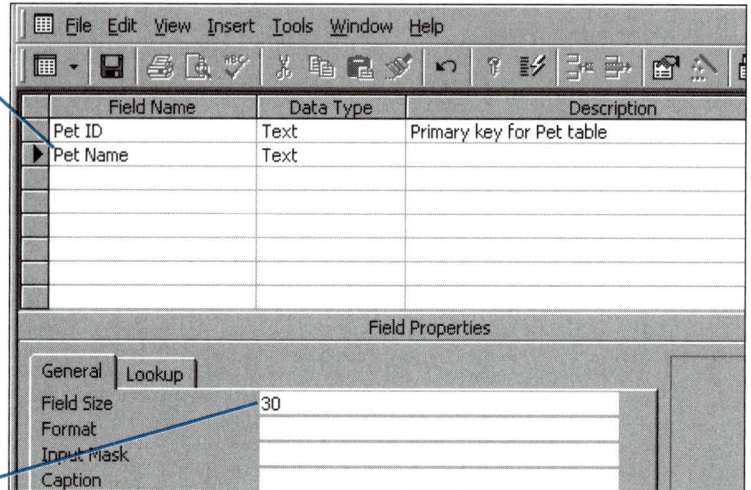

Field Name	Data Type	Description
Pet ID	Text	Primary key for Pet table
Pet Name	Text	

Field Properties

General | Lookup

Field Size	30
Format	
Input Mask	
Caption	

5. Follow the steps in the preceding illustration to create the next four fields, as shown in the following illustration. Set the Field Size to 30 for all of the fields except the Gender field. Set the size of the Gender field to 10.

Field Name	Data Type	Description
Pet ID	Text	Primary key for Pet table
Pet Name	Text	
Pet Type	Text	
Breed	Text	
Gender	Text	
Color	Text	

Define Date Fields

In the next few steps, you will define two fields that will eventually contain dates. You will set the Data Type to Date for these fields. Setting the Data Type to Date is useful because Access will identify the contents of the fields as dates. Dates can be used in calculations. For example, you could have Access calculate the number of days an account is past due by subtracting the invoice date from the current date.

6. Follow these steps to define a date field.

Ⓐ *Click in the next **Field Name** box, and type* **Date of Birth**.

Ⓑ *Tap the* `TAB` *key, and click the drop-down button in the **Data Type** box. A list of data types will appear, as shown here.*

Ⓒ *Choose* Date/Time *from the drop-down list.*

Ⓓ *Notice the **Field Properties** section does not contain a Field Size box. You cannot set the field size for date fields. The options on the Field Properties list change for each data type.*

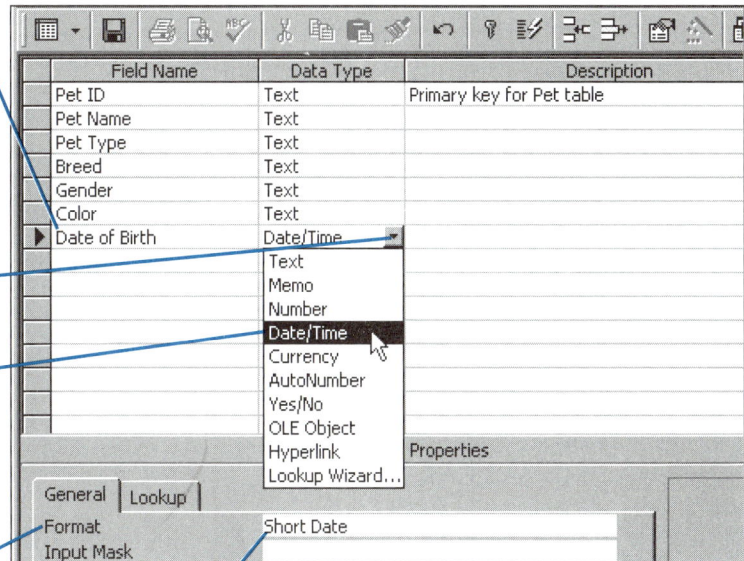

Field Name	Data Type	Description
Pet ID	Text	Primary key for Pet table
Pet Name	Text	
Pet Type	Text	
Breed	Text	
Gender	Text	
Color	Text	
Date of Birth	Date/Time	

Text
Memo
Number
Date/Time
Currency
AutoNumber
Yes/No
OLE Object
Hyperlink
Lookup Wizard...

Properties

General | Lookup
Format   Short Date
Input Mask

Ⓔ *Click in the **Format** box, click the drop-down button, and then choose* Short Date, *as shown here. The Short Date format will force all dates in the field to appear in the indicated format.*

7. Now define another date field named **Last Visit**, as shown in the following illustration. Set the Format to Short Date, as shown at the bottom of the illustration.

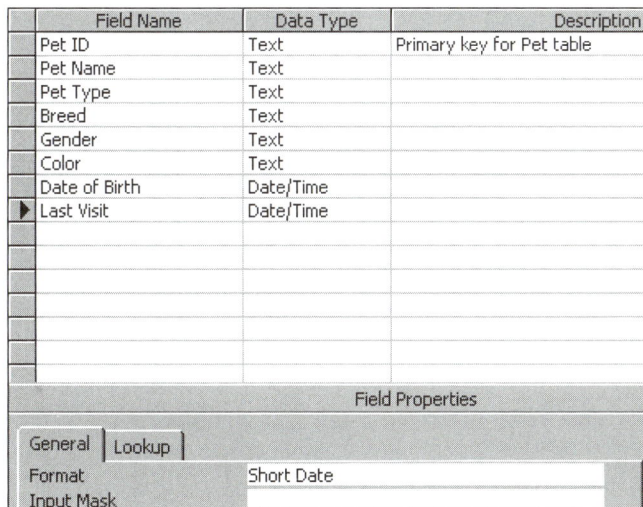

Field Name	Data Type	Description
Pet ID	Text	Primary key for Pet table
Pet Name	Text	
Pet Type	Text	
Breed	Text	
Gender	Text	
Color	Text	
Date of Birth	Date/Time	
Last Visit	Date/Time	

Field Properties

General | Lookup
Format   Short Date
Input Mask

(Continued on the next page)

Define Currency and Number Fields

In the next few steps, you will define two more fields. You will set the Data Type to Currency for one of the fields and Number for the other. Currency and number fields can be used in calculations. Furthermore, fields that are formatted with the Currency data type will display a dollar sign, a decimal point, and decimals whenever you enter data into the fields.

8. Follow this step to define the Expenditures and Number of Visits fields.

Ⓐ *Define the* Expenditures *and* Number of Visits *fields as shown here. Set the Data Types as shown, and enter the descriptions as shown. Leave the Field Properties at the bottom of the dialog box set to the default settings. Number fields normally have a* **Field Size** *of* Long Integer *as shown here. Keep in mind that choosing* **Field Properties** *can be an involved process that often requires extensive knowledge of Access.*

	Field Name	Data Type	Description
	Pet ID	Text	Primary key for Pet table
	Pet Name	Text	
	Pet Type	Text	
	Breed	Text	
	Gender	Text	
	Color	Text	
	Date of Birth	Date/Time	
	Last Visit	Date/Time	
	Expenditures	Currency	Total expenditures on this pet from time of first visit
▶	Number of Visits	Number	Total number of visits for this pet

Field Properties

General	Lookup
Field Size	Long Integer
Format	

9. Now continue with the next topic; you will define a primary key for the table.

Primary Keys

Every Access table must have one field defined as the primary key. The primary key field uniquely identifies each record in the table. For this reason, each record must have a unique entry in the primary key field. Most tables use numbers or codes in the primary key field. For example, the Pet ID field will be the primary key in the Pets table. A unique Pet ID will identify each pet. In table Design view, you specify a primary key by clicking in the desired field and clicking the Primary Key button on the Access toolbar. Access will also prompt you to choose a primary key field if you close a table that has not been assigned a primary key.

Hands-On 1.4 **Choose a Primary Key**

1. Follow these steps to choose a primary key.

A *Click in the* Pet ID *Field Name box.* **B** *Click the Primary Key button on the Access toolbar.*

C *Notice that a* key icon *appears on the Pet ID field. This icon identifies Pet ID as the primary key field.*

	Field Name	Data Type		De:
🔑▶	Pet ID	Text	Primary ke Primary Key le	
	Pet Name	Text		
	Pet Type	Text		
	Breed	Text		

Saving Database Objects

An Access database is a "container" that holds tables and other types of objects. The entire database is saved as a single file onto a hard disk or diskette. However, you must also save the objects within the database. Database objects are assigned names when they are saved. This allows you to identify the objects at a later time. A database object name can be up to 64 characters in length and may contain letters, numbers, spaces, and other types of characters.

From the Keyboard

(CTRL)+S to save an open object

You save an open object by clicking the Save 🖫 button on the Access toolbar. Access will also prompt you to save an object if you attempt to close the object without saving the changes.

Hands-On 1.5 **Save the Table**

1. Click the Save 🖫 button on the Access toolbar.

2. Type the name **Pets** in the Save As box, and click OK.

3. Follow these steps to close the table.

	Field Name	Data Type	Description
🔑▶	Pet ID	Text	Primary key for Pet table
	Pet Name	Text	
	Pet Type	Text	
	Breed	Text	
	Gender	Text	
	Color	Text	

A *Notice that there are two Close buttons in the Access window. The top button is used to close the entire Access program. The bottom button is used to close the open object (a table in this case).*

B *Click the bottom Close button, and the table will close.*

A "Pets icon" will appear in the Tables section of the Access window. You have completed the process of setting up a table. At this point, you could set up additional tables or other types of objects. However, you will enter data into the Pets table in the next exercise. To accomplish this, you will use Datasheet view.

Selecting Objects with the Objects Bar

From the Keyboard

(ENTER) to open a selected object

(CTRL)+(ENTER) to open a selected object in Design view

The Access Database window provides access to all database objects. You can select any object by clicking the appropriate objects button and then clicking the desired object. Once you select an object, you can open the object or display it in Design view.

*You can open a selected object by double-clicking it or clicking the **Open** button.*

*You use this button to display a selected object in **Design** view.*

You select an object by clicking an object button and then choosing the desired object.

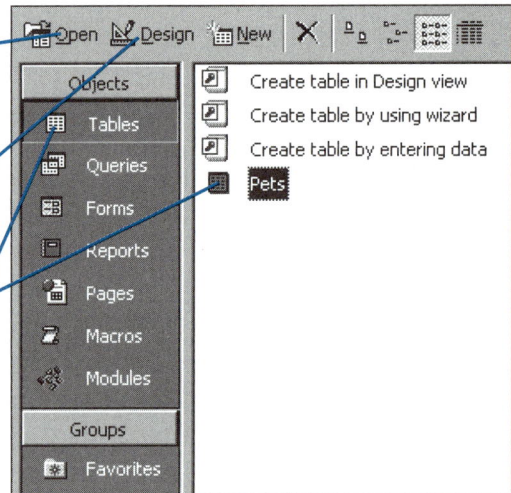

Datasheet View

In the previous exercises, you used Design view to set up the Pets table. Design view lets you set up or modify the structure of tables. However, to enter data into a table, you must display the table in Datasheet view. You can open a table in Datasheet view from the Access Database window as discussed in the previous topic.

Hands-On 1.6 Enter Data

1. Follow these steps to open the Pets table in Datasheet view.

Ⓐ *Make sure the **Tables** button is chosen, and click the Pets table icon.*

Ⓑ *Click the **Open** button. You could also have opened the Pets table by double-clicking the Pets icon.*

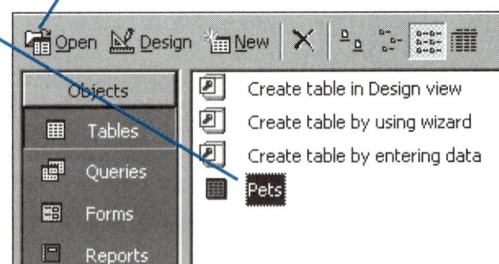

2. Follow these steps to explore the Datasheet view window.
Keep in mind that your window may have different dimensions than shown here.

Ⓐ *Notice that many of the toolbar buttons are different from those in the Design view window.*

Ⓑ *Notice that the field names are displayed as column headings.*

Ⓒ *Data is entered into the rows (although you will only see one row at this point). Each row is a record. For example, each row will contain all of the data for one pet. You use the* TAB *key to move the insertion point from one field to the next within a row (or you can click in the desired row or field).*

Pet ID	Pet Name	Pet Type	Breed	Gender	Color

Record: 1 of 1
Primary key for Pet table
NUM

Ⓓ *The record navigation buttons and the horizontal scroll bar are used to move between records and to scroll from left to right through the fields.*

3. Follow these steps to begin entering a record.

Ⓐ *Type* **DG12** *as the Pet ID, and Access will add a new row in preparation for the next record.*

Ⓑ *Tap the* TAB *key to move to the next field and type the pet name* **Wolfy**.

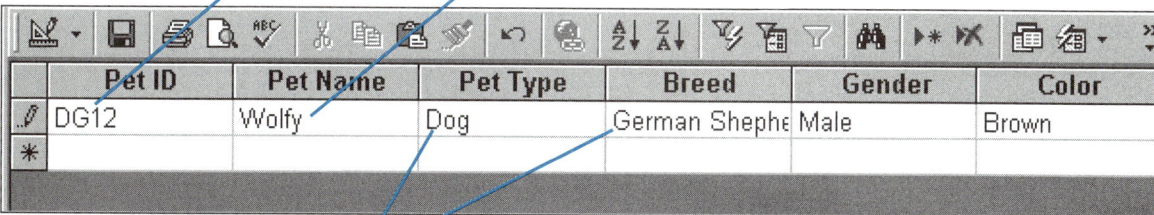

Pet ID	Pet Name	Pet Type	Breed	Gender	Color
DG12	Wolfy	Dog	German Shephe	Male	Brown
*					

Ⓒ *Continue entering the data shown here using the* TAB *key to move between fields. When you get to the* Breed *field, type the phrase* **German Shepherd** *even though the text is wider than the column. Access will scroll the column allowing you to enter the text.*

4. Follow this step to display the remaining fields.

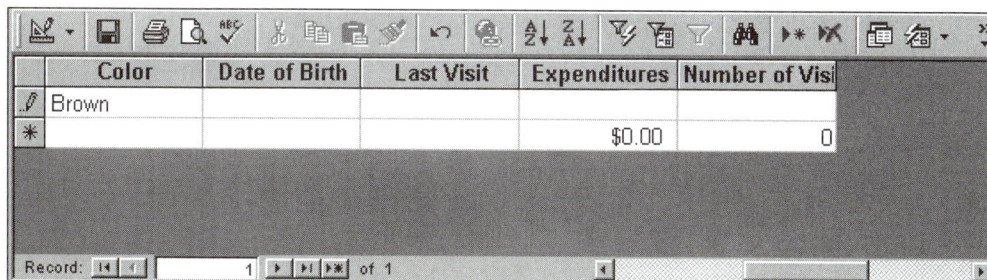

Color	Date of Birth	Last Visit	Expenditures	Number of Visi
Brown				
*			$0.00	0

Record: 1 of 1

Ⓐ *If necessary, use the horizontal scroll bar to scroll to the right until the fields shown here are visible.*

(Continued on the next page)

5. Follow these steps to enter data in the remaining fields.

Ⓐ *Make sure the insertion point is in the* Date of Birth *field, and type* **6/6/91**. *Access will display an error message if you enter a number (or text) that is not a valid date. For this reason, you must use the forward slashes (/) while entering dates, or enter dates using another valid date format such as 6-Jun-91.*

Ⓑ *Tap the* (TAB) *key, and enter* **7/15/99** *in the* Last Visit *field.*

	Color	Date of Birth	Last Visit	Expenditures	Number of Visi
✎	Brown	6/6/91	7/15/99	$450.00	7
∗				$0.00	0

Record: |◄ ◄ 1 ► ►| ►∗ of 1

Ⓒ *Tap the* (TAB) *key, and type* **450** *in the* Expenditures *field. Tap* (TAB) *again, and Access will format the number with a dollar sign ($), a decimal place, and two zeros to the right of the decimal. Access formats the number this way because you chose the Currency format for this field when you set up the table.*

Ⓓ *Type* **7** *in the* Number of Visits *field, and then tap* (TAB) *to move to the* Pet ID *field in the next record.*

Also notice that Access right-aligned the dates and numbers in the last four fields. Access always right-aligns entries that can be used in calculations.

6. Follow these guidelines to enter the records shown below into the table.

   ▪ Use the (TAB) key to move between fields.

   ▪ Make sure you use forward slashes / when entering the dates.

   ▪ **Do not** type dollar signs when entering numbers in the Expenditures field. However, **do** type a decimal point followed by the indicated decimals.

Pet ID	Pet Name	Pet Type	Breed	Gender	Color	Date of Birth	Last Visit	Expenditures	Number of Visits
DG13	Dillon	Dog	Mutt	Male	Black	10/5/94	7/7/99	150.55	3
CT89	Puffy	Cat	Siamese	Female	White with patches	12/12/96	7/7/99	30.00	1
RB23	Bugs	Rabbit	Jack	Unknown	Brown	6/7/95	9/7/99	600.50	4
CT02	Max	Cat	Unknown	Male	White	1/7/86	9/7/99	1450.55	20
CT16	Stripes	Cat	Tortoise shell	Male	Black and brown	10/8/90	7/15/99	450.00	9

7. Check your data carefully to make sure it is error-free. Accuracy is extremely important when entering data.

8. When you have finished checking your work, choose **File→Close** from the menu bar.
   Access will close the table, and the Database window will be displayed. You can close objects with either the File→Close command or by clicking the Close button (as you did in an earlier exercise). Notice that Access did not prompt you to save the table. Access automatically saves data entered into a table.

Changing the Structure of a Table

You can change the structure of a table after it has been set up. For example, you may need to change the size or name of a field or add a new field. Structural changes are made to a table in Design view.

Impact on Data

You must be careful when changing the structure of a table, especially if data has already been entered. For example, imagine that a field has a length of 30 and you have already entered records into the table. If you reduce the field length to 20, you may delete up to 10 characters from some records. Access will usually provide a warning message if you attempt to make a change that has the potential of destroying data in a field.

Switching Between Object Views

The Datasheet View [icon] button appears on the left end of the Access toolbar whenever you are in Design view. You can switch from Design view to Datasheet view by clicking the Datasheet View button.

Likewise, the Design View [icon] button appears on the left end of the Access toolbar when you are in Datasheet view. You can switch to Design view by clicking the Design View button.

Setting the Default Value of Fields

NOTE!

Only set a default value if the field will have that value 50% or more of the time.

Access lets you set default values for fields. The default value is automatically entered in new records when you enter data in Datasheet view. This can be convenient if a field is typically set to a certain value. For example, you will set the default value of the Number of Visits field to 1. Pets will be entered into the database when they make their first visit to the clinic. By setting the Number of Visits field to 1, you will be able to skip over the Number of Visits field when entering data for a new pet. In Design view, default values are set in the Field Properties area at the bottom of the dialog box.

Change a Field's Properties

1. Click the ▦ **Pets** icon in the Access window, and then click the ⬛ Design button on the Database toolbar. The Database toolbar is located just above the Objects bar.
   The Pets table will open in Design view.

2. Follow these steps to change the default value for the Number of Visits field.

Ⓐ *Click anywhere in the Number of Visits row (you may need to scroll down).*

Ⓑ *Change the default value to **1**.*

	Field Name	Data Type	
🔑	Pet ID	Text	Primary key for Pet table
	Pet Name	Text	
	Pet Type	Text	
	Breed	Text	
	Gender	Text	
	Color	Text	
	Date of Birth	Date/Time	
	Last Visit	Date/Time	
	Expenditures	Currency	Total expenditures on th
▶	Number of Visits	Number	Total number of visits fo

Field Properties

General	Lookup
Field Size	Long Integer
Format	
Decimal Places	Auto
Input Mask	
Caption	
Default Value	1
Validation Rule	

Add a Field

In the next few steps, you will add a Customer ID field to the table. The Customer ID field will eventually link the Pets table to a Customers table.

3. Follow these steps to add the Customer ID field.

Ⓐ *Click in the box below Number of Visits, and type the name* **Customer ID**. *Make sure you include a space between Customer and ID. The space is necessary because the name will eventually need to match the name in the Customers table.*

	Field Name	Data Type	
🔑	Pet ID	Text	Primary key for Pet
	Pet Name	Text	
	Pet Type	Text	
	Breed	Text	
	Gender	Text	
	Color	Text	
	Date of Birth	Date/Time	
	Last Visit	Date/Time	
	Expenditures	Currency	Total expenditures
	Number of Visits	Number	Total number of visi
▶	Customer ID	Number	

Field Properties

General	Lookup
Field Size	Long Integer
Format	
Decimal Places	Auto

Ⓑ *Set the **Data Type** to Number.*

Ⓒ *Take a moment to check the spelling of every field name. Make sure the spelling is correct and matches the spelling of the field names in this illustration. It is important that the field names be spelled correctly because they will be used in other objects throughout this course.*

4. Click the Datasheet View [icon] button on the left end of the Access toolbar, and then click the **Yes** button when the Office Assistant asks if you want to save the table.
   Notice that the order of the records has changed in the table. The records should now be sorted in alphabetical order based upon the primary key field. The records were sorted when you closed the table and then reopened it. One of the benefits of choosing a primary key field (such as Pet ID) is that Access will sort the records based upon the primary key field.

5. Now add the Customer IDs shown below into the table. Make sure you enter the correct Customer ID in each record. You may need to scroll to the left and right in the table to ensure that the correct Customer ID has been entered for each Pet ID. As you can see from this example, it can be difficult to add data to records after changing the structure of a table. For this reason, you should spend as much time as necessary designing and planning a database to minimize the number of changes that are required.

Pet ID	Pet Name	Pet Type	Breed	Gender	Color	Date of Birth	Last Visit	Expenditures	Number of Visits	Customer ID
CT02	Max	Cat	Unknown	Male	White	1/7/86	9/7/99	$1,450.55	20	2
CT16	Stripes	Cat	Tortoise shell	Male	Black and brown	10/8/90	7/15/99	$450.00	9	3
CT89	Puffy	Cat	Siamese	Female	White with patches	12/12/96	7/7/99	$30.00	1	1
DG12	Wolfy	Dog	German Shepherd	Male	Brown	6/6/91	7/15/99	$450.00	7	3
DG13	Dillon	Dog	Mutt	Male	Black	10/5/94	7/7/99	$150.55	3	1
RB23	Bugs	Rabbit	Jack	Unknown	Brown	6/7/95	9/7/99	$600.50	4	2

Make sure each Pet ID *has the correct* Customer ID.

6. Leave the table in Datasheet view, and continue with the next topic.
   You will add a record and make other changes in the next exercise.

Record Management

In Datasheet view, the Access toolbar has several buttons that let you manage records. The following quick reference table defines three of these buttons.

[Quick Reference icon]

RECORD MANAGEMENT BUTTONS

Button	Function
[icon] Find	Lets you locate a record by searching for a word or phrase. The Replace option lets you replace a word or phrase with another word or phrase.
[icon] New Record	Adds a new record at the end of the table.
[icon] Delete Record	Deletes the current record.

Navigating Within a Table

In Datasheet view, a record navigation bar appears at the bottom of the Access program window. The following illustration defines the buttons on the navigation bar.

Go to the first record in the table. — *Move forward one record.*

Move back one record. — *Go to the last record in the table.* — *Add a new record.*

Notice the Back One Record button is "ghosted out" in this illustration. This is because the insertion point is in the first record as shown in the center of the navigation bar. In other words, there is no record to move back to.

Hands-On 1.8 Manage Records

The Pets table should be in Datasheet view from the previous exercise.

Add a Record

1. Click the New Record ▸✳ button on the Access toolbar.
   The insertion point will move to a new record at the end of the table.

2. Enter the following data into the new record.

Pet ID	Pet Name	Pet Type	Breed	Gender	Color	Date of Birth	Last Visit	Expenditures	Number of Visits	Customer ID
CT92	Tony	Cat	Unknown	Male	Brown with black stripes	4/3/97	7/7/99	145	6	1

Navigate to Records

3. Follow these steps to navigate to various records.

Ⓐ *Notice the Pencil icon shown in this illustration. The Pencil icon indicates that the current record is being edited.*

Ⓑ *If necessary, scroll to the left until the Pet ID field is visible.*

Pet ID	Pet Name	Pet Type	Breed	Gender	C
CT02	Max	Cat	Unknown	Male	White
CT16	Stripes	Cat	Tortoise shell	Male	Black
CT89	Puffy	Cat	Siamese	Female	White
DG12	Wolfy	Dog	German Shephe	Male	Brown
DG13	Dillon	Dog	Mutt	Male	Black
RB23	Bugs	Rabbit	Jack	Unknown	Brown
CT92	Tony	Cat	Unknown	Male	Brown

Record: ◀◀ ◀ 7 ▶ ▶▶ ▶✳ of 7

Ⓒ *Click the various navigation buttons to browse through the records. The navigation buttons are useful when you have a large database with many records.*

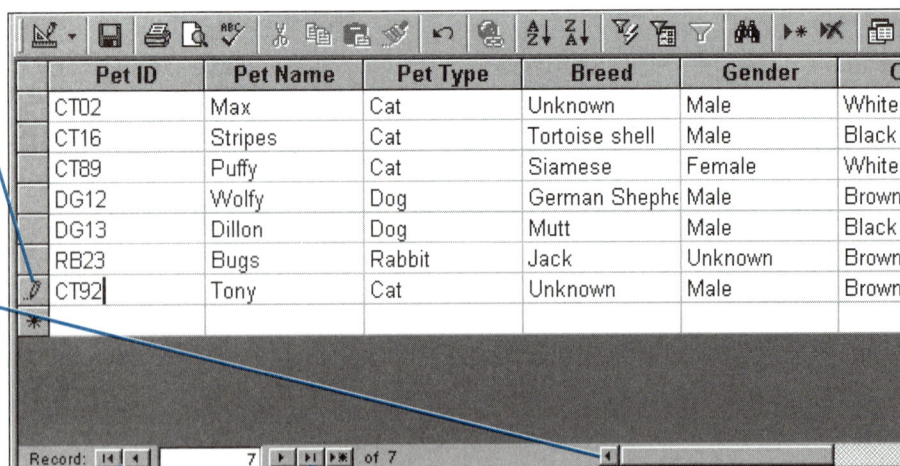

Delete a Record

4. Follow these steps to delete a record.

A *Click the record selector box (square box) to the left of the CT89 record to select the entire record. The vertical column of boxes to the left of the records is called the Selection bar.*

B *Click the **Delete Record** button on the Access toolbar.*

C *Click the **Yes** button on the warning box that appears to confirm the deletion.*

Pet ID	Pet Name	Pet Type	Breed	Gender	Color
CT02	Max	Cat	Unknown	Male	White
CT16	Stripes	Cat	Tortoise shell	Male	Black and br
CT89	Puffy	Cat	Siamese	Female	White with p
DG12	Wolfy	Dog	German Shephe	Male	Brown
DG13	Dillon	Dog	Mutt	Male	Black

In the preceding steps, you selected the CT89 record prior to deleting it. You could actually have deleted the record by clicking anywhere in the CT89 row and then clicking the Delete Record button. The Selection bar is most useful when you want to delete several records. You can select several records by dragging the mouse down the Selection bar.

Find Records

5. Click on any Pet ID in the Pet ID column.
   In the following steps, you will search for Pet IDs. You must position the insertion point somewhere in the column that you wish to search through prior to initiating the search.

6. Click the Find 🔍 button on the Access toolbar.

7. Follow these steps to conduct the search.

A *Type **ct92** in the **Find What** box.*

B *Notice that the **Look In** field indicates that you are searching for a Pet ID. In a large database, narrowing the search to a particular field can speed up the search.*

C *If the **More** button is available, click it to display additional options. The More button will turn into a **Less** button, as shown here.*

Find and Replace

Find | Replace

Find What: ct92   Find Next
                         Cancel

Look In: Pet ID
Match: Whole Field   << Less

Search: All   ☐ Match Case
              ☐ Search Fields As Formatted

D *Notice the **Match Case** box. It should be unchecked for the current search as shown here. This is because you typed the search string in lowercase (ct92) but the actual Pet ID in the database is in uppercase (CT92). Access will still find the Pet ID because the **Match Case** box is unchecked.*

E *Click the **Find Next** button, and the Pet ID CT92 will become selected.*

8. Use the preceding steps to find Pet ID **DG12**.
   Keep in mind that the Find feature is most useful when you have a large database and the item you are searching for is not visible on the screen.

(Continued on the next page)

9. Click the **Replace** tab at the top of the dialog box.

10. Notice that a Replace With box and several replace buttons appear.
You can use the Replace options to replace data in a table. For example, you could enter a word or phrase in the Find What box, type a replacement word or phrase in the Replace With box, and click the Replace All button to make the replacement in all records of the table.

11. Click the **Cancel** button to close the dialog box.

12. Leave the table open in Datasheet view, and continue with the next topic.

Cut, Copy, and Paste

Cut, Copy, and Paste are available in all Office 2000 applications. With Cut, Copy, and Paste you can move or copy data from one table cell to another. Copying data can be useful especially when a cell's contents are lengthy. You can even use Cut, Copy, and Paste to move or copy entire rows and columns. In addition, Copy and Paste can be used to copy objects in the Database window.

Quick Reference

CUT, COPY, AND PASTE

Command	Discussion	Procedure
Cut	The Cut command removes entries from table cells and places them on the Office clipboard.	Click the Cut button or press CTRL+X.
Copy	The Copy command also places entries on the Office clipboard, but it leaves a copy of the entries in the original table cells.	Click the Copy button or press CTRL+C.
Paste	The Paste command pastes entries from the Office clipboard to table cells.	Click the Paste button or press CTRL+V.

The Office 2000 Clipboard

NOTE!
Use the View→Toolbars →Clipboard command to display the Clipboard toolbar.

Office 2000 introduces a new clipboard that can hold up to 12 cut or copied items. The Clipboard toolbar uses icons to display cut or copied items. You can paste any item by choosing it from the Clipboard toolbar. You can paste all items from the toolbar by clicking the Paste All button. The items are pasted in the order in which they were cut or copied to the toolbar.

*This **Clipboard** toolbar has had two items copied to it. The Clipboard can hold items from all Office programs.*

When you point at an item, a ScreenTip pops up. When you click an item, it is pasted into the table.

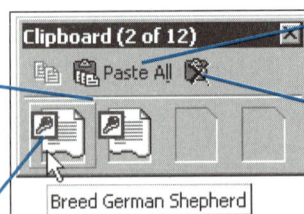

This button pastes all items into the table.

This button clears the Clipboard contents.

Hands-On 1.9 Use Copy and Paste

In this exercise, you will use Copy and Paste to assist you in entering a new record.

1. Click the New Record ▶※ button on the Access toolbar to add a new record to the table.

2. Follow these steps to enter data and to copy and paste data.

A *Type* **DG14** *in the* Pet ID *field, type* **Fetch** *in the* Pet Name *field, and type* **Dog** *as the* Pet Type, *as shown here.*

B *Position the mouse pointer on the left edge of the* Breed *cell for Wolfy the dog, and the pointer will have a thick cross shape as shown here.*

C *Click the mouse button to select the text in the* Breed *cell. You could also have selected the text by dragging over the cell's contents.*

Pet ID	Pet Name	Pet Type	Breed
CT02	Max	Cat	Unknown
CT16	Stripes	Cat	Tortoise shell
DG12	Wolfy	Dog	⊹German Shephe
DG13	Dillon	Dog	Mutt
RB23	Bugs	Rabbit	Jack
CT92	Tony	Cat	Unknown
▶ DG14	Fetch	Dog	

D *Click the* **Copy** *button on the Access toolbar.*

E *Position the mouse pointer on the left edge of the* Breed *cell for the new record, and click when the thick cross appears. The entire blank cell will be selected.*

F *Click the* **Paste** *button on the Access toolbar. The phrase* German Shepherd *will be pasted into the cell.*

3. Type **Male** in the Gender field.

4. Use Copy 🗐 and Paste 🗐 to copy the color information from the "Stripes the cat" record to the new record for "Fetch the dog."

5. Complete the new record by entering the data shown below.

Date of Birth	Last Visit	Expenditures	Number of Visits	Customer ID
6/12/96	9/10/99	345.00	3	3

Printing Tables

It is very important that you enter data accurately. There are few things more upsetting to customers and other business contacts than misspelling their names and careless data entry errors. For this reason, it is important to check your data for accuracy after it has been entered. Perhaps the best way to check data accuracy is to print out the contents of your tables. Proofreading hard copy (paper printout) is usually the best way to spot errors.

From the Keyboard

(CTRL)+P to display the Print dialog box

The Print 🖨 button on the Access toolbar sends the entire contents of a table open in Datasheet view to the current printer. You must display the Print dialog box if you want to change printers, adjust the number of copies to be printed, or to set other printing options. You display the Print dialog box with the **File→Print** command. The illustration on the following page highlights the most frequently used options available in the Print dialog box.

You choose printers from this drop-down list.

Print

Printer

Name: HP LaserJet 6P   Properties

Status: Default printer; Ready
Type: HP LaserJet 6P
Where: LPT1:
Comment: ☐ Print to File

*You can specify the number of copies here. The **Collate** option is useful when you are printing more than one copy of a multiple-page table. If the Collate box is checked, all pages of the first copy are printed before the second copy begins printing, etc.*

Print Range

◉ All

○ Pages From: ___ To: ___

○ Selected Record(s)

Copies

Number of Copies: 1

☑ Collate

You can choose to print all pages, a range of pages, or selected records.

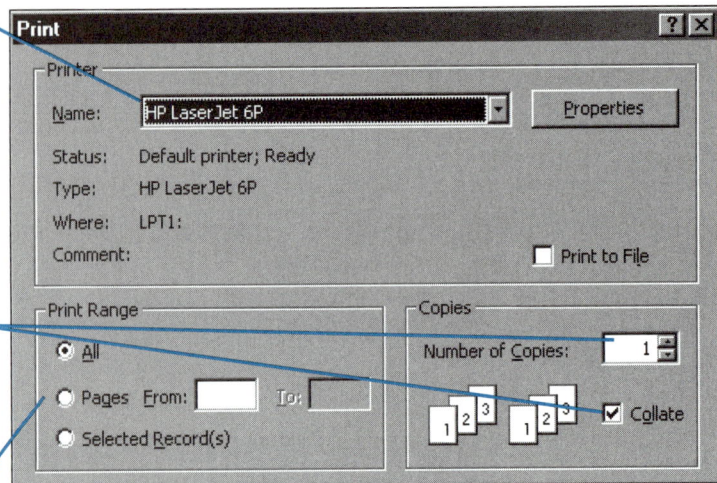

Print Preview

The Print Preview 🔍 button on the Access toolbar displays the Print Preview window. Print Preview lets you see exactly how a table will look when it is printed. Print Preview can save time, paper, and wear-and-tear on your printer. Print Preview is especially useful when printing a table with a large number of records. It is always wise to preview a large table before sending it to the printer. When you display the Print Preview window, the Access toolbar is replaced by the Print Preview toolbar.

Hands-On 1.10 Use Print Preview

1. Click the Print Preview 🔍 button on the Access toolbar.

2. Zoom in by clicking anywhere on the table.

3. Zoom out by clicking anywhere on the table.
   Notice that only six of the table's columns are visible in the Print Preview window. It is a good thing that you used Print Preview before printing the table. You will hold off on printing the table until you change the page orientation and margins.

4. Click the **Close** button on the Print Preview toolbar to exit without printing.

Adjusting Column Widths

You may need to adjust table column widths in order to see the entire contents of table cells on a printout. In Datasheet view, you can use several techniques to adjust column widths, as described in the following table.

Quick Reference

ADJUSTING COLUMN WIDTHS

Adjustment Technique	Procedure
Manually adjust column widths.	Drag the border between two column headings.
AutoFit a column to fit the widest entry in the column.	Double-click the border between two column headings, or choose Format→Column Width, and click the Best Fit button.
Set a precise column width.	Choose Format→Column Width, and enter the desired width.
Set column widths to the default standard width.	Choose Format→Column Width, check the Standard Width box, and click OK.

Hands-On 1.11 Adjust Column Widths

1. Follow these steps to manually adjust the width of the Pet ID column.

   A *Position the mouse pointer on the border between the Pet ID and Pet Name column headings, and the Adjust pointer will appear.*

Pet ID	Pet Name	Pet Type
CT02	Max	Cat
CT16	Stripes	Cat
DG12	Wolfy	Dog

   B *Drag the border to the left until the Pet ID column is just wide enough to display the column heading (Pet ID).*

2. Follow this step to AutoFit a column to the width of the column heading.

   A *Position the mouse pointer on the border between the Pet Name and Pet Type columns, and double-click when the adjust pointer appears. This technique can be tricky, so keep trying until the Pet Name column shrinks to the width of the heading. If the column has entries wider than the heading, then the width will adjust to fit the widest entry in the column.*

Pet ID	Pet Name	Pet Type
CT02	Max	Cat
CT16	Stripes	Cat
DG12	Wolfy	Dog

3. Follow these steps to AutoFit the width of all columns.

   A *Position the mouse pointer on the Pet ID column heading, and press and hold the left mouse button. The column selection pointer will appear, as shown here.*

   B *Drag the mouse over all 11 column headings in the table so that all columns are selected.*

   C *Choose **Format→Column Width** from the menu bar and click the **Best Fit** button.*

Pet ID	Pet Name	Pet Type
CT02	Max	Cat
CT16	Stripes	Cat
DG12	Wolfy	Dog

4. Click anywhere in the table to deselect the columns.

5. Scroll to the left, and notice that all column widths fit the widest entry (or heading) in the columns.

Margins and Page Orientation

Many tables are quite wide and may not fit on a single printed page. Fortunately, most printers can print text vertically in **portrait** orientation or horizontally in **landscape** orientation. Landscape orientation may allow a wide table (such as the Pets table) to print on a single page. You set the orientation of a page by issuing the **File→Page Setup** command, clicking the Page tab, and choosing the desired orientation. The margins can also be adjusted in the Page Setup dialog box.

Hands-On 1.12 Set Page Orientation and Margins, and Print

1. Choose **File→Page Setup** from the Access menu bar.

2. Make sure the Margins tab is active, and set all four margins to **0.25"** (that's 0.25 not 25).

3. Click the **Page** tab, and choose the **Landscape** option.

4. Click **OK** to complete the changes.

5. Click the Print Preview button on the Access toolbar.

6. If necessary, zoom in by clicking anywhere on the table. Scroll left or right to view all columns in the table.
   Notice that the page orientation is now horizontal (landscape). All columns should be visible on the page.

7. Print the table by clicking the Print button on the Print Preview toolbar.

8. Click the **Close** button on the Print Preview toolbar when you have finished.

9. Now close the table by choosing **File→Close** from the Access menu bar.

10. Click the **Yes** button when Access asks if you want to save the changes.
    In the next topic, you will set up another table using the Table Wizard.

The Table Wizard

Access provides a Table Wizard to help you set up common tables. The Table Wizard provides a variety of sample tables and sample fields for each table. You can choose the sample fields to include in a table and the Wizard will then build the table for you. In the next exercise, you will use the Table Wizard to set up a Customers table. Thus, you will have experience setting up tables in Design view and with the Table Wizard. In the future, you can use whichever method you prefer.

To start the Table Wizard, you click the New button on the Access Database toolbar, and choose Table Wizard from the New Table box. You can also double-click the **Create table by using wizard** option that appears in the Tables section of the Access Database window.

Use the Table Wizard to Create a New Table

1. Click the New [New] button on the Access Database toolbar (located just above the Objects bar).

2. Choose **Table Wizard,** and click **OK.**

3. Use the following steps to begin setting up a table.

Ⓐ *Make sure the **Business** category is chosen. The **Wizard** provides sample tables for both business and personal use.*

Ⓑ *Choose the Customers sample table.*

Ⓒ *Notice the list of **Sample Fields** for the Customers table. Each sample table contains a different set of sample fields.*

Ⓓ *Make sure the CustomerID field is selected in the **Sample Fields** list; then click this Add button. The CustomerID field will move to the Fields in my new table list, as shown here.*

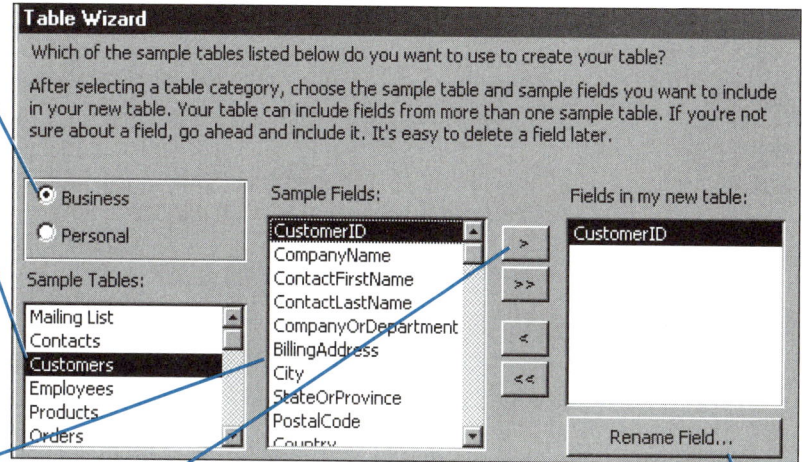

Table Wizard

Which of the sample tables listed below do you want to use to create your table?

After selecting a table category, choose the sample table and sample fields you want to include in your new table. Your table can include fields from more than one sample table. If you're not sure about a field, go ahead and include it. It's easy to delete a field later.

- ⦿ Business
- ○ Personal

Sample Tables:

- Mailing List
- Contacts
- Customers
- Employees
- Products
- Orders

Sample Fields:

- CustomerID
- CompanyName
- ContactFirstName
- ContactLastName
- CompanyOrDepartment
- BillingAddress
- City
- StateOrProvince
- PostalCode
- Country

Fields in my new table:

- CustomerID

[>] [>>] [<] [<<]

[Rename Field...]

Ⓔ *Click the **Rename Field** button, and insert a space in the name to make it Customer ID; then click OK. This is necessary so that the spelling of the field name matches the Customer ID field in the Pets table.*

4. Now add the **ContactFirstName, ContactLastname, BillingAddress, City, StateOrProvince, PostalCode,** and **PhoneNumber** fields by choosing them one at a time and clicking the Add button. Change the names of the fields as you add them, as shown in the following table.

Change this Field Name . . .	to This Name
ContactFirstName	Firstname
ContactLastName	Lastname
BillingAddress	Address
City	Leave as is
StateOrProvince	State
PostalCode	Zip
PhoneNumber	Phone

(Continued on the next page)

Fields in my new table:

Customer ID
Firstname
Lastname
Address
City
State
Zip
Phone

5. Use the Remove Field ◄ button if you mistakenly added a field and wish to remove it. Your completed **Fields in my new table** list should match the example shown to the right (although your Phone field should be completely visible).

6. Click the Next button at the bottom of the dialog box.
The next screen will propose the table name Customers and offer to set the primary key for you.

7. Leave the options set as they are by clicking the **Next** button.
The next screen will ask you about relationships between tables.

8. Leave the option set to **not related to Pets** by clicking the **Next** button.
The next screen will ask how you wish to display the completed table.

9. Choose the **Modify the table design** option and click the **Finish** button.
Access will create the table for you, and display it in Design view.

Modify the Table Structure

You may find Access wizards most useful for setting up tables and other objects. Once objects are set up, you can modify them to suit your particular needs. In the next few steps, you will use this approach by modifying the structure of the Customers table.

10. Follow these steps to explore the table you just created.

Field Name	Data Type
Customer ID	AutoNumber
Firstname	Text
Lastname	Text
Address	Text
City	Text
State	Text
Zip	Text
Phone	Text

General	Lookup
Field Size	50
Format	

Ⓐ *Notice that the data type of the Customer ID field has been set to AutoNumber. The AutoNumber field type is often used with primary key fields. AutoNumbering automatically assigns sequential numbers (beginning with 1) to records as you add them to a table. For example, the first customer you add will be assigned a Customer ID of 1, and the next customer will be assigned the Customer ID 2, and so on.*

Ⓑ *Click anywhere on the Address field.*

Ⓒ *Change the field size from 255 to **50**.*

11. Follow these steps to change the default value of the State field.

Field Name	Data Type
🔑 Customer ID	AutoNumber
Firstname	Text
Lastname	Text
Address	Text
City	Text
▶ State	Text
Zip	Text
Phone	Text

Ⓐ *Click anywhere on the* State *field.*

General | Lookup

Field Size	20
Format	
Input Mask	
Caption	
Default Value	CA
Validation Rule	

Ⓑ *Change the default value to CA (even if you do not live in California). Each new record that you add to the database will display CA as the default state.*

12. Follow these steps to check out the Input Mask property for the phone field.

Field Name	Data Type
🔑 Customer ID	AutoNumber
Firstname	Text
Lastname	Text
Address	Text
City	Text
State	Text
Zip	Text
▶ Phone	Text

Ⓐ *Click anywhere on the* Phone *Field.*

General | Lookup

Field Size	30
Format	
Input Mask	!\(999") "000\-0000
Caption	

Ⓑ *Notice these characters in the* **Input Mask** *box. An input mask displays characters in a field to assist you in entering data. For Example, the input mask shown here will display parentheses as you enter data in the phone field. The parentheses are displayed so that you know where to type the area code. The input mask can also restrict the characters that you are allowed to enter in a field. Some input masks will let you enter only the digits 0–9. The Table Wizard set up this Input Mask for the Phone field. You can also apply input masks to fields by choosing the desired mask in the Input Mask box. However, you would need to install the Input Mask Wizard in Microsoft Office before doing this.*

Add new Fields

13. Follow these steps to insert a new date field.

Ⓐ *Click below the Phone field, and type* **Last Visit**.

Ⓑ *Click in the Data Type box, and choose* Date/Time *from the drop down list.*

Ⓒ *Choose* Short Date *as the format.*

Zip	Text	
Phone	Text	
▶ Last Visit	Date/Time	

Field Properties

General | Lookup

Format	Short Date
Input Mask	

14. Now add a field named **Current Balance**, and set the Data Type to **Currency**.
At this point, you have finished setting up the Customers table. In the next steps you will add data to the table.

(Continued on the next page)

Add Data to the Table

15. Click the Datasheet View ▦ button on the Access toolbar.

16. Click **Yes** when Access asks if you wish to save the table.
Notice the word (AutoNumber) is selected in the first empty record. This field is formatted with the AutoNumber data type so you will bypass it in the next step. Access will automatically assign the number 1 to the record when you begin entering data in the Firstname field.

17. Tap the ⟮TAB⟯ key to bypass the Customer ID field.

18. Type the name **Mark** in the Firstname field, and the number 1 will appear in the Customer ID field.

19. Tap ⟮TAB⟯, and type **Roth** in the Lastname field.

20. Tap ⟮TAB⟯, and type **760 Maple Avenue** in the Address field.

21. Tap ⟮TAB⟯, and type **Fremont** in the City field.

22. Tap ⟮TAB⟯, and notice that the State field is set to CA.
This is because you set CA as the default value for this field.

23. Tap ⟮TAB⟯ to bypass the State field (CA is correct) and type **94538** in the Zip field.
You will notice that a hyphen appears to the right of the digits. This is because the Zip field has also been formatted with an input mask. The input mask inserts a hyphen between the first five and last four digits (if you use nine digits).

24. Tap ⟮TAB⟯ to bypass the last four digits of the zip code.

25. Type the area code **510** in the Phone field, and the input mask will surround the number with parenthesis.

26. Complete the phone number by typing **2349090**.
Access will format the number by inserting a hyphen between the 4 and the 9.

27. Tap ⟮TAB⟯, and type **7/7/99** in the Last Visit field.

28. Tap ⟮TAB⟯, and type **235** in the Current Balance field.

29. Now add the following two records to the table.
The AutoNumber feature will insert numbers in the Customer ID field, so just tap ⟮TAB⟯ when you reach that field. Also, do not type parenthesis in the phone numbers because the input mask will automatically apply parenthesis for you.

Customer ID	Firstname	Lastname	Address	City	State	Zip	Phone	Last Visit	Current Balance
2	Tony	Simpson	312 York Lane	Richmond	CA	94804	(510) 238-2233	9/7/99	185
3	Jason	Jones	2233 Crystal Street	San Mateo	CA	94403	(415) 312-2312	7/15/99	48

Print the Table

30. Adjust the width of all columns to fit the widest entry/heading in the columns. You can accomplish this by double-clicking the borders between the column headings. You can also select all of the columns by dragging the mouse pointer across the column headings and then double-clicking the border between the column headings of any two selected columns. Finally, you can also select all columns and use the **Format→Column Width** command, and then click the **Best Fit** button.

31. Use the **File→Page Setup** command to set all four margins to 0.5".

32. Notice that the Print Headings box is checked on the Margins tab.
    In a moment when you preview the table printout, you will notice a header and footer appear at the top and bottom of the page. The Print Headings box displays the header and footer. The Table Wizard turned on this option.

33. Set the orientation to **Landscape** using the Page tab in the Page Setup dialog box, and click **OK.**

34. Use Print Preview to preview the table, and then print the table if desired.

35. Close Print Preview, and feel free to experiment with any of the topics that you have learned in this lesson.

36. Close the table when you have finished experimenting, and save any changes.

37. Close Access by choosing **File→Exit** from the Access menu bar.

38. Now continue with the end-of-lesson questions and exercises on the following pages.

Concepts Review

True/False Questions

1. An Access database can have a maximum of 1 table.   TRUE   FALSE

2. Datasheet view is used to set up the structure of tables.   TRUE   FALSE

3. If you are in Design view and you want to switch to Datasheet view, you must close the table and reopen it in Datasheet view.   TRUE   FALSE

4. A database is like a container because it can hold several types of objects, including tables.   TRUE   FALSE

5. Changing the structure of a table will never result in lost data.   TRUE   FALSE

6. The page orientation can be changed with the File→Print command.   TRUE   FALSE

7. Portrait orientation causes a table to print horizontally on a page.   TRUE   FALSE

8. The Table Wizard is used to automate data entry in a table.   TRUE   FALSE

Multiple Choice Questions

1. What is the maximum number of characters that a field name may contain?
   a. 8
   b. 32
   c. 64
   d. 255

2. What is the first step that you should take if you want to delete a record?
   a. Click in the desired record, or select the record.
   b. Click the Delete Record button on the toolbar.
   c. Narrow the column width.
   d. Delete all text from the cells.

3. Which of the following commands is used to change the page orientation?
   a. File→Print
   b. File→Page Setup
   c. Format→Page Orientation
   d. Format→Print Preview

4. What happens when you double-click the border between two column headings in Datasheet view?
   a. The table is closed.
   b. The column width is set to the default column width.
   c. A new column is inserted.
   d. The column width is AutoFit to the widest entry.

Skill Builders

Skill Builder 1.1 Set Up a Table in Design View

In this exercise, you will set up a new database for the Tropical Getaways travel company. Tropical Getaways is an exciting new travel company that specializes in inexpensive vacations to tropical locations worldwide. You have been asked to set up a database to track clients and trips. In this exercise, you will create the first table for the database.

1. Start Access, choose the **Blank Access** database option, and click **OK.**

2. Assign the name **Tropical Getaways** to your new database, and save it on your exercise diskette.
   The Tables object list should be displayed in the Access Database window.

3. Double-click the **Create table in Design view** option to begin setting up a new table in Design view.

4. Type **Customer ID** as the first field name, and tap the TAB key.

5. Click the drop-down ⊡ button in the Data Type box, and choose **AutoNumber**.
   Access will automatically assign sequential Customer IDs when you enter data in this table.

6. Click the Primary Key 🔑 button on the toolbar to make Customer ID the primary key.

7. Set up the remainder of this table using the field names, data types, and options shown in the following table. Keep in mind that you have already set up the Customer ID field.

Field Name	Data Type	Field Size	Primary Key	Description
Customer ID	AutoNumber		Yes	
Firstname	Text	30		
Lastname	Text	30		
Address	Text	50		
City	Text	30		
State	Text	2		
Zip	Text	5		
Profile	Text	20		The profile indicates the category of trips the customer prefers

8. When you have finished, click the Datasheet View 🔲 button on the Access toolbar.

9. Click **Yes** when Access asks if you wish to save the table.

(Continued on the next page)

10. Type the name **Customers**, click **OK**, and then enter the following four records. The Customer ID numbers should be entered automatically because Customer ID has an AutoNumber data type.

Customer ID	Firstname	Lastname	Address	City	State	Zip	Profile
1	Debbie	Thomas	450 Crestwood Lane	Austin	TX	78752	Adventure
2	Wilma	Boyd	855 State Street	Richmond	NY	12954	Leisure
3	Ted	Wilkins	900 C Street	Fort Worth	TX	76104	Adventure
4	Alice	Simpson	2450 Ridge Road	Fort Worth	TX	76105	Family

11. When you have finished, choose **File→Close** from the Access menu bar to close the table. *Access automatically saves the data you entered. You will set up another table in the next Skill Builder exercise.*

Skill Builder 1.2 Set Up a Table in Design View

In this exercise, you will set up another table for the Tropical Getaways database.

1. Double-click the **Create table in Design view** option to begin setting up a new table in Design view.

2. Set up the table using the following structure.

Field Name	Data Type	Field Size/Format	Primary Key	Description
Trip ID	Text	8	Yes	Four- to eight-character unique identifier for each trip
Customer ID	Number	Long Integer		ID number from Customers table
Destination	Text	50		
Category	Text	30		All trips have a category such as Adventure, Leisure etc.
Departure Date	Date/Time	Short Date		
Return Date	Date/Time	Short Date		
Cost	Currency			

3. Switch to Datasheet, view and save the table as **Trips**.

4. Enter the following data into the Trips table. Do not type the dollar signs and commas when entering the Cost numbers. Access will add the dollar signs and commas for you because you chose the Currency data type when setting up the Cost field.

Trip ID	Customer ID	Destination	Category	Departure Date	Return Date	Cost
Adv01	1	Kenyan Safari	Adventure	8/5/97	9/4/97	$6,600
Lei01	2	Caribbean Cruise	Leisure	9/19/98	9/28/98	$2,390
Adv02	1	Amazon Jungle Trek	Adventure	8/7/98	9/14/98	$7,765
Fam01	4	Orlando	Family	3/4/99	3/10/99	$3,400

5. Close the Trips table when you have finished.
   The Tables objects list should now display both the Customers and Trips table icons. In the next exercise, you will print the Customers table.

Skill Builder 1.3 Print the Table

The Tropical Getaways database should be open, and the Customers and Trips tables should be visible in the Access Database window.

1. Double-click the **Customers** table to open it in Datasheet view.
   You can always open a table in Datasheet view by double-clicking it.

2. Adjust the widths of all columns to display the widest entries in the columns.

3. Use the Print Preview button to preview the table.

4. Zoom in on the table by clicking anywhere on it.

5. Feel free to print the table and check your data for accuracy.

6. Close Print Preview when you have finished.

7. Close the table and choose **Yes** when Access asks if you want to save the changes.

8. Now open the **Trips** table, and adjust the column widths to fit the widest entries in the columns.

9. Print the table, and check your data for accuracy.

10. Close the table, and save the changes when you have finished.

11. Exit from Access by choosing **File→Exit** from the menu bar.

Assessment

Assessment 1.1 Create a Table

In this assessment, you will begin creating a database for Classic Cars. Classic Cars is an organization devoted to tracking, categorizing, and preserving classic automobiles. You will begin by creating tables to track collectors and cars.

1. Start Access, and create a new database named **Classic Cars**.

2. Create a new table with the following structure.

Field Name	Data Type	Field Size	Primary Key	Description
Collector ID	AutoNumber	Yes	Yes	
Firstname	Text	30		
Lastname	Text	30		
Address	Text	50		
City	Text	30		
State	Text	2		
Zip	Text	5		
Era of Interest	Text	20		This field identifies the time period that the collector is most interested in
Collection Size	Number	Long Integer		Number of cars in collection

3. Enter the following records into the table, and name the table **Collectors**.

Collector ID	Firstname	Lastname	Address	City	State	Zip	Era of Interest	Collection size
1	Cindy	Johnson	4220 Edward Street	Northlake	IL	60164	1950's	42
2	Tammy	Olson	1200 Big Pine Drive	Moses Lake	WA	98837	1960's	6
3	Ed	Larkson	2300 Watson Street	Cainesville	OH	43701	Early 1900's	34
4	Bob	Barker	6340 Palm Drive	Rockridge	FL	32955	1950's	7

4. AutoFit the width of all columns to fit the largest entry/heading in the columns.

5. Use Print Preview to preview the table. If necessary, switch the orientation to landscape and reduce the margins until the table fits on one page.

6. Print the table.

7. Close the table when you have finished, and save any changes that you have made.

8. Create another new table with the following structure.

Field Name	Data Type	Field Size/ Format	Primary Key	Description
Car ID	Text	15	Yes	Up to 15 characters to uniquely identify each car
Collector ID	Number	Long Integer		ID number from Collectors table
Year	Text	20		
Make	Text	30		
Model	Text	50		
Color	Text	30		
Condition	Text	30		
Value	Currency			Estimated value

9. Enter the following records into the table and name the table **Cars**.

Car ID	Collector ID	Year	Make	Model	Color	Condition	Value
CJ01	1	58	Chevrolet	Corvette	Red and white	Mint	$65,000
TO05	2	62	Chevrolet	Corvette	Blue	Excellent	$30,000
CJ22	1	59	Ford	Thunderbird	Tan	Good	$20,000
BB03	4	58	Chevrolet	Corvette	Black	Excellent	$35,000

10. AutoFit the width of all columns to fit the largest entry/heading in the columns.

11. Use Print Preview to preview the table.

12. Print the table.

13. Close the table when you have finished, and save any changes that you have made.

14. Exit from Access when you have finished.

Forms and Reports

In this lesson, you will enhance the Pinnacle Pet Care database with forms and reports. You will create forms that will make it easy to view, enter, and edit data in the Customers and Pets tables. You will also create reports to present your data in a variety of ways.

In This Lesson

Case Study

Most of the employees at Pinnacle Pet Care have little computer experience and even less experience using Microsoft Access. For this reason, Penny Johnson must make it easy for employees to enter and extract data from the database. Penny decides to set up data entry forms that let employees enter customer information and pet information. Penny also works closely with her employees to determine the types of reports they require. Penny realizes that her employees require an outstanding customer balance report that includes the customer names and telephone numbers. Another report will list the expenditures and number of visits for each pet. This report will be sorted by expenditures so that the customers spending the most on their pets will appear at the top of the report.

*Form for **Customers** table*

Outstanding balances report for customers

Outstanding Balances

Firstname	*Lastname*	*Phone*	*Current Balance*
Mark	Roth	(510) 234-9090	$235.00
Tony	Simpson	(510) 238-2233	$185.00
Jason	Jones	(415) 312-2312	$48.00
Jacob	Samuels	(404) 367-8002	$250.50

The Office Assistant

The Office Assistant is an interactive Help tool available in all Office 2000 applications. The Assistant monitors your activities and provides tips, suggestions, and alert messages whenever it assumes you need assistance. For example, the Assistant may display a **speech balloon** asking if you want to save a table when you switch from table Design view to Datasheet view.

Office Assistant

Using the Assistant to Get Help

The Assistant's speech balloon contains a search box where you can enter phrases and questions. When you click the Search button, the Assistant interprets the phrase or question in the search box and displays a list of topics relating to the search box text. When you click a topic, Access displays a Help window providing you with detailed help information.

Controlling the Assistant

You can control all aspects of the Assistant. For example, you may not want the Assistant to display a tip of the day, or you may want to turn the Assistant off. You set options for the Assistant in the Office Assistant dialog box. The following Quick Reference table outlines various methods of controlling the Assistant.

Quick Reference

CONTROLLING THE OFFICE ASSISTANT

Task	Procedure
Display the Assistant's speech balloon (four different methods).	■ Click anywhere on the Assistant. ■ Press F1. ■ Click the Help button on the Standard toolbar. ■ Choose Microsoft Access Help from the Help menu.
Close the speech balloon.	Click anywhere in the Access window or tap ESC.
Display Office Assistant dialog box.	Display the speech balloon, and click the Options button.
Change animated character.	Display the Office Assistant dialog box, click the Gallery tab, use the Next button to browse the available characters, choose a character, and click OK.
Temporarily hide the Assistant.	Choose Help→Hide the Office Assistant, or right-click the Assistant, and choose Hide from the pop-up menu.
Turn Assistant off completely.	Display the Office Assistant dialog box and uncheck the Use the Office Assistant box.
Unhide the Assistant, or turn the Assistant back on.	Choose Help→Show the Office Assistant.

Forms

In the previous lesson, you learned that an Access database is composed of various objects. A form is a type of object that lets you view, edit, and enter data. The benefit of a form is that it allows you to focus on a single record in the database. This is in contrast to Datasheet view where you are able to view many records at the same time. The following illustration shows a form for the Customers table in the Pinnacle Pet Care database.

Notice that the form displays one complete record from the database. Forms let you focus on a single customer, pet, etc.

*Fields such as **Phone, Last Visit,** and **Current Balance** are automatically formatted with symbols (as they are in Datasheet view).*

The form also contains navigation buttons to let you browse through the database.

🔡 Customers	_ □ ✕
Customer ID	1
Firstname	Mark
Lastname	Roth
Address	760 Maple Avenue
City	Fremont
State	CA
Zip	94538-
Phone	(510) 234-9090
Last Visit	7/7/99
Current Balance	$235.00

Record: |◄ | ◄ | 1 | ► | ►| | ►* | of 3

Creating Forms with AutoForm

You can use AutoForm to automatically create simple forms. AutoForm creates a form that displays all fields from a particular table. The form in the preceding illustration was created from the Customers table using AutoForm. More complex forms can be created using form Design view or with the Form Wizard.

Quick Reference

CREATING FORMS WITH AUTOFORM

- Choose the desired table in the Access Database window.
- Click the New Object 🗗 ▾ drop-down button near the right end of the Access toolbar.
- Choose AutoForm from the drop-down list.
- Close the form when you have finished using it, and assign it a name.

Hands-On 2.1 Use AutoForm

In this exercise, you will open the Pinnacle Pet Care database from your exercise diskette. You will continue to enhance the Pinnacle Pet Care database throughout this course. If you have not satisfactorily completed the Hands-On exercises in the previous lesson, then ask your instructor to copy the file named Pinnacle Pet Care - Lesson 2 to your exercise diskette. This file provides the Pinnacle Pet Care database in the state it should be in after completing Lesson 1. If necessary, your instructor can provide you with files to give you a fresh starting point whenever you begin a new lesson in this book.

A *If the Pinnacle Pet Care database is listed in the dialog box that appears, then choose it from the list as shown here, and click OK. If it is not listed, then skip this illustration, and continue with the next step.*

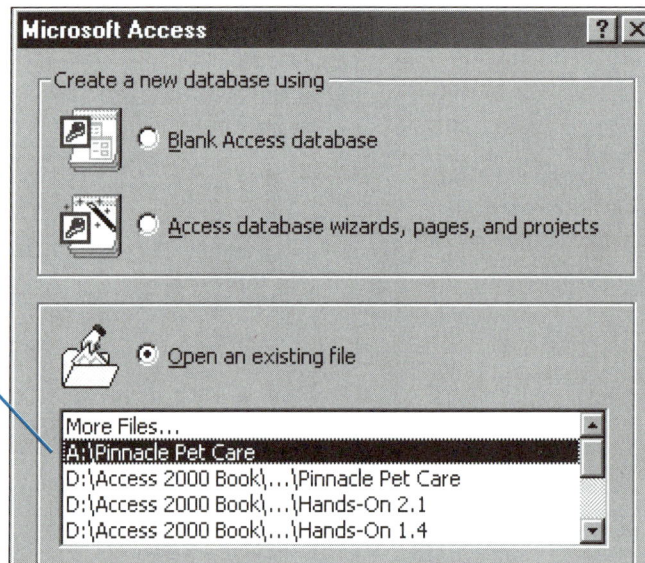

1. Start Access, and follow this step to open the Pinnacle Pet Care database.

2. If the Pinnacle Pet Care database was not listed as shown above, then click the **Cancel** button on the dialog box, click the **Open** button on the Access toolbar, navigate to your exercise diskette, and open the Pinnacle Pet Care file.

A *Choose the Customers table from the list of tables. You must choose the desired table before creating a form.*

B *Click the drop-down button on the **New Object** button, and choose AutoForm, as shown here.*

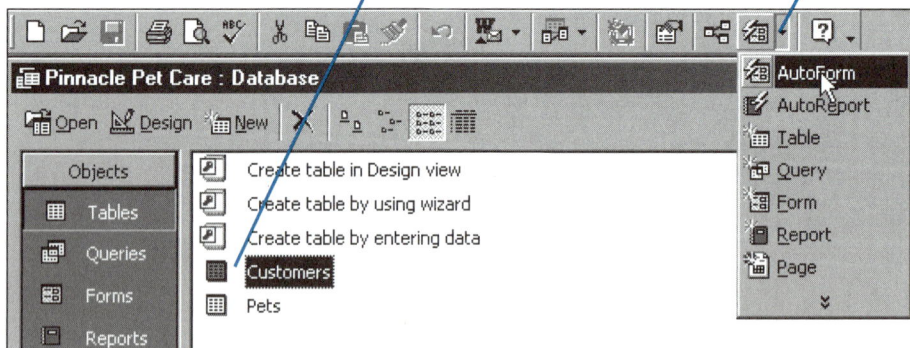

3. Follow these steps to create a form for the Customers table.
Access will create the form, and the Mark Roth record will be displayed. This is because the Mark Roth record is the first record in the table.

Entering Data and Navigating Records in Forms

Forms are used for viewing and entering data one record at a time. When you enter data using a form, the data is stored in the underlying table that the form is based upon. Forms also make it easy to navigate to various records. The navigation bar at the bottom of a form lets you navigate to records in the underlying table. The form navigation bar has the same buttons that appear on the navigation bar in Datasheet view.

Go to the first record in the table.

Move forward one record.

Move back one record.   *Go to the last record in the table.*   *Add a new record.*

Hands-On 2.2 Enter Data and Navigate

1. Follow these steps to prepare to enter a new record.

A *Click the New Record button, and a new record will appear, as shown here.*

B *Tap the (TAB) key to bypass the Customer ID field, and move the insertion point to the Firstname field.*

Customers

Customer ID	(AutoNumber)
Firstname	
Lastname	
Address	
City	
State	CA
Zip	
Phone	
Last Visit	
Current Balance	$0.00

Record: 4 of 4

(Continued on the next page)

2. Follow this step to enter the data.

Ⓐ *Enter the data shown here using the* (**TAB**) *key to move from one field to the next. Notice that you must change the entry in the **State** field from CA to GA. You can always change the default value for a record by typing a new value. You set the default value to CA when you created the table in the previous lesson. Also, the dollar sign will not appear in the **Current Balance** field until you go to another field or record after typing the entry in the Current Balance field.*

Customers	
Customer ID	4
Firstname	Jacob
Lastname	Samuels
Address	2300 North Pratt Street
City	Atlanta
State	GA
Zip	30309-
Phone	(404) 367-8002
Last Visit	10/8/97
Current Balance	$250.50

Record: ◄◄ ◄ 4 ► ►► ►* of 4

In the next few steps, you will close the form and assign a name to it. You name forms as you name tables and all other database objects.

3. Follow this step to close the form.

Customers	
Customer ID	4
Firstname	Jacob
Lastname	Samuels

Ⓐ *Click the Close button on the form, and Access will ask if you want to save the form.*

4. Click the **Yes** button, and Access will propose the name Customers.

5. Click **OK** to accept the proposed name.

6. Follow these steps to confirm that the form has been created and to reopen the form.

Ⓐ *Click the **Forms** button on the **Objects** bar, and the **Customers** icon will be visible as shown here.* ———

Pinnacle Pet Care : Database

📂Open 📐Design 📑New ✕ ▯▯ ▫▫ ▦ ▦

Objects	
Tables	Create form in Design view
Queries	Create form by using wizard
Forms	Customers
Reports	

Ⓑ *Double-click the Customers icon to open it. (You also could have clicked the form and then clicked the **Open** button on the Database toolbar just above the **Objects** bar).* ———

7. Use the navigation bar at the bottom of the form to browse through the records.
Notice that the Jacob Samuels record you just added is visible as the last record. The data you entered for Jacob Samuels has been entered into the Customers table.

8. Now close the Customers form again by clicking its Close ✕ button.

Deleting and Editing Records with Forms

The Delete Record ⊠ button on the Access toolbar deletes the current record displayed in a form. The record is deleted from the underlying table. You can also use a form to edit data in an underlying table. Keep in mind that you must first navigate to a record before you can edit the data or delete the record.

Hands-On 2.3 Create a New Form and Work with Records

1. Follow these steps to create a new form for the Pets table.

Ⓐ *Click the Tables button on the Objects bar.*

Ⓑ *Choose the Pets table.*

Ⓒ *Click the AutoForm button (not the drop-down button) to create the form. The New Objects button always displays the most recent object type created on the face of the button.*

Notice that the new form is based upon the fields in the Pets table.

2. Click the New Record ▶* button on the navigation bar at the bottom of the form.

3. Enter the following records, stopping at the Breed field for Slinky the Snake.

Pet ID	Pet Name	Pet Type	Breed	Gender	Color	Date of Birth	Last Visit	Expenditures	Number of Visits	Customer ID
DG24	Ben	Dog	Terrier	Male	Black	6/1/92	10/8/99	480	3	4
DG25	Spike	Dog	Chow	Male	Brown	4/3/84	10/8/99	890	12	4
SN01	Slinky	Snake								

4. It turns out that snakes are not welcome in the Pinnacle Pet Care clinic, so click the Delete Record ⊠▾ button on the Access toolbar.

5. Click **Yes** to confirm the deletion of Slinky the Snake.

6. Use the navigation bar to navigate backwards through the records, and notice that the Ben the dog record and the Spike the dog record are still there.

7. Click the Close ⊠ button on the form.

8. Click **Yes** when Access asks if you want to save the form.

9. Click **OK** on the Save As box to accept the name Pets.
Both the Customers and Pets form icons should be visible in the Database window.

Printing Forms

You can print the records in a table by clicking the **Print** 🖨 button from an open form. Access will print a copy of the form with displayed data for each record in the database. This technique can be useful if there are a large number of fields in a table. Printing a datasheet with a large number of fields is often difficult because the fields can't be displayed on a single page. A form, however, will often fit on a single page. On the other hand, printing forms may not be wise if the table has a large number of records. Forms typically take a large amount of space on the printed page, and you will use a lot of paper if you print a table with many records.

Hands-On 2.4 Preview the Pets Form

1. Click the **Forms** button on the Objects bar.

2. Double-click the Pets icon in the Forms section of the database window.

3. Click the **Print Preview** 🔍 button on the Access toolbar.

4. If necessary, maximize 🔲 the Print Preview window.

5. Click anywhere on the page in the Print Preview window to zoom in.
   Notice that a copy of the form is displayed for each record in the Pets table.

6. Use the navigation bar at the bottom of the Print Preview window to browse through the pages.
   As you can see, printing data via a form may require a lot of paper.

7. Close the Print Preview window without printing.

8. Click the **Restore** 🗗 button near the top right corner of the window to restore the Pets form (not the Access program window).

9. Click the **Close** ☒ button on the Pets form.

Reports

You can create reports to present data in a printed format. You can specify the fields to include in reports and you can format reports using built-in report styles. In the next exercise, you will create the report shown below. Notice that the report lists just four fields from the Customers table.

Outstanding Balances

Firstname	Lastname	Phone	Current Balance
Mark	Roth	(510) 234-9090	$235.00
Tony	Simpson	(510) 238-2233	$185.00
Jason	Jones	(415) 312-2312	$48.00
Jacob	Samuels	(404) 367-8002	$250.50

Complexity of Reports

In this lesson, you will use the Report Wizard to create simple reports. However, Access reports can be quite complex. For example, reports can include calculated fields that sum up columns of numbers and grouping levels to organize records in logical groups.

AutoReport and the Report Wizard

In the previous exercises, you used AutoForm to create forms. AutoForm creates a form using all fields from a table. This is acceptable, because you will normally want all fields from a table on a form. Reports, on the other hand, usually require a subset of a table's fields. For example, the report shown in the previous illustration uses just four fields from the Customers table. AutoReport has limited use because it inserts all fields from a table into a report. Fortunately, Access provides a Report Wizard that gives you flexibility when setting up reports. The Report Wizard lets you choose the fields to include in the report. The Report Wizard also lets you specify various formatting options.

USING THE REPORT WIZARD

- Click the **Reports** button on the Objects bar in the Database window.

- Double-click the **Create report by using wizard** option. You can also click the New button on the Access Database toolbar and choose Report Wizard from the dialog box.

- Choose the desired table or query that you wish to base the report on from the Tables/Queries list, and click **OK**.

- Follow the Report Wizard steps to create the desired report.

Previewing and Printing Reports

The **Preview** ⬚Preview button appears on the Access Database toolbar whenever the Reports button is pressed on the Objects bar and a report is chosen. You can open the report in Print Preview mode by clicking the Preview button. The Print Preview window functions the same way with reports as it does with other objects.

The **Print** 🖨 button can be used to print reports directly from the Database window. The Print button also appears on the Print Preview toolbar when a report is chosen. You can print all pages of a report by clicking the Print button. You must use the **File→Print** command to display the Print dialog box if you want to print a range of pages or set other print options.

1. Follow these steps to launch the Report Wizard.

Ⓐ *Click the* **Reports** *button on the Objects bar.*

Ⓑ *Double-click the* Create report by using wizard *option.*

Pinnacle Pet Care : Database

Preview   Design   New

Objects
Tables
Queries
Forms
Reports
Pages

Create report in Design view
Create report by using wizard

2. Follow these steps to choose the Customers table as the basis for the report and to add the Firstname field to the Selected Fields list.

Ⓐ *Make sure* Customers *is chosen from the* **Tables/Queries** *list.*

Ⓑ *Choose* Firstname *from the* **Available Fields** *list.*

Ⓒ *Click the* **Add Field** *button.*

Tables/Queries

Table: Customers

Available Fields:

Customer ID
Firstname
Lastname
Address

Selected Fields:

>
>>

3. Now add the **Lastname**, **Phone**, and **Current Balance** fields. The completed Selected Fields list is shown to the right.

Firstname
Lastname
Phone
Current Balance

4. Click **Next** to display the Grouping Levels screen.

5. Click **Next** to bypass the Grouping Levels screen and display the Sort Order screen.

6. Click **Next** to bypass the Sort Order screen and display the Layout screen. Make sure the layout options are set as shown on the next page.

7. Click **Next** to display the Style screen.

8. Choose **Corporate**, click **Next**, and follow these steps to set the final report options.

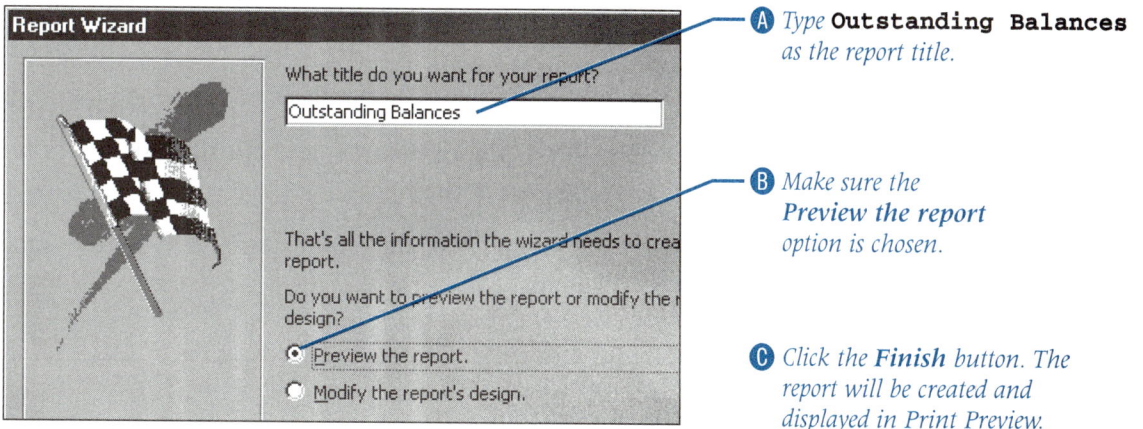

Ⓐ *Type* **Outstanding Balances** *as the report title.*

Ⓑ *Make sure the* **Preview the report** *option is chosen.*

Ⓒ *Click the* **Finish** *button. The report will be created and displayed in Print Preview.*

9. If necessary, maximize the Print Preview window by clicking its **Maximize** 🔲 button.

10. Zoom in or out on the report by clicking the mouse pointer anywhere on it.

The top section of your report should match the following example (although the sort order may be differ-ent). You will sort reports in the Skill Builder exercises.

Outstanding Balances

Firstname	Lastname	Phone	Current Balance
Mark	Roth	(510) 234-9090	$235.00
Tony	Simpson	(510) 238-2233	$185.00
Jason	Jones	(415) 312-2312	$48.00
Jacob	Samuels	(404) 367-8002	$250.50

(Continued on the next page)

11. Click the **Design View** button on the left end of the Print Preview toolbar.
The report will display in Design view with a report header, page header, detail section, etc. In Design view, you can change the position of objects, add and remove objects, and change the properties of objects. However, you won't work in Design view at this time.

12. Click the Print Preview button on the left end of the toolbar to switch back to Print Preview.

13. Feel free to print the report by clicking the **Print** button on the Print Preview toolbar.

14. Choose **File→Close** from the menu bar to close the report.
The Report will automatically be assigned the name Outstanding Balances, and an Outstanding Balances icon will appear in the Reports section of the database window. As you can see from this example, creating simple reports is quite easy if you use the Report Wizard. Now continue with the next exercise, where you will create a report to accompany the Pets table.

Hands-On 2.6 **Create a Report for the Pets Table**

1. Make sure the Reports button is pressed on the Objects bar, and double-click the **Create report by using wizard** option.

2. Choose the **Pets** table from the Tables/Queries list.

3. Add the **Pet Name**, **Pet Type**, **Expenditures**, and **Number of Visits** fields to the Selected Fields list as shown at the right.

Selected Fields:

Pet Name
Pet Type
Expenditures
Number of Visits

4. Click the **Finish** button to accept all of the remaining default settings, and the completed report shown below will appear.
Once again, the sort order may be different than shown here.

Pets

Pet Name	Pet Type	Expenditures	Number of Visits
Wolfy	Dog	$450.00	7
Dillon	Dog	$150.55	3
Bugs	Rabbit	$600.50	4
Max	Cat	$1,450.55	20
Stripes	Cat	$450.00	9
Tony	Cat	$145.00	6
Fetch	Dog	$345.00	3
Ben	Dog	$480.00	3
Spike	Dog	$890.00	12

5. Notice the alignment of the fields within the columns.
Fields have the same left or right alignment in a report as they do in the table the report is based on.

6. Close the report with the **File→Close** command.
The Reports section should now have an Outstanding Balance report and a Pets report.

Copying Objects

From the Keyboard

CTRL+C to copy
CTRL+V to paste

You can copy tables, forms, reports, and other types of objects. Objects can be copied and then pasted into the same database, to a different database, or to other applications. Copying an object to the same database can be useful if you intend to modify the object. By making a copy, you will have a backup of the object in case you damage the original. You copy objects with the **Copy** and **Paste** buttons on the Access toolbar.

Deleting Objects

From the Keyboard

DELETE to delete
selected object

Objects can also be deleted from an Access database. However, you must be careful when deleting objects because they are permanently deleted from the database. Deleting objects can be useful, especially when using Wizards and tools like AutoForm. If you make a mistake or are unhappy with the results that one of these automated tools produces, you can delete the object and start over. You delete an object by choosing the desired object in the database window and issuing the **Edit→Delete** command.

Hands-On 2.7 Copy a Report, and Then Delete the Copy

Copy the Report

1. Choose the Pets icon in the Reports section of the database window.

2. Click the **Copy** button on the Access toolbar.

3. Click the **Paste** button on the toolbar, and the Paste As box will appear.

4. Type the name **Copy of Pets** in the Paste As box, and click **OK**.
   The Copy of Pets report will appear in the Reports section.

5. Double-click the **Copy of Pets** report, and it will open.
   Notice that this report is identical to the Pets report.

6. Close the report with the **File→Close** command.

Delete the Report

7. Make sure the Copy of Pets report is chosen.

8. Choose **Edit→Delete** from the menu bar.

9. Click **Yes** to confirm the deletion.
   Keep in mind that you can delete a report (or other object) whenever you want to "get a fresh start." This technique is useful when using wizards and other automated tools. You may need to use this technique in the Skill Builder and Assessment exercises on the following pages. You will create several reports in these exercises that are more complex than the reports you just created. If you make a mistake, remember to delete the report and recreate it with the Report Wizard.

10. Close the Pinnacle Pet Care database with the **File→Close** command.

Concepts Review

True/False Questions

1. Forms can be used to enter data in tables.   TRUE   FALSE

2. The main benefit of forms is that they allow you to view several records   TRUE   FALSE
   simultaneously.

3. The navigation buttons at the bottom of a form can be used to move between records.   TRUE   FALSE

4. Forms do not display currency symbols $ and other formatting characters.   TRUE   FALSE

5. AutoForm creates a form for the table that is selected in the Tables section of the   TRUE   FALSE
   Access window.

6. The Report Wizard lets you choose the fields that you wish to include in a report.   TRUE   FALSE

7. Reports can be printed.   TRUE   FALSE

8. The Report Wizard lets you choose portrait or landscape orientations.   TRUE   FALSE

Multiple-Choice Questions

1. Which of the following statements is/are
   accurate?
   a. Forms can be used to enter records into
      a table.
   b. Forms can be used to browse through the
      records in a table.
   c. Forms let you focus on one record at a time.
   d. All of the above

2. Which of the following commands can you
   issue through the navigation buttons on a form?
   a. Add a new record.
   b. Delete a record.
   c. Change the size of a field.
   d. All of the above

3. Which of the following statements is true?
   a. The Report Wizard lets you choose portrait or
      landscape orientations.
   b. The Report Wizard lets you choose the fields
      to include in a report.
   c. The Report Wizard lets you choose a title for
      the report.
   d. All of the above

4. The Report Wizard is initiated from which
   section of the database window?
   a. The Tables section
   b. The Reports section
   c. The Forms section
   d. Any of the above

Skill Builders

Skill Builder 2.1 Create Forms

The Access window should be open from the previous exercise, and all databases should be closed. In this exercise, you will open the Tropical Getaways database from your exercise diskette. You will continue to enhance this database as you progress through the Skill Builder exercises in this course. If you did not accurately complete the Skill Builder exercises in the previous lesson, then ask your instructor to copy the file named Tropical Getaways—Lesson 2 to your exercise diskette. This file provides the Tropical Getaways database as it should be after completing Lesson 1.

Create a Form for the Customers Table

1. Click the Open ☞ button on the Access toolbar, navigate to your diskette, and open the **Tropical Getaways** database.

2. Make sure the Tables button is pressed on the Objects bar.

3. Choose the Customers table, click the New Object 🗗 drop-down button, and choose AutoForm.

   Access will create the form shown below. The form uses all of the fields in the Customers table.

Customers	
Customer ID	1
Firstname	Debbie
Lastname	Thomas
Address	450 Crestwood Lane
City	Austin
State	TX
Zip	78752
Profile	Adventure

Record: 1 of 4

4. Click the **New Record** ▶✳ button on the form's navigation bar, and add the following records.

Customer ID	Firstname	Lastname	Address	City	State	Zip	Profile
5	Victor	Thomas	2311 Wilmont Street	Danvers	MA	01923	Adventure
6	Lisa	Simms	100 Westside Drive	Batavia	NY	14020	Leisure
7	Ted	Carter	250 Smith Street	Charlton	MA	01507	Family

5. Click the Close ✕ button on the form, and choose **Yes** when Access asks you to save the form.

6. Click **OK** to accept the proposed name Customers.

(Continued on the next page)

Create a Form for the Trips Table

7. Use AutoForm to create a form for the Trips table.

8. Use the form to add the following records to the Trips table.

TripID	Customer ID	Destination	Category	Departure Date	Return Date	Cost
Adv03	1	Swiss Alps	Adventure	10/10/98	11/5/98	$3,500
Adv04	5	Rocky Mountains	Adventure	5/6/99	5/22/99	$2,190
Adv05	5	Baja California	Adventure	8/8/99	8/18/99	$2,900
Lei02	6	Hawaii	Leisure	2/5/99	2/15/99	$4,500
Fam02	7	Hawaii	Family	3/7/99	3/15/99	$5,300

9. Close the form, and save it with the proposed name Trips.
Leave the Tropical Getaways database open. You will continue to use it in the next exercise.

Skill Builder 2.2 Create Reports

In this Skill Builder exercise, you will create reports for the Tropical Getaways database. You will use the sort option in the Report Wizard to sort the records in the reports.

Create a Customer Profiles Report

1. Click the Reports button on the Objects bar.

2. Double-click the **Create report by using wizard** option.

3. Choose **Customers** from the Tables/Queries list.

4. Add the **Firstname**, **Lastname**, **State**, and **Profile** fields to the Selected Fields list.

5. Click the **Next** button twice to display the Sorting screen.

6. Click the drop-down button on the first sorting box, and choose **State** as shown to the right.
This will group all records with the same state together in the report. Notice that you could set additional sort options. For example, imagine that you had a large database and you wanted the records sorted first by state and then by zip code within the states. In that situation, you would set the second sort key to zip code.

7. Click the **Next** button twice to display the Report Style screen.

8. Choose the Soft Gray style and click **Next.**

9. Type the name **Customer Profiles by State** in the title box of the last screen.

10. Click the **Finish** button to complete the report.

The completed report is shown below. Notice that the State field appears first in the report, and the records for each state are grouped together. The State field appears first because you sorted on that field.

Customer Profiles by State

State	Firstname	Lastname	Profile
MA	Ted	Carter	Family
MA	Victor	Thomas	Adventure
NY	Wilma	Boyd	Leisure
NY	Lisa	Simms	Leisure
TX	Alice	Simpson	Family
TX	Ted	Wilkins	Adventure
TX	Debbie	Thomas	Adventure

11. Close the report when you have finished viewing it.

Access will automatically name the report Customer Profiles by State.

Create a Report for the Trips Table

12. Now create the report shown below for the Trips table. You will need to start the Report Wizard and choose the appropriate fields from the Trips table. Also, sort the report on the Category field, choose the Soft Gray style, and use the report title Trips by Category.

Trips by Category

Category	Destination	Cost
Adventure	Baja California	$2,900.00
Adventure	Rocky Mountains	$2,190.00
Adventure	Swiss Alps	$3,500.00
Adventure	Amazon Jungle Trek	$7,765.00
Adventure	Kenyan Safari	$6,600.00
Family	Hawaii	$5,300.00
Family	Orlando	$3,400.00
Leisure	Hawaii	$4,500.00
Leisure	Caribbean Cruise	$2,390.00

(Continued on the next page)

13. Close the report when you have finished viewing it.
Your Tropical Getaways database should now have two reports: Customer Profiles by State *and* Trips by Category.

14. Use the **File→Close** command to close the database. The Access program window should remain open.

Assessment

Assessment 2.1 Create Forms and Reports

1. Open the Classic Cars database.

   You began setting up this database in the assessments in the previous lesson.

2. Use AutoForm to create the form shown below for the Collectors table.

Collectors

Collector ID	1
Firstname	Cindy
Lastname	Johnson
Address	4220 Edward Street
City	Northlake
State	IL
Zip	60164
Era of Interest	1950's
Collection Size	42

Record: 1 of 4

3. Use the form to enter the following new record into the Collectors table.

Collector ID	Firstname	Lastname	Address	City	State	Zip	Era of Interest	Collection Size
5	Jake	Johnson	840 Edgewood Drive	Arcadia	FL	33821	1920s	3

4. Close the form, and save it with the proposed name *Collectors*.

5. Use AutoForm to create the form shown below for the *Cars* table.

Cars

Car ID	BB03
Collector ID	4
Year	58
Make	Chevrolet
Model	Corvette
Color	Black
Condition	Excellent
Value	$35,000.00

Record: 1 of 4

(Continued on the next page)

6. Use the form to enter the following new records into the table.

Car ID	Collector ID	Year	Make	Model	Color	Condition	Value
CJ04	1	48	Packard	Custom Eight Sedan	White	Fair	$15,000
JJ01	5	27	Ford	Model A	Black	Mint	$75,000
BB04	4	57	Chevrolet	Corvette	Red	Excellent	$42,000

7. Close the form, and save it with the proposed name *Cars*.

8. Create the report shown below for the Collectors table. The report sorts the records by the Era of Interest field, and it uses the Compact style. Also notice the title is Era of Interest.

9. Print the report, and then close it.

Era of Interest

Era of Interest	Firstname	Lastname	Collection Size
1920's	Jake	Johnson	3
1950's	Bob	Barker	7
1950's	Cindy	Johnson	42
1960's	Tammy	Olson	6
Early 1900's	Ed	Larkson	34

10. Create the report shown below for the Cars table. When adding the fields in the first Report Wizard screen, you will need to add them in the order shown on the report. For example, add the Model field first, the Year field second, the Condition field third, etc. This report is sorted on the Model field, and it uses the Compact style.

Models Report

Model	Year	Condition	Color	Value
Corvette	57	Excellent	Red	$42,000.00
Corvette	58	Excellent	Black	$35,000.00
Corvette	62	Excellent	Blue	$30,000.00
Corvette	58	Mint	Red and white	$65,000.00
Custom Eight Sedan	48	Fair	White	$15,000.00
Model A	27	Mint	Black	$75,000.00
Thunderbird	59	Good	Tan	$20,000.00

11. Print the report, and then close it.

12. Close the Classic Cars database when you have finished, and continue with the next lesson.

Getting Answers with Queries

In this lesson, you will learn how to set up and use queries. Queries are an essential part of any Access database. Queries allow you to extract and combine data from tables. You will learn how to specify criteria in queries to extract only the records you desire. You will create calculated fields, work with statistical functions, and sort and group query results.

In This Lesson

Case Study

The staff at Pinnacle Pet Care has used their new database for some time, and now they want answers to a variety of questions. For example,

- What is the current balance of each customer in California?

- Which customers have a current balance that is greater than $200?

- Which customers in California have a current balance that is greater than $200?

- What is the average amount of money that customers spend on cats and dogs?

Penny Johnson sets up queries in the Pinnacle Pet Care database to answer these questions. The following illustration shows a query, the Customers table, and the resulting recordset.

Field:	Firstname	Lastname	Phone	Current Balance
Table:	Customers	Customers	Customers	Customers
Sort:				Descending
Show:	☑	☑	☑	☑
Criteria:				>200

A *A query contains fields and criteria that are used to select records from a table.*

	Customer ID	Firstname	Lastname	Address	City	State	Zip	Phone	Last Visit	Current Balance
	1	Mark	Roth	760 Maple Avenue	Fremont	CA	94538-	(510) 234-9090	7/7/99	$235.00
	2	Tony	Simpson	312 York Lane	Richmond	CA	94804-	(510) 238-2233	9/7/99	$185.00
	3	Jason	Jones	2233 Crystal Street	San Mateo	CA	94403-	(415) 312-2312	7/15/99	$48.00
	4	Jacob	Samuels	2300 North Pratt Str	Atlanta	GA	30309-	(404) 367-8002	10/8/99	$250.50

	Firstname	Lastname	Phone	Current Balance
	Jacob	Samuels	(404) 367-8002	$250.50
	Mark	Roth	(510) 234-9090	$235.00

B *Access produces a recordset when the query is run.*

What Are Queries?

Queries are an essential part of any Access database. Most people use queries to get answers to questions and to extract data from one or more tables. When you run a query, Access creates a temporary table using the fields and criteria you specify in the query. The temporary table is known as a **recordset.** The recordset is composed of data from one or more tables in your database. A query's recordset can even be used as the basis for forms and reports. Thus, queries give you the ability to produce forms and reports using data from multiple tables.

Select Queries

Select queries are the most common type of query. Select queries let you selectively extract data from one or more tables in a database. When designing select queries, you specify the fields that you wish to include in the recordset. You can also specify **criteria** that are used to select records from the table(s) in your database. The following illustration shows the Customers table from the Pinnacle Pet Care database and the resulting recordset. Take a few moments to study the illustration.

Customer ID	Firstname	Lastname	Address	City	State	Zip	Phone	Last Visit	Current Balance
1	Mark	Roth	760 Maple Avenue	Fremont	CA	94538-	(510) 234-9090	7/7/99	$235.00
2	Tony	Simpson	312 York Lane	Richmond	CA	94804-	(510) 238-2233	9/7/99	$185.00
3	Jason	Jones	2233 Crystal Street	San Mateo	CA	94403-	(415) 312-2312	7/15/99	$48.00
4	Jacob	Samuels	2300 North Pratt Str	Atlanta	GA	30309-	(404) 367-8002	10/8/99	$250.50

Firstname	Lastname	Phone	Current Balance
Jacob	Samuels	(404) 367-8002	$250.50
Mark	Roth	(510) 234-9090	$235.00

A query is run that instructs Access to only choose the Firstname, Lastname, Phone, and Current Balance fields from the Customers table for those customers with a Current Balance > $200.

The query produces the recordset shown here. Notice that the recordset only includes the specified fields for customers with a Current Balance > $200.

Setting Up Queries

You can use the **Query Wizard** to assist you in setting up queries, or you can set them up yourself using the **query design grid.** The design grid gives you complete flexibility in determining the fields, criteria, and other options that you wish to use in the query. The following Quick Reference table describes how to display the Query window and how to add tables to the query. You must add table(s) to the Query window so that you can use the desired fields from the table(s) in the query.

Quick Reference

ADDING TABLES TO THE QUERY WINDOW

■ Open the desired database, and make sure the Queries button is pressed on the Objects bar.

■ Double-click the Create query in Design view option.

■ Choose a table that you want the query to extract data from in the Show Table box, and click Add.

■ Add any other tables from which you wish to extract data.

■ Click the Close button on the Show Table box.

In this exercise, you will begin setting up a query. You will display the Query window, and you will add the Customers table in the Pinnacle Pet Care database to the Query window.

Display the Query window

1. Start Access, and open the **Pinnacle Pet Care** database.

2. Click the **Queries** button on the Objects bar.

3. Double-click the **Create query in Design view** option.
   The Query window will appear, and the Show Table dialog box will be displayed. The Show Table dialog box lets you choose the table(s) that you wish to use in the query. In this exercise, you will add just the Customers table to the Query window.

TIP!

You can also double-click the table name.

4. Choose **Customers,** and click the **Add** button.
   A Customers field list will appear above the design grid. The field names in the list are taken from the Customers table. In a moment, you will use the Customers field list to add fields to the query.

5. Click the **Close** button on the Show Table dialog box.
   You won't be using the Pets table in this exercise.

Set Up the Window

6. Make sure that the Access window is maximized 🔲 and that the Query window is maximized within the Access window.

7. Follow these steps to adjust the size of the design grid and the Customers field list.

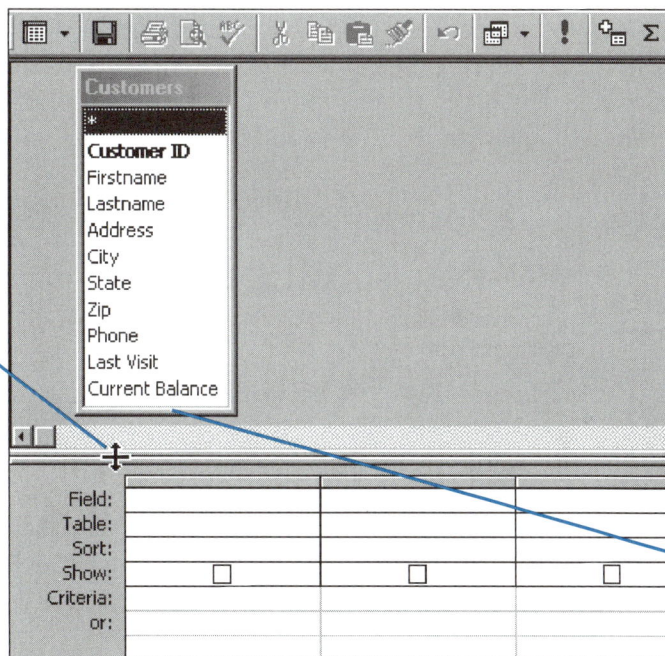

Ⓐ *Position the mouse pointer on the top border of the design grid and a double-headed arrow will appear.*

Ⓑ *Drag the border down to allocate more space to the top-half of the window.*

Ⓒ *If possible, drag the bottom border of the Customers field list down until all field names are visible.*

The Query Design Grid

The design grid appears when you begin setting up a new query. The design grid lets you specify the fields to include in the query. You can also use the design grid to specify criteria and other parameters that affect the query recordset. The following illustration displays the design grid and the recordset for the sample query shown. You will develop the query shown in the illustration as you progress through the next few exercises.

The Table row indicates the table from which each field is taken. In this example, all fields are taken from the Customers table.

*Fields such as **Firstname, Lastname, Phone,** and Current Balance are added to the columns of the design grid. These fields will be displayed in the recordset.*

Field:	Firstname	Lastname	Phone	Current Balance
Table:	Customers	Customers	Customers	Customers
Sort:		Ascending		
Show:	☑	☑	☑	☑
Criteria:				>200
or:				

*The **Sort** row lets you specify one or more fields for sorting the selected records. In this example, the recordset will be sorted in Ascending order (A-Z) by the Lastname field.*

You can use criteria to select records from the table(s). In this example, only customer records with a Current Balance greater than $200 will be selected.

The recordset includes customer records with a Current Balance greater than $200. Only the fields specified in the query appear in the recordset.

Firstname	Lastname	Phone	Current Balance
Mark	Roth	(510) 234-9090	$235.00
Jacob	Samuels	(404) 367-8002	$250.50

Adding Fields to the Design Grid

The first step in defining a query is to add fields to the design grid. The fields you add to the design grid will appear in the recordset. Once you have added fields to the design grid, you can specify sorting options, criteria, and other options that affect the recordset. The following Quick Reference table describes the techniques you can use to add fields to the design grid.

Quick Reference

ADDING FIELDS TO THE QUERY DESIGN GRID

Technique	Description
Double-click	You can add a single field to the design grid by double-clicking the desired field in the field list.
Drop-down list	You can add a single field by clicking in a field cell, clicking the drop-down button that appears, and then choosing the desired field from the drop-down menu.
Drag	You can add a single field or multiple fields to the design grid by dragging them from a field list to the desired cell in the design grid. You can select multiple fields prior to dragging by pressing and holding the (CTRL) key while clicking the desired field names in the field list.
All fields	You can add all fields to the design grid by double-clicking the asterisk * symbol at the top of the desired field list.

1. Follow these steps to add the Firstname field to the design grid.

A *Double-click the Firstname field in the field list and it will appear in the first cell of the design grid.*

B *Notice the **Table** row specifies that the field is taken from the Customers table. Knowing which table the field is taken from can be important especially when the same field name is used in more than one table.*

2. Now add the *Lastname, Phone,* and *Current Balance* fields to the design grid by double-clicking them on the field name list. The design grid should match the following illustration when you have finished adding the fields.

Field:	Firstname	Lastname	Phone	Current Balance
Table:	Customers	Customers	Customers	Customers
Sort:				
Show:	☑	☑	☑	☑
Criteria:				
or:				

Removing Fields from the Design Grid

You can remove fields from the design grid by clicking in the desired column and choosing **Edit→Delete Columns** from the menu bar. You may need to remove fields from time to time as you develop queries. Remember to use this technique if you make a mistake and add an incorrect field to the design grid.

1. Click anywhere in the Current Balance column in the design grid.

2. Choose **Edit→Delete Columns** from the menu bar, and the field will be removed.

3. Follow these steps to reinsert the Current Balance field using the drop-down list technique.

*Ⓐ Click in the empty Field box to the right of the Phone field.
A drop-down button will appear on the right side of the box.*

Field:	Firstname	Lastname	Phone	
Table:	Customers	Customers	Customers	Lastname
Sort:				Address
Show:	☑	☑	☑	City
Criteria:				State
or:				Zip
				Phone
				Last Visit
				Current Balance

Ⓑ Click the drop-down button and the field list from the Customers table will appear.

Ⓒ Scroll to the bottom of the list and choose Current Balance.

The Current Balance field should be returned to the grid. As you can see, there are several ways to add fields to the design grid. Once again, feel free to remove fields from the design grid whenever you make a mistake or wish to change the order of the fields in the grid.

Running Queries

You can run a query by clicking the Run 🔲 button on the Access toolbar. When you run a select query, Access selects records and fields from tables in your database and displays the recordset. You can navigate through the recordset or print it if desired. The recordset will always reflect the current data stored in the database.

Editing Data In a Recordset

When you run a select query, the recordset is connected to the underlying table(s) that the query is based upon. If you edit data in the recordset, then the data in the underlying tables is changed as well. However, most select queries are only used for viewing selective data.

Hands-On 3.4 **Run the Query**

1. Click the Run ▣ button on the Access toolbar.
   The query will run, and the recordset shown below will appear. Keep in mind that your query is quite basic. This query simply displays four fields from each record in the Customers table.

Firstname	Lastname	Phone	Current Balance
Mark	Roth	(510) 234-9090	$235.00
Tony	Simpson	(510) 238-2233	$185.00
Jason	Jones	(415) 312-2312	$48.00
Jacob	Samuels	(404) 367-8002	$250.50

2. Now continue with the next topic, where you will learn how to sort the query results.

Sorting the Query Results

You can instruct Access to sort the rows in a recordset using one or more fields as sort keys. For example, you may want to view the recordset with the largest current balances displayed first. You sort recordsets by setting the sort box to Ascending or Descending for one or more fields in the design grid. If you set the sort box for more than one field, then the first field is used as the primary sort key, followed by the next field, and so on.

Hands-On 3.5 **Sort the Results**

The recordset should be displayed from the previous exercise.

1. Notice that the records in the recordset do not appear to be sorted in any particular order.
   However, the records are actually sorted on the Customer ID field, which is the primary key for the Customers table. In the next few steps, you will set the sort key for the Lastname field in the design grid. You will run the query again, and the recordset will be sorted by last name with the Jones record first, followed by the Roth record, and so on.

2. Click the Design View ▣ button on the left end of the Access toolbar.
   The design grid will reappear. You can always use the view button to switch back and forth between the recordset and the design grid.

3. Follow these steps to set a sort key.

Field:	Firstname	Lastname	Phone	Current Balance
Table:	Customers	Customers	Customers	Customers
Sort:				
Show:	☑	Ascending	☑	☑
Criteria:		Descending		
or:		(not sorted)		

Ⓐ *Click in the Sort box for the Lastname field.*

Ⓑ *Click the drop-down button and choose* Ascending *from the list. The word Ascending will appear in the Sort box.*

(Continued on the next page)

4. Click the Run ▣ button, and the recordset shown below will appear.
Notice that the records are sorted by the Lastname field.

Firstname	Lastname	Phone	Current Balance
Jason	Jones	(415) 312-2312	$48.00
Mark	Roth	(510) 234-9090	$235.00
Jacob	Samuels	(404) 367-8002	$250.50
Tony	Simpson	(510) 238-2233	$185.00

5. Click the Design View ▣ button to display the design grid.

6. Follow these steps to remove the Lastname sort key and to set the sort order to descending based upon the Outstanding Balance field.

A *Click in the Sort box for the Lastname field.*

Field:	Firstname	Lastname	Phone	Current Balance
Table:	Customers	Customers	Customers	Customers
Sort:		Ascending ▼		Descending
Show:	☑	Ascending	☑	☑
Criteria:		Descending		
or:		(not sorted)		

B *Click the drop-down button and choose (not sorted). The Sort box will be cleared.*

C *Choose Descending as the sort order for the Current Balance field.*

7. Click the Run ▣ button, and the recordset shown below will appear.
Notice that the records with the largest Current Balance are displayed first.

Firstname	Lastname	Phone	Current Balance
Jacob	Samuels	(404) 367-8002	$250.50
Mark	Roth	(510) 234-9090	$235.00
Tony	Simpson	(510) 238-2233	$185.00
Jason	Jones	(415) 312-2312	$48.00

8. Click the Design View ▣ button to display the design grid.

Using Criteria to Select Records

One of the most important benefits of queries is that you can select specific records by specifying **criteria.** This gives you the ability to select the precise data you desire from a database. For example, you may want to know how many customers have an outstanding balance that is greater than $200. Or, perhaps you are interested in viewing only those records where the state is equal to CA (California). These and other questions are easily answered by specifying criteria in the query design grid.

Equality Criteria

You can use *equality criteria* to choose only those records where a field has a specific value. For example, you may want to display only those records where the state field is equal to CA. You accomplish this by entering the value that you want the field to equal in the Criteria row of the design grid. The following illustration shows how this is accomplished.

Field:	Firstname	Lastname	Phone	Current Balance	State
Table:	Customers	Customers	Customers	Customers	Customers
Sort:				Descending	
Show:	☑	☑	☑	☑	☑
Criteria:					CA
or:					

This is a **Criteria** *row.*

Entering CA *in the* State **Criteria** *box instructs Access to select only those records where the state is CA.*

As expected, only records where the state is CA appear in the recordset.

Firstname	Lastname	Phone	Current Balance	State
Mark	Roth	(510) 234-9090	$235.00	CA
Tony	Simpson	(510) 238-2233	$185.00	CA
Jason	Jones	(415) 312-2312	$48.00	CA

Comparison Criteria

You can use the comparison operators > (greater than), < (less than), >= (greater than or equal), <= (less than or equal), and NOT (not equal) when specifying criteria. Access will select only those records matching the criteria. For example, placing the criterion >200 in the Current Balance field instructs Access to select only records where the Current Balance is greater than 200.

The Show Check Box

The Show row in the design grid contains a check box ☑ for each field. You can prevent a field from displaying in the recordset by removing the check from the Show box. This can be useful in many situations. For example, in the preceding illustration, the State field is used to select only records where the state is equal to CA. The State field must be present in the design grid in order to specify this criteria. However, you may not want the State field to be displayed in the recordset. You could prevent the State field from being displayed in the recordset by removing the check from the State field in the design grid.

The design grid should be displayed from the previous exercise.

Use an Equality Criterion

1. Double-click the **State** field on the Customers field list to add the field to the design grid.
   The State field should be in the fifth column of the design grid.

2. Follow these steps to set an equality criterion for the State field.

   A *Click in the **Criteria** box for the State field.*   **B** *Type **CA** as shown here. You can type it in uppercase (CA) or lowercase (ca).*

Field:	Firstname	Lastname	Phone	Current Balance	State
Table:	Customers	Customers	Customers	Customers	Customers
Sort:				Descending	
Show:	☑	☑	☑	☑	☑
Criteria:					CA
or:					

   C *Click in the box below CA and Access will surround CA with quotation marks "CA". The quotation marks indicate that this is a text criterion (as opposed to a number or date).*

3. Click the Run ▣ button.
   The three records with the State field equal to CA should appear in the recordset.

4. Click the Design View ▣ button to display the design grid.

Use Comparison Criteria

5. Follow these steps to create a "greater than" comparison criterion for the Current Balance field.

Field:	Firstname	Lastname	Phone	Current Balance	State
Table:	Customers	Customers	Customers	Customers	Customers
Sort:				Descending	
Show:	☑	☑	☑	☑	☑
Criteria:				>200	

   A *Click in the **Criteria** box for the Current Balance field and type **>200**.*   **B** *Click in the **Criteria** box for the State field and delete the "CA" criterion.*

6. Click the Run ▣ button, to produce the recordset shown below.
   Notice that the current balance is greater than $200 for each record.

Firstname	Lastname	Phone	Current Balance	State
Jacob	Samuels	(404) 367-8002	$250.50	GA
Mark	Roth	(510) 234-9090	$235.00	CA

7. Click the Design View ▣ button again to display the design grid.

8. Change the >200 criterion to **<200** and run the query again.
   Only records with current balances less than $200 will appear in the recordset.

Uncheck the Show box

In the next few steps, you will prevent the State field from appearing in the recordset by removing the check from the Show box.

9. Click the Design View ![button] button to display the design grid.

10. Follow these steps to set up the query.

Field:	Firstname	Lastname	Phone	Current Balance	State
Table:	Customers	Customers	Customers	Customers	Customers
Sort:				Descending	
Show:	☑	☑	☑	☑	☐
Criteria:				<200	

Ⓐ *Make sure the* Current Balance *criterion is set to* <200.

Ⓑ *Click the* **Show** *check box for the* State *field to remove the check.*

11. Click the Run ![button] button and the State field will be removed from the recordset.

12. Take 10 minutes to experiment with the query you have been using. Try entering various criteria and perhaps adding and removing fields from the design grid. Continue with the next topic when you have finished experimenting.

Clearing the Design Grid

You can clear all entries from the design grid with the **Edit→Clear Grid** command. This command can be used to give you a "fresh start" when working in the design grid.

Hands-On 3.7 Clear the Grid and Add All Fields

1. If necessary, click the Design View ![button] button to display the design grid.

2. Choose **Edit→Clear Grid** to remove all fields from the grid.

3. Follow these steps to add all fields from the Customers table to the design grid.

Ⓐ *Double-click the asterisk * at the top of the* **Customers** *field list.*

Customers
*
Customer ID
Firstname
Lastname
Address
City
State
Zip
Phone
Last Visit
Current Balance

Ⓑ *Notice that a* Customers.* *entry is inserted in the grid. This entry indicates that all fields from the Customers table will be displayed when the query is run.*

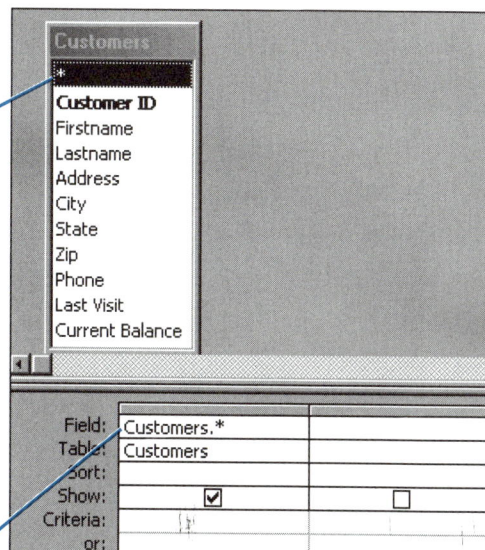

Field:	Customers.*	
Table:	Customers	
Sort:		
Show:	☑	☐
Criteria:		
or:		

(Continued on the next page)

4. Click the Run ![Run button] button. All records from the Customers table should appear in the recordset.

Use a Criterion to Select the Records

In the next few steps, you will add the Current Balance field to the design grid and specify a criterion for that field.

5. Click the Design View ![icon] button to display the design grid.

6. Follow these steps to add the Current Balance field to the grid and to specify a criterion.

Ⓐ *Double-click the Current Balance field on the Customers field list. The Current Balance will be added to the design grid as shown in the lower section of this illustration.*

Ⓑ *Enter the expression >100 in the Criteria box of the Current Balance field.*

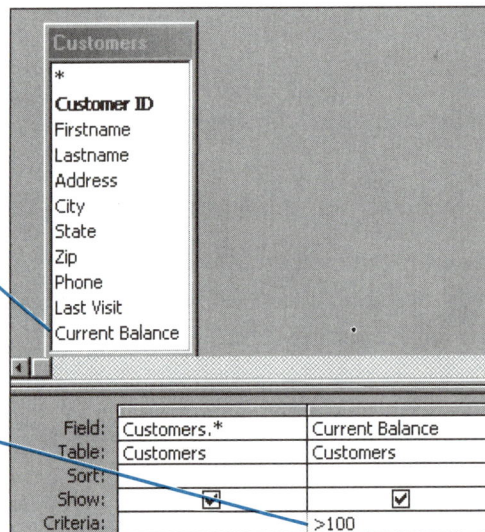

	Customers
	*
	Customer ID
	Firstname
	Lastname
	Address
	City
	State
	Zip
	Phone
	Last Visit
	Current Balance

Field:	Customers.*	Current Balance
Table:	Customers	Customers
Sort:		
Show:	☑	☑
Criteria:		>100

7. Run ![Run button] the query to produce the recordset shown in the following illustration.

Notice that the last two columns of the recordset contain a Customers.Current Balance *field and a* Field0 *field. This unusual nomenclature was used because the Current Balance field was included twice in the query design grid. It was included once as part of the Customers.* entry and again as a separate field in the second column. Access cannot display the same field name twice in a table or recordset, therefore, Access changed the names of the column headings in the recordset. You will correct this by removing the check from the Show box in the next few steps.*

Customer ID	Firstname	Lastname	Address	City	State	Zip	Phone	Last Visit	Customers.Curre	Field0
1	Mark	Roth	760 Maple Avenue	Fremont	CA	94538-	(510) 234-9090	7/7/99	$235.00	$235.00
2	Tony	Simpson	312 York Lane	Richmond	CA	94804-	(510) 238-2233	9/7/99	$185.00	$185.00
4	Jacob	Samuels	2300 North Pratt Str	Atlanta	GA	30309-	(404) 367-8002	10/8/97	$250.50	$250.50

8. Switch to Design View ![icon], and remove the check from the Show box of the Current Balance field. The design grid should match the example to the right.

Field:	Customers.*	Current Balance
Table:	Customers	Customers
Sort:		
Show:	☑	☐
Criteria:		>100

9. Run the query; only one Current Balance field will be visible.

The >100 criterion in the Current Balance field selects the appropriate records. However, the field is not displayed in the recordset because the Show box is unchecked.

10. Choose **File→Close** from the menu bar, and click the **Yes** button to save the query.

11. Type the name **Current Balance** in the Save As box, and click **OK.**

Compound Criteria

Thus far, you have worked with relatively simple queries containing one criterion. However, you will sometimes need to use more than one criterion. Criteria that are composed of two or more criteria are known as *compound criteria*. There are two types of compound criteria: *AND* criteria and *OR* criteria.

AND Criteria

AND criteria let you select records based on logical AND expressions. In the next exercise, you will use AND criteria to select records in the Pets table. For example, you will use an AND expression to select all records where the pet type is dog *and* the number of visits is greater than 5. With AND criteria, Access will only select records when all of the criteria are true.

OR Criteria

OR criteria allow you to select records based on logical OR expressions. For example, you will use an OR expression to select all records where the pet type is dog *or* the pet type is cat. With OR criteria, Access will select records if any of the criteria are true.

Setting up Compound Criteria

You set up compound criteria in the design grid. AND criteria are set up by placing two or more criterion in different fields within the same Criteria row. OR criteria are set up by placing two or more criteria on different rows within the design grid. The following illustration shows the compound criteria you will set up in the next exercise.

Field:	Pet Name	Pet Type	Last Visit	Expenditures	Number of Visits
Table:	Pets	Pets	Pets	Pets	Pets
Sort:					
Show:	☑	☑	☑	☑	☑
Criteria:		"dog"			>5

*In this example, the criterion "dog" and >5 are on the same **Criteria** row. This creates an AND condition. Only records where the Pet Type is dog and the Number of Visits > 5 will be chosen.*

In this example, the criteria are on different rows within the Pet Type field. This creates an OR condition as indicated by the or heading at the left end of the second Criteria row. All records where the Pet Type = dog or the Pet Type = cat will be chosen.

Field:	Pet Name	Pet Type	Last Visit	Expenditures	Number of Visits
Table:	Pets	Pets	Pets	Pets	Pets
Sort:					
Show:	☑	☑	☑	☑	☑
Criteria:		"dog"			
or:		"cat"			

Hands-On 3.8 Use Compound Criteria

In this exercise, you will set up a new query using the Pets table from the Pinnacle Pet Care database. You will use compound criteria to query the database in various ways.

Set Up the Query Window

1. Make sure the queries are displayed in the Database window.

2. Double-click the **Create query in Design view** option.

3. Choose **Pets** from the Show Table box, and click the **Add** button.

4. Click the **Close** button on the Show Table dialog box.

5. If necessary, maximize ⬜ the query window. Also, you may want to adjust the size of the design grid and the Pets field list to allow you to see the entire content of the Pets field list. You used this technique in the first exercise in this lesson with the Customers field list.

Create an AND Criterion

6. Double-click the **Pet Name**, **Pet Type**, **Last Visit**, **Expenditures**, and **Number of Visits** fields on the Pets field list to add those fields to the design grid.

7. Enter the criteria shown below into the Pet Type and Number of Visits boxes in the Criteria row.

Field:	Pet Name	Pet Type	Last Visit	Expenditures	Number of Visits
Table:	Pets	Pets	Pets	Pets	Pets
Sort:					
Show:	☑	☑	☑	☑	☑
Criteria:		"dog"			>5

8. Click the Run 🔲 button to produce the following recordset.
   Notice that each record has Dog as the Pet Type and that the Number of Visits is greater than 5.

Pet Name	Pet Type	Last Visit	Expenditures	Number of Visits
Wolfy	Dog	7/15/99	$450.00	7
Spike	Dog	10/8/99	$890.00	12

Create an OR Criterion

9. Switch to Design View 🔲, and remove the >5 criterion from the Number of Visits criteria box.

10. Add the cat criterion to the row below the dog criterion as shown below. It isn't necessary to type the quotation marks shown in the illustration. Access will add the quotation marks as soon as you click outside of the field after typing the criterion.

TIP!

When using OR criteria, you can use as many rows as necessary. Each row that you add creates one more condition in the OR expression.

Field:	Pet Name	Pet Type	Last Visit	Expenditures	Number of Visits
Table:	Pets	Pets	Pets	Pets	Pets
Sort:					
Show:	☑	☑	☑	☑	☑
Criteria:		"dog"			
or:		"cat"			

11. Click the Run ▣ button to produce the following recordset (although the sort order may be different than shown here).

Notice that all records have a Pet Type of Dog or Cat.

Pet Name	Pet Type	Last Visit	Expenditures	Number of Visits
Wolfy	Dog	7/15/99	$450.00	7
Dillon	Dog	7/7/99	$150.55	3
Max	Cat	9/7/99	$1,450.55	20
Stripes	Cat	7/15/99	$450.00	9
Tony	Cat	7/7/99	$145.00	6
Fetch	Dog	9/10/99	$345.00	3
Ben	Dog	10/8/99	$480.00	3
Spike	Dog	10/8/99	$890.00	12

Use a Combination of AND and OR Compound Criteria

12. Switch to Design View ▨, but do not change the "dog" and "cat" criteria.

13. Add the >5 criteria to the Number of Visits field as shown below.

This compound criteria will choose all records where the Pet Type is dog and *the Number of Visits is greater than 5* or *the Pet Type is cat* and *the Number of Visits is greater than 5.*

Field:	Pet Name	Pet Type	Last Visit	Expenditures	Number of Visits
Table:	Pets	Pets	Pets	Pets	Pets
Sort:					
Show:	☑	☑	☑	☑	☑
Criteria:		"dog"			>5
or:		"cat"			>5

14. Click the Run ▣ button to produce the following recordset.

Pet Name	Pet Type	Last Visit	Expenditures	Number of Visits
Wolfy	Dog	7/15/99	$450.00	7
Max	Cat	9/7/99	$1,450.55	20
Stripes	Cat	7/15/99	$450.00	9
Tony	Cat	7/7/99	$145.00	6
Spike	Dog	10/8/99	$890.00	12

15. Switch to Design view and take 10 minutes to experiment with compound criteria.

Be creative; query the Pets table for answers to any questions that may come to mind.

16. When you have finished experimenting, choose **File→Close** from the menu bar, and click the **Yes** button when Access asks if you want to save the query.

17. Type the name **Compound Criteria** in the Save As box, and click **OK**.

Calculated Fields

Access lets you create *calculated fields* within queries. Calculated fields perform calculations using values from other fields within the query or from fields in the underlying table(s). For example, in the next exercise, you will set up a new query that will be based upon the Pets table. The Pets table contains an Expenditures field that represents the total expenditures for a particular pet. The Pets table also contains a Number of Visits field that represents the total number of visits by the pet. You will create a calculated field within the query named Expenditures Per Visit. The Expenditures Per Visit will be calculated as the Expenditures divided by the Number of Visits. The following illustration shows the design grid with the Pet Name and Pet Type fields and the Expenditures Per Visit calculated field.

Field:	Pet Name	Pet Type	Expenditures Per Vis
Table:	Pets	Pets	
Sort:			
Show:	☑	☑	☑
Criteria:			

Expenditures Per Visit is a calculated field, and it is too wide to be completely visible in the cell. The complete content of the cell is Expenditures Per Visit: [Expenditures]/[Number of Visits].

The following illustration discusses the syntax that must be used with calculated fields.

A descriptive name for the calculated field is entered into an empty field cell. You can use spaces in the name.

A colon : must follow the name. The colon identifies the field as a calculated field.

*An expression follows the colon. The expression can include field names, numbers, and operators such as +, -, *, and /. The various parts of the expression are surrounded with square brackets.*

Expenditures Per Visit: [Expenditures]/[Number of Visits]

The Zoom Dialog Box

Calculated field expressions can be quite long and complex. For this reason, you may not be able to see the entire expression as you enter it in a cell. Fortunately, Access provides a Zoom command that displays a Zoom dialog box. When you enter the desired expression into the Zoom dialog box, you can see the entire expression as it is entered. In the following exercise, you will use the Zoom dialog box to enter an expression. You display the Zoom dialog box by right-clicking the cell where the expression will be entered and choosing Zoom from the pop-up menu.

Hands-On 3.9 Create a Calculated Field

The Queries section of the Database window should be displayed from the previous exercise.

1. Create a new query in Design view, and add the **Pets** table to the query.

2. Close the **Show Tables** dialog box.

3. Add the **Pet Name** and **Pet Type** fields to the design grid.

4. Follow these steps to display the Zoom dialog box.

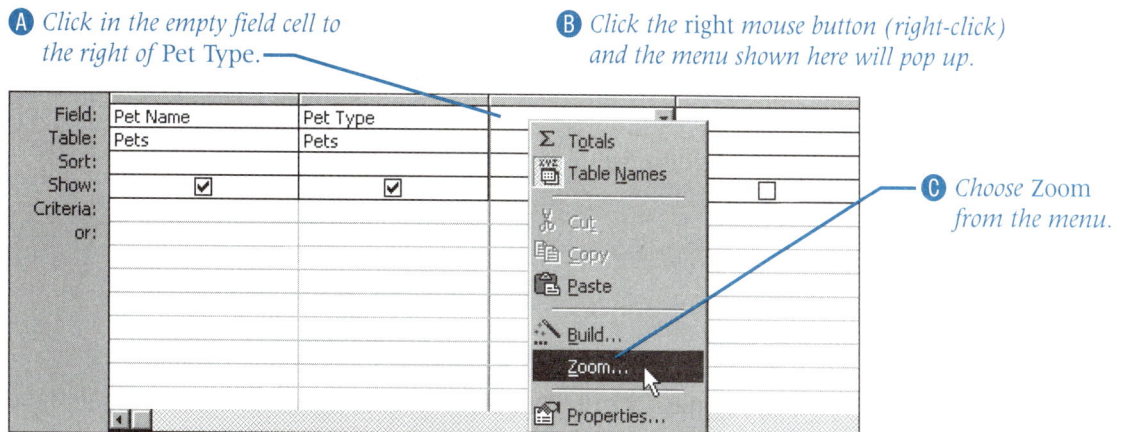

Ⓐ *Click in the empty field cell to the right of* Pet Type.

Ⓑ *Click the* right *mouse button (right-click) and the menu shown here will pop up.*

Field:	Pet Name	Pet Type	
Table:	Pets	Pets	
Sort:			
Show:	☑	☑	☐
Criteria:			
or:			

Σ Totals
Table Names
✂ Cut
Copy
Paste
Build...
Zoom...
Properties...

Ⓒ *Choose* Zoom *from the menu.*

5. Enter the calculated field expression shown in the following illustration into the Zoom box. Make sure you enter the expression exactly as shown. In particular, make sure you use a colon : (not a semicolon ;), correctly spell the field names, use the correct open and closed brackets [ ], and use the forward slash / symbol to represent division. Access is lenient when it comes to spaces, so you can omit the spaces that come after the colon and before and after the forward slash / if you desire.

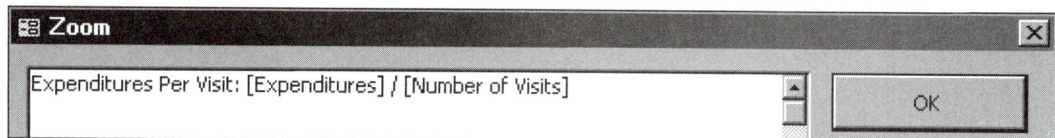

Zoom ✕

Expenditures Per Visit: [Expenditures] / [Number of Visits]

OK

6. Click **OK** to insert the expression in the field.

7. Use the ← and → keys on your keyboard to scroll through the expression within the cell. Make sure the syntax is correct as shown above. If necessary, you can edit the expression within the cell or redisplay the Zoom dialog box and make any necessary changes.

8. Click the Run button to produce the following recordset.
The numbers shown in the Expenditures Per Visit field represent the average expenditure for each pet on each visit. Notice the excessive number of decimal places that are displayed in the calculated field. In the next exercise, you will reduce the number of displayed decimal places by changing one of the properties of the Expenditures Per Visit field.

Pet Name	Pet Type	Expenditures
Max	Cat	72.5275
Stripes	Cat	50
Tony	Cat	24.1666666667
Wolfy	Dog	64.2857142857
Dillon	Dog	50.1833333333
Fetch	Dog	115
Ben	Dog	160
Spike	Dog	74.1666666667
Bugs	Rabbit	150.125

9. Switch to Design View , and continue with the next topic.

Modifying Query Properties

The Properties ![icon] button on the Access toolbar displays the Properties dialog box. You can use the Properties dialog box to change the properties of any Access object, including fields within queries. Properties can affect the appearance and format of objects. For example, in the following exercise, you will set the Format property of the Expenditures Per Visit field to Currency. The Currency format will reduce the number of displayed decimal places in the recordset.

Hands-On 3.10 Set the Format Property

The query design grid should be displayed from the previous exercise.

1. Click in the **Expenditures Per Visit** box, and then click the Properties ![icon] button on the toolbar.
   The Field Properties dialog box will appear.

2. Follow these steps to set the format of this field to Currency.
   When the query is run, the Currency format will display a dollar sign and two decimal places in the Expenditures Per Visit field.

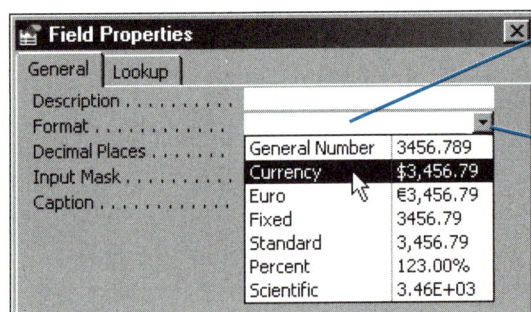

Ⓐ *Click in the **Format** box.*

Ⓑ *Click the drop-down button and choose Currency.*

Ⓒ *Click the Close ✕ button to close the **Field Properties** box.*

3. Click the Run ![icon] button.
   The numbers in the Expenditures Per Visit field should now be formatted with the Currency format, which includes a dollar sign and two decimal places.

4. Switch to Design View ![icon].

Insert a Criterion

5. Click in the Criteria box for the Pet Type field, and type **dog** as shown below.

Field:	Pet Name	Pet Type	Expenditures Per Vis
Table:	Pets	Pets	
Sort:			
Show:	✔	✔	✔
Criteria:		dog	

6. Click the Run ![icon] button.
   The Pet Name, Pet Type, and Expenditures Per Visit will be displayed for records where the Pet Type is Dog. As you can see, Access allows you to combine criteria, calculated fields, and other parameters within a query.

7. Choose **File→Close** to close the query, and save it as **Expenditures Per Visit.**

Statistical Functions

Access provides built-in statistical functions for calculating statistical information within a query. The built-in statistical functions include SUM (summation), AVG (average), MIN (minimum), MAX (maximum), COUNT, VAR (variance), FIRST, and LAST. For example, you could use the AVG function to compute the average expenditures on pets, or you may want to use the COUNT function to count the number of dogs that attend the Pinnacle Pet Care clinic.

The Total Row

To use the statistical functions, you must first click the **Totals** button to display a Total row in the query design grid. Once the Total row is displayed, you can choose statistical function(s) for the desired field(s) in the query. Queries that use statistical functions will normally have just one or two fields.

*Statistical functions are entered in the **Total** row of the query design grid.*

Field:	Expenditures
Table:	Pets
Total:	Avg
Sort:	
Show:	☑
Criteria:	

Hands-On 3.11 Use Statistical Functions

1. Set up a new query in Design view, and add the **Pets** table to the query.

2. Close the Show Tables dialog box.

3. Add the **Expenditures** field to the design grid.

4. Click the Totals ∑ button on the toolbar, and a Total row will appear below the Table row.
   The Total row lets you choose statistical functions and set grouping for fields. You will learn about grouping later in this lesson.

5. Follow these steps to choose the Average function for the Expenditures field.

Field:	Expenditures
Table:	Pets
Total:	Avg
Sort:	
Show:	☑
Criteria:	

   Ⓐ *Click in the **Total** box and a drop-down button will appear.*

   Ⓑ *Click the drop-down button and choose* Avg.

   When you run the query, Access will determine the average expenditure for all pets. Access will display a single cell in the recordset containing the result of the average calculation.

6. Click the Run ▫ button.
   The result should be $551.29. In other words, each pet has been responsible for an average of $551.29 in revenue.

7. Switch to Design View ▫, and click in the **Totals** box that currently contains the Avg function.

8. Click the drop-down button, scroll to the top of the list, and choose **Sum.**

9. Run ▫ the query again. This time the result should be $4,961.60.
   This number represents the summation of the expenditures for all pets.

10. Switch to Design View ▫, and continue with the next topic.

Using Criteria with Statistical Functions

You can combine criteria with statistical functions to refine your statistical calculations. For example, imagine you are interested in determining the total expenditures for dogs at Pinnacle Pet Care. The answer can be found by summing the Expenditures of all records where the Pet Type is dog. The following illustration shows how this is expressed in the design grid.

*The Pet Type field is added to the design grid and the Where function is chosen in the **Total** cell.*

The Expenditures field uses the Sum function.

The word dog is entered in the criteria cell for the Pet Type field.

Field:	Expenditures	Pet Type
Table:	Pets	Pets
Total:	Sum	Where
Sort:		
Show:	☑	☐
Criteria:		dog

These settings will sum the expenditures of all records where the Pet Type is equal to dog.

Hands-On 3.12 Use Criteria with Statistical Functions

1. Double-click the **Pet Type** field on the Pets field list to add it to the design grid.

2. Follow these steps to specify criteria for the Pet Type field.

Field:	Expenditures	Pet Type
Table:	Pets	Pets
Total:	Sum	Where
Sort:		
Show:	☑	☐
Criteria:		dog

Ⓐ *Click in the **Total** box, click the drop-down button that appears, scroll to the bottom of the list, and choose Where.*

Ⓑ *Click in the **Criteria** box and type **dog**.*

3. Run the query. The result should be $2,315.55.
   This number represents the total expenditures on dogs.

4. Switch back to Design view, and continue with the last topic.

Using Grouping with Statistical Functions

The Total row in the design grid has a Group By option that can be used in conjunction with statistical functions. If you choose Group By for a field and run the query, then Access will group all records together that have the same value in the Group By field. For example, if the Pet Type field is set to Group By, then all records that have cat as the pet type will be in one group. Likewise, all records with a pet type of dog will be in another group. If you are performing a statistical calculation as well, then the statistical calculation will be performed on each group. For example, if you use the Sum function to calculate the expenditures for the groups mentioned above, then the total expenditures for cats will be calculated, as will the total expenditures for dogs.

1. Follow these steps to set grouping for the Pet Type field.

A *Click in the Total box, click the drop-down button, scroll up, and choose* Group By.

Field:	Expenditures	Pet Type
Table:	Pets	Pets
Total:	Sum	Group By
Sort:		
Show:	☑	☑
Criteria:		

B *Click in the Criteria box and delete the dog criteria.*

C *Make sure the Show box is checked.*

2. Run the query to produce the following recordset.
   The recordset displays the total expenditures for each pet type.

SumOfExpend	Pet Type
$2,045.55	Cat
$2,315.55	Dog
$600.50	Rabbit

3. Switch back to Design view.

4. Practice using all of the querying techniques you have learned in this lesson.

5. When you have finished practicing, close the query, and save it as **Expenditures by Pet Type.**

6. Now use the **File→Close** command again to close the Pinnacle Pet Care database.

7. Continue with the end-of-lesson questions and exercises on the following pages.

Concepts Review

True/False Questions

1. Criteria determine the records that are selected by a query. TRUE FALSE

2. The query design grid is where you define a query. TRUE FALSE

3. You can add fields to the design grid by double-clicking the desired fields on the field list(s) above the design grid. TRUE FALSE

4. You can add all fields to the design grid by double-clicking any field in the field list. TRUE FALSE

5. Changing data in the recordset has no impact on the underlying data in the table(s) that the query is based upon. TRUE FALSE

6. You must type criteria in the same case (uppercase or lowercase) as the data in the tables you are querying or Access will not select the desired records. TRUE FALSE

7. If a field has been entered into the design grid, then there is no way to prevent the field from appearing in the recordset. TRUE FALSE

8. The two types of compound criteria are Sum and Avg. TRUE FALSE

Multiple-Choice Questions

1. Which of the following commands can be used to remove fields from the design grid?
   a. Field→Remove
   b. Edit→Delete Columns
   c. Edit→Delete Rows
   d. File→Delete Columns

2. Which of the following symbols is used to represent greater than in query criteria?
   a. <
   b. >
   c. <=
   d. >=

3. Which of the following commands is used to clear the design grid?
   a. File→Clear All
   b. File→Clear Grid
   c. Edit→Clear Grid
   d. The grid cannot be cleared.

4. Which symbol(s) must be placed after the field name when creating a calculated field?
   a. A colon :
   b. A semicolon ;
   c. Parenthesis ( )
   d. Brackets [ ]

Skill Builders

Skill Builder 3.1 Use Comparison Criteria and Compound Criteria

In this exercise, you will use comparison criteria and compound criteria to query the Customers table in the Tropical Getaways database.

1. Open the Tropical Getaways database on your exercise diskette, and click the **Queries** button on the Objects bar.

2. Double-click the **Create query in Design view** option.

3. Choose **Customers** in the Show Table box, and click the **Add** button.

4. Click the **Close** button to close the Show Table dialog box.

5. If necessary, maximize the Query window, and adjust the height of the design grid and the Customers field list box.

6. Add the **Firstname**, **Lastname**, and **Profile** fields to the design grid by double-clicking them on the Customers field list.

7. Type the word **adventure** in the Criteria box of the Profile field as shown below.

Field:	Firstname	Lastname	Profile
Table:	Customers	Customers	Customers
Sort:			
Show:	✔	✔	✔
Criteria:			adventure

8. Run 🔲 the query. Only records with the Adventure profile will be displayed, as shown below.

Firstname	Lastname	Profile
Debbie	Thomas	Adventure
Ted	Wilkins	Adventure
Victor	Thomas	Adventure

9. Switch back to Design 📝 view.

10. Add the **State** field to the design grid.

11. Set the criteria for the State field to **TX** and the sort order of the Lastname field to **Ascending** as shown below.

Field:	Firstname	Lastname	Profile	State
Table:	Customers	Customers	Customers	Customers
Sort:		Ascending		
Show:	✔	✔	✔	✔
Criteria:			"adventure"	TX

(Continued on the next page)

12. Run the query. Only records where the profile is Adventure *and* the state is TX will be displayed, as shown below.

Firstname	Lastname	Profile	State
Debbie	Thomas	Adventure	TX
Ted	Wilkins	Adventure	TX

13. Close the query, and save it as **Adventure Profiles.**

Skill Builder 3.2 **Nest Calculated Fields**

In this exercise, you will use calculated fields in the Tropical Getaways database.

1. Set up a new query in Design view, and add the Trips table to the query.

2. Close the Show Tables dialog box.

3. Add the **Destination**, **Category**, and **Cost** fields to the design grid.

4. Set the Sort box for the Category field to **Ascending.**

5. Follow these steps to display the Zoom box for a new calculated field.

🅐 *Click in the empty field cell to the right of the Cost field.*

🅑 *Click the right mouse button (right-click) and the menu shown here will pop up.*

🅒 *Choose* **Zoom** *from the menu.*

Field:	Destination	Category	Cost		Σ Totals
Table:	Trips	Trips	Trips		Table Names
Sort:		Ascending			
Show:	☑	☑	☑		✂ Cut
Criteria:					Copy
or:					Paste
					Build...
					Zoom...
					Properties...

6. Enter the expression shown below into the Zoom box. Make sure you type the expression exactly as shown, including the colon after the word *Duration*.
When you run the query, this expression will calculate the duration of each trip. You can perform calculations using dates in Access and Excel.

Zoom

Duration: [Return Date] - [Departure Date]

7. Click **OK.** If necessary, use the left arrow and right arrow keys on your keyboard to check your new calculated field for errors. Correct any errors that you find.

8. Run the query to produce the following recordset.

Destination	Category	Cost	Duration
Baja California	Adventure	$2,900.00	10
Rocky Mountains	Adventure	$2,190.00	16
Swiss Alps	Adventure	$3,500.00	26
Amazon Jungle Trek	Adventure	$7,765.00	38
Kenyan Safari	Adventure	$6,600.00	30
Hawaii	Family	$5,300.00	8
Orlando	Family	$3,400.00	6
Hawaii	Leisure	$4,500.00	10
Caribbean Cruise	Leisure	$2,390.00	9

In the next few steps, you will add another calculated field that calculates the average daily cost of each trip. The average daily cost will be calculated as the Cost / Duration. This new calculated field will use the Duration calculated field as part of the calculation. Access allows you to "nest" calculated fields in this manner.

9. Switch to Design view.

10. Right-click in the empty cell to the right of the Duration cell, and choose **Zoom** from the pop-up menu.

11. Enter the following expression into the Zoom box.

⊞ Zoom

Cost per day: [Cost] / [Duration]

12. Click **OK** to insert the Cost per day calculated field into the cell.

13. Run the query to produce the following recordset.
Notice that the Cost per day numbers are not formatted with the Currency format. You will correct this in the next few steps.

Destination	Category	Cost	Duration	Cost per day
Baja California	Adventure	$2,900.00	10	290
Rocky Mountains	Adventure	$2,190.00	16	136.875
Swiss Alps	Adventure	$3,500.00	26	134.615384615
Amazon Jungle Trek	Adventure	$7,765.00	38	204.342105263
Kenyan Safari	Adventure	$6,600.00	30	220
Hawaii	Family	$5,300.00	8	662.5
Orlando	Family	$3,400.00	6	566.666666667
Hawaii	Leisure	$4,500.00	10	450
Caribbean Cruise	Leisure	$2,390.00	9	265.555555556

(Continued on the next page)

14. Switch to Design view.

15. Right-click on the Cost per day field, and choose **Properties** from the pop-up menu.

16. Click in the Format box, click the drop-down button, and choose **Currency.**

17. Close ☒ the Properties box.

18. Run the query. The Cost per day numbers should be formatted as Currency with two decimal places.

19. Close the query, and save it as **Cost per day.**

Skill Builder 3.3 Use Statistical Functions

In this exercise, you will create a query to perform statistical calculations in the Tropical Getaways database.

1. Create a new query that uses the Trips table.

2. Add the **Cost** field to the design grid.

3. Display the Total row by clicking the Totals Σ button on the toolbar.

4. Choose the **Avg** function in the Total box, as shown below.

Field:	Cost
Table:	Trips
Total:	Avg
Sort:	
Show:	☑
Criteria:	

5. Run the query. The average cost of a trip should be calculated as $4,282.78.

6. Switch to Design view.

7. Add the **Category** field to the design grid.
   The Total box will automatically be set to Group By as shown below. When you run the query, the Avg function in the Cost field will calculate the average cost for each category of trip.

Field:	Cost	Category
Table:	Trips	Trips
Total:	Avg	Group By
Sort:		
Show:	☑	☑
Criteria:		

8. Run the query to produce the following recordset.

AvgOfCost	Category
$4,591.00	Adventure
$4,350.00	Family
$3,445.00	Leisure

9. Close the query, and save it as **Cost by Category.**

10. Close the Tropical Getaways database.

Assessment

Assessment 3.1 Create Queries

1. Open the **Classic Cars** database.

2. Create a new query, and add the **Collectors** table to the query.

3. Set up the query to produce the recordset shown below. Notice that this query simply chooses the indicated fields and sorts the records in descending order by Collection Size.

Firstname	Lastname	Era of Interest	Collection Size
Cindy	Johnson	1950's	42
Ed	Larkson	Early 1900's	34
Bob	Barker	1950's	7
Tammy	Olson	1960's	6
Jake	Johnson	1920's	3

4. Run the query, print the recordset, close the query, and save it as **Collection Sizes.**

5. Create a new query, and add the **Cars** table to the query.

6. Set up the query to produce the recordset shown below. Notice that this query only selects records where the model is **Corvette** and the condition is **Excellent.** The query also sorts the records by Value, with the largest values appearing first.

Make	Model	Year	Color	Condition	Value
Chevrolet	Corvette	57	Red	Excellent	$42,000.00
Chevrolet	Corvette	58	Black	Excellent	$35,000.00
Chevrolet	Corvette	62	Blue	Excellent	$30,000.00

7. Run the query, print the recordset, close the query, and save it as **Excellent Corvettes.**

8. Create a new query, and add the **Cars** table to the query.

9. Set up the query to produce the recordset shown in the following illustration. Notice that this query calculates the average value of each group of models. In other words, the query groups the records on the Model field and then calculates the average value of each group. The query also sorts the records by Value, with the largest values appearing first.

Model	AvgOfValue
Model A	$75,000.00
Corvette	$43,000.00
Thunderbird	$20,000.00
Custom Eight Sedan	$15,000.00

10. Run the query, and then adjust the width of the Model column as shown in the preceding illustration to fit the widest entry in the column. You can accomplish this by double-clicking the border between the Model and AvgOfValue column headings.

11. Print the recordset, close the query, and save it as **Average Value of Model Groups.**

12. Close the Classic Cars database when you have finished, and exit from Access.

Relationships, Hyperlinks, and Customizing Objects

Access provides tools, such as the AutoForm tool and Wizards, to help you easily create forms and reports. However, many forms and reports require customization. Design view is available for forms, reports, queries, and other objects to enable you to customize the objects to suit your specific needs. In this lesson, you will customize both forms and reports. In addition, you will set up queries that select data from multiple tables. These queries will also contain pop-up box criteria that prompt the user to enter a criteria range. These queries will be used as the basis for reports. Hyperlinks are also introduced in this lesson. Hyperlinks allow you to jump between database objects or to pages on the World Wide Web.

In This Lesson

Case Study

The office staff at Pinnacle Pet Care has asked Al Smith to include the pet owner's names and phone numbers on the Pets form. This way, the owner's name will be visible when the staff members view the record for a pet. In addition, the staff has asked Al to include links on the Pets form and the Customers form to allow them to easily switch back and forth between the forms. Al also wants to create an Overdue for Visit report that will allow the staff to easily call customers who have not visited the clinic in awhile.

This form displays data from both the Pets and Customers Tables. The fields from the Customers table are "ghosted out" to prevent data entry from occurring.

New Pets

Pet ID	DG13		Firstname	Mark
Pet Name	Dillon		Lastname	Roth
Pet Type	Dog		Phone	(510) 234-9090
Breed	Mutt			
Gender	Male			GoTo Customers Form
Color	Black			Overdue For Visit
Date of Birth	10/5/94			
Last Visit	7/7/99			
Expenditures	$150.55			
Number of Visits	3			
Customer ID	1			

Record: |◄ ◄ 1 ► ►| ►* of 9

When you click a hyperlink, another form or report is opened.

The second hyperlink displays the **Overdue for Visit** *report, which is based upon a query. The query displays a pop up box requesting user input. The resulting report displays only those records where the Last Visit date is prior to the date entered in the pop-up box.*

Enter Parameter Value

Before which date?

9/1/99

[OK] [Cancel]

Overdue For Visit

Last Visit	Pet Name	Pet Type	Firstname	Lastname	Phone
7/15/99	Wolfy	Dog	Jason	Jones	(415) 312-2312
7/7/99	Dillon	Dog	Mark	Roth	(510) 234-9090
7/15/99	Stripes	Cat	Jason	Jones	(415) 312-2312
7/7/99	Tony	Cat	Mark	Roth	(510) 234-9090

Relationships

In a properly designed Access database, each type of data is stored in a separate table. For example, all customer data is stored in a Customers table. Storing data in separate tables is essential if you want to create a "clean" and flexible database system. However, it is also important to have a mechanism that allows you to "bring the data back together." For example, you may need to create a report that displays data from both the Customers and Pets tables. In order to accomplish this, you must create a relationship between the tables. Relationships determine how the records in one table are related to the records in another table. For example, each pet in the Pinnacle Pet Care database is related to a customer in the Customers table.

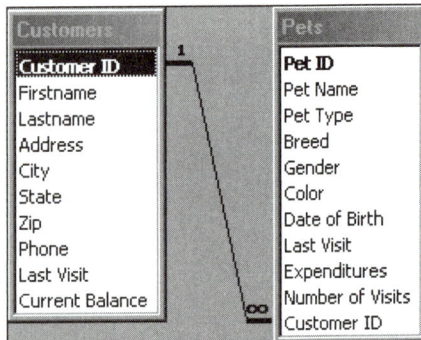

*The relationship between the **Customers** and **Pets** tables is established through the Customer ID field, which appears in both tables. Each customer can have many pets. Thus, a one-to-many relationship will be established between the tables.*

Establishing Table Relationships

You create relationships between tables by matching key fields in the tables. The key fields are typically the *primary key* in one table and a *foreign key* in the other table. The key fields typically have the same name and they must have the same data type. For example, the relationship used in the illustration above matches the CustomerID field in the Customers table with the CustomerID field in the Pets table. The CustomerID field determines the relationship that the two tables have with one another. The primary purpose of the relationship is to synchronize the records. For example, imagine that you create a report that lists each pet in the database along with the pet owner. In this example, the relationship between the CustomerID fields in the tables will ensure that the proper customer is displayed for each pet.

Enforcing Referential Integrity

When you create a relationship, Access will give you the option of enforcing referential integrity between the tables. Referential integrity will prevent you from using a value in the foreign key of one table unless the same value exists as a primary key in the other table. For example, in the Pinnacle Pet Care database, referential integrity will allow you to enter a CustomerID in the Pets table only if that CustomerID has been used in the Customers table. In other words, referential integrity will ensure that every pet is associated with a customer. Referential integrity will also prevent you from deleting a customer record from the Customers table if a record in the Pets table uses that CustomerID.

ESTABLISHING RELATIONSHIPS

To establish table relationships:

- Open the desired database and click the Relationships ⊞ button or choose *Tools→Relationships* from the menu bar.

- Use the Show Table box to add the tables between which you wish to establish relationships.

- Close the Show Table box.

- Drag the field that will be used to establish the relationship from one table to the field that it will be linked to in another table.

- If desired, use the Join button to change the join or relationship type.

- If desired, use the Enforce Referential Integrity box to enforce referential integrity.

- Click the *Create* button to create the relationship and then close the Relationships window.

Hands-On 4.1 Establish a Relationship and Enforce Referential Integrity

In this exercise, you will establish a relationship between the Customers and Pets tables in the Pinnacle Pet Care database.

1. Start Access and open the Pinnacle Pet Care database.

2. Click the Relationships ⊞ button on the Access toolbar.
   The Relationships window will open and the Show Table box will appear.

3. Choose the Customers table and click the **Add** button.
   The Customers table will be added to the Relationships window.

4. Now add the Pets table to the Relationships window and close the Show Table box.

5. Follow these steps to adjust the size of the Customers and Pets field lists.

Ⓐ *Position the mouse pointer on the bottom edge of the* **Customers** *field list and a double-headed arrow will appear.*

Ⓑ *Drag the bottom edge of the list down until all fields are visible.*

Ⓒ *Extend the* **Pets** *field list until all fields are visible.*

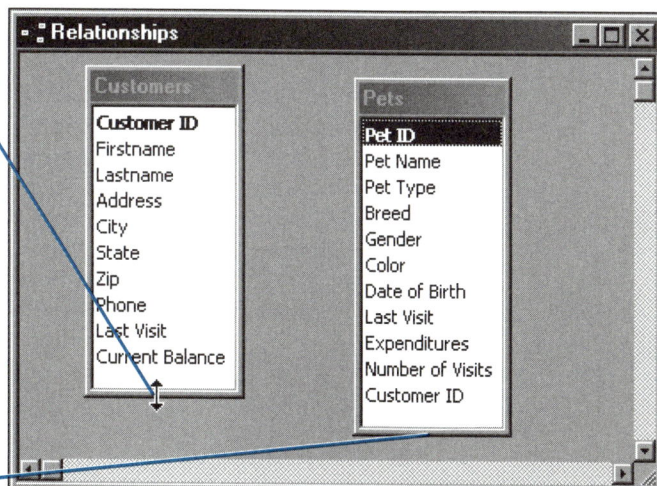

(Continued on the next page)

6. Follow these steps to establish a relationship between the Customer ID fields.

Ⓐ *Position the mouse pointer on the* Customer ID *field in the **Customers** table and press and hold the left mouse button.*

Ⓑ *Drag the mouse pointer until it is over the* Customer ID *field in the **Pets** table and a rectangular icon will be visible, as shown here.*

Ⓒ *Release the mouse button, and the **Edit Relationships** box will appear.*

The Edit Relationships box lets you choose the desired relationship type. The default relationship type is one-to-many, which is the most common type of relationship.

7. Follow these steps to enforce referential integrity and to examine the options in the Edit Relationships box.

Ⓐ *Check this box to* Enforce Referential Integrity.

Ⓑ *Notice this check box (but don't check it). If the **Cascade Update Related Fields** box were checked, then Access would automatically change the values in the Customer ID fields in the Pets table, but only if the corresponding Customer IDs were changed in the Customers table. If the box is unchecked, then you cannot change Customer IDs in the Customers table.*

Ⓒ *Notice this check box (but don't check it). If the **Cascade Delete Related Records** box were checked, then Access would automatically delete records in the Pets table when the corresponding Customer record in the Customers table was deleted. If the box is unchecked, you cannot delete records from the Customers table.*

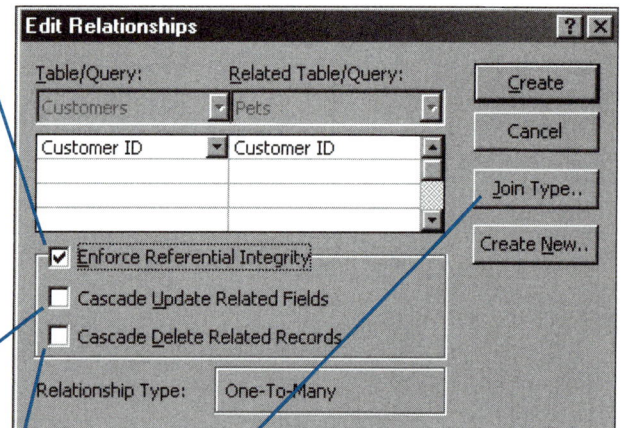

Ⓓ *The **Join Type** button is used to choose other types of relationships when a one-to-many relationship is not acceptable.*

8. Click the **Create** button to complete the relationship.
A join line will connect the Customer ID fields in the tables.

9. Follow these steps to understand the relationship.

Ⓐ *Notice that the* Customer ID *field in the* **Customers** *table is marked with a 1 symbol. This symbol indicates that this is the* one *side of the relationship. In other words, each Customer ID in the Customers table will be unique. There will only be one occurrence of each Customer ID in the Customers table.* ——

Ⓑ *Notice that the* Customer ID *field in the* **Pets** *table is marked with an infinity symbol (∞). This symbol indicates that this is the* many *side of the relationship. There can be many records in the* **Pets** *table with the same Customer ID. In other words, many pets can have the same owner/Customer ID.* ——

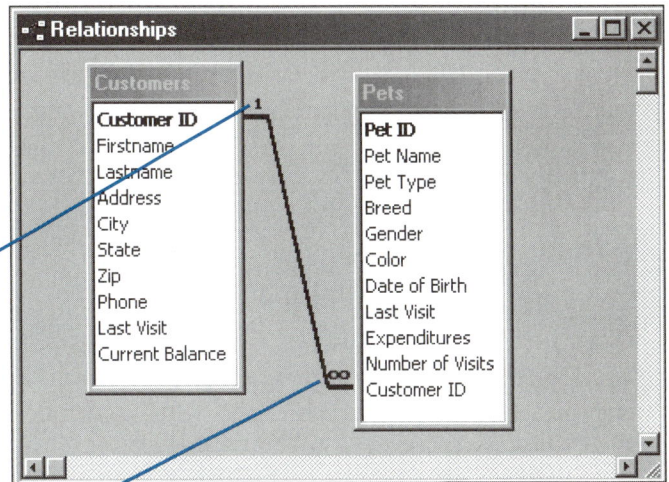

The relationship is now established, and it can be used to help you develop queries, forms, and reports.

10. Leave the Relationships window open and continue with the next topic.

Printing Relationships

The **File→Print Relationships** command is available whenever the Relationships window is open. When you choose this command, Access prepares a report that displays the same relationships that are displayed in the Relationships window. You can then print the relationships by clicking the Print button on the Access toolbar.

Hands-On 4.2 Print Relationships

The Relationships window should be displayed from the previous exercise.

1. Choose **File→Print Relationships** from the menu bar.
   Access will require a few moments to prepare the report.

2. If desired, click the Print 🖨 button on the toolbar to print the report.

3. Close the report window without saving the report.

4. Close the Relationships window and click **Yes** if Access asks you to save the changes to the Relationships.

The Form Wizard

The Form Wizard guides you step-by-step through the creation of a form. You can choose the fields to include in the form, various layout options, and a design style for the form. Unlike the AutoForm tool, the Form Wizard gives you flexibility when setting up a form. The Form Wizard is initiated by choosing the *Create form by using Wizard* option in the Forms section of the Access database window.

Using Fields from Multiple Tables in a Form

The Form Wizard lets you choose fields from more than one table. You can use fields from multiple tables in a form provided that a relationship has been established between the tables. The relationship keeps the tables synchronized so that the form always displays the appropriate records.

Hands-On 4.3 Create a Form Using Fields From Two Tables

In this exercise, you will create a new Pets form that includes the customer name and telephone number. The Pinnacle Pet Care database window should be displayed from the previous exercise.

1. Click the **Forms** button on the Objects bar.

2. Double-click the *Create form by using Wizard* option.
   In the next few steps, you will choose the fields that will be displayed on the form. It is important that you choose the fields in the order specified in this exercise. This will make it easy for you to modify the form later in this lesson.

3. Follow these steps to add fields from the Pets table.

   Ⓐ *Choose the* **Pets** *table from the* **Tables/Queries** *list. You can base a form on one or more tables or even on a query.*

   Ⓑ *Click the* Add all fields *button to move all fields to the* **Selected Fields** *list.*

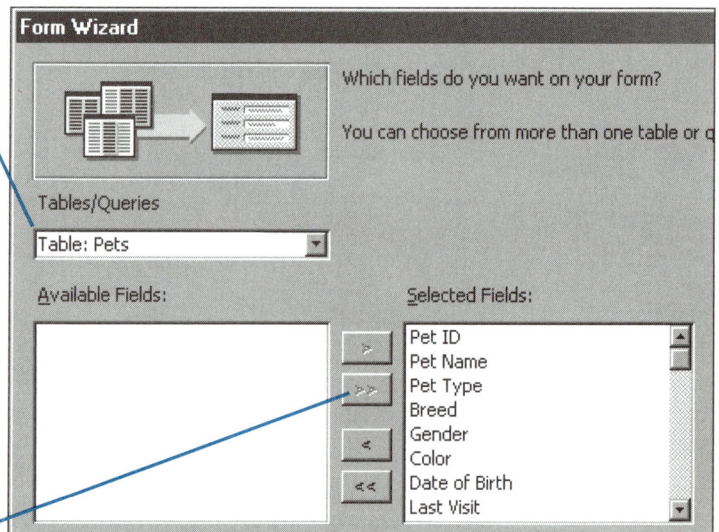

4. Follow these steps to add three fields from the Customers table.

Ⓐ *Choose the* Customers *table from the* **Tables/Queries** *list.*

Ⓑ *Add the* FirstName, LastName *and* Phone *fields to the* **Selected Fields** *list by choosing them one at a time and clicking the* **Add field** *button. The fields will appear at the bottom of the* **Selected Fields** *list.*

Form Wizard

Which fields do you want on your form?

You can choose from more than one table or

Tables/Queries

Table: Customers

Available Fields:

Customer ID
Address
City
State
Zip
Last Visit
Current Balance

Selected Fields:

Date of Birth
Last Visit
Expenditures
Number of Visits
Customer ID
Firstname
Lastname
Phone

5. Click the **Next** button to display the next wizard screen.

6. Make sure the view data option is set to *by Pets* and the *Single form* radio button is chosen.
   The by Pets *option instructs Access to base the form upon the Pets table. The customer data for a particular pet is then displayed on the form along with the pet data.*

7. Click the **Next** button.

8. Make sure the Columnar option is chosen and click the **Next** button.

9. Choose Standard as the style and click the **Next** button.

10. Type the name **New Pets** as the title and click the **Finish** button.
    Access will create the form as shown to the right; however, your form may have a slightly different layout. Notice that the form displays the data for Dillon the dog and Dillon's owner, Mark Roth. The relationship between the Customer ID fields in the Pets and Customers tables will ensure that Access displays the appropriate customer for each pet.

New Pets

Pet ID	DG13
Pet Name	Dillon
Pet Type	Dog
Breed	Mutt
Gender	Male
Color	Black
Date of Birth	10/5/94
Last Visit	7/7/99
Expenditures	$150.55
Number of Visits	3
Customer ID	1

Firstname	Mark
Lastname	Roth
Phone	(510) 234-9090

Record: 1 of 9

11. Use the record navigation buttons at the bottom of the form to browse through the records in the New Pets form.
    Notice that a customer name and phone number is displayed for each pet. Once again, the correct customer information is displayed for each pet because of the relationship between the CustomerID fields in the Pets and Customers tables.

12. Leave the form open because you will continue to use it in the next exercise.

Filtering Records

Filters are used with forms to let you temporarily view only those records that meet the criteria specified in the filter. The two most common types of filtering are *filtering by selection* and *filtering by form*. In both cases, the end result of applying a filter is that certain records are filtered out leaving only those records that meet the filter criteria. The difference between the two filter types is the method that is used to apply the filter.

- **Filtering by selection**—The Filter By Selection ▧ button is used to filter by selection. To filter by selection, you navigate to a record and click in a field that has the desired filter value. For example, if you are interested in seeing only records where the pet type is equal to dog, you should navigate to a record where the pet type is dog and click in the pet type field. When the Filter By Selection button is clicked, Access will only display records where the pet type is equal to dog.

- **Filtering by form**—The Filter By Form ▧ button is used to filter by form. To filter by form, you first click the Filter By Form button and Access displays a form with blank fields. Then, type the desired filter value(s) into the blank field(s). You can also click in the blank fields and choose the desired values from drop-down lists. Access applies the filter when you click the Apply/Remove Filter button.

- **Applying and removing filters**—The Apply/Remove Filter ▽ button is used to apply filtering by form. In addition, you can remove filters by clicking the Apply/Remove Filter button. Access redisplays all records once a filter has been removed.

Hands-On 4.4 Apply and Remove Filters

The New Pets form should still be displayed from the previous exercise.

Filter by Selection

1. Use the record navigation buttons at the bottom of the form to navigate to any record where the Pet Type is dog.

2. Click in the Pet Type field.
   The first record should have a pet type of Dog.

3. Click the Filter By Selection ▧ button on the Access toolbar.
   Notice the navigation bar now indicates that you are viewing record 1 of 5 (Filtered).

4. Use the navigation bar to browse through the records and notice that only records with a Pet Type of dog are visible.

5. Click the Remove Filter ▽ button.
   The Navigation bar should once again indicate that nine records are available.

Add a Filter to a Filter

You can use the Filter By Selection button to filter records that have already been filtered.

6. Use the Navigation bar to navigate to any record where the pet type is cat.

7. Click in the Pet Type field and click the Filter By Selection 🄵 button.

8. Navigate through the records and notice that only three cat records are visible.

9. If necessary, navigate to a record where the Breed field is set to unknown.

10. Click in the Breed field and click the Filter By Selection 🄵 button.
    Only two filtered records should now be available.

11. Click the Remove Filter 🔽 button to remove the filtering.

Filter by Form

12. Click the Filter By Form 🄵 button.

13. Follow these steps to enter the desired criteria in the Filter By Form box.

Ⓐ *Click in the **Pet Type** box and a drop-down button will appear.*

Ⓑ *Click the drop-down button and a list of all values that have been entered into the **Pet Type** field will appear. Choose Dog from the list and "Dog" will appear in the **Pet Type** box, as shown here.*

Ⓒ *Click in the **Breed** box and delete the word Unknown.*

Ⓓ *Click in the **Color** box, click the drop-down button, and choose Black.*

New Pets: Filter by Form	
Pet ID	Firstname
Pet Name	Lastname
Pet Type	"Dog" ▾Phone
Breed	
Gender	
Color	"Black"
Date of Birth	
Last Visit	

14. Click the Apply Filter 🔽 button.
    Browse through the filtered records and notice that they both have a Pet Type of Dog and a Color of Black. Entering two values in the Filter by Form box has the same effect as applying a filter to a filter using the Filter by Selection tool.

15. Click the Remove Filter 🔽 button to remove the filter.

16. Feel free to experiment with filters. Remove all filtering when you have finished and continue with the next topic.

Hyperlinks

Access 2000 lets you insert hyperlinks in forms and other objects. Hyperlinks can be used to open forms and reports, navigate to Web pages, and to prepare email messages for delivery. When you click a hyperlink, Access opens the form, report, or Web page to which the hyperlink points.

Inserting Hyperlinks

From the Keyboard

(CTRL)+K to display the Insert Hyperlink box

The Design View ![icon] button appears on the left end of the Access toolbar when a form is open in Form view. You must switch to Design view to insert hyperlinks and to modify forms. Hyperlinks are inserted using the Insert Hyperlink box. The Insert Hyperlink box is displayed by choosing **Insert→Hyperlink** or by clicking the Insert Hyperlink button on the Access toolbar. The following illustration describes the options available in the Insert Hyperlink box.

The object type that you wish to link to is chosen from the Link to *list.*

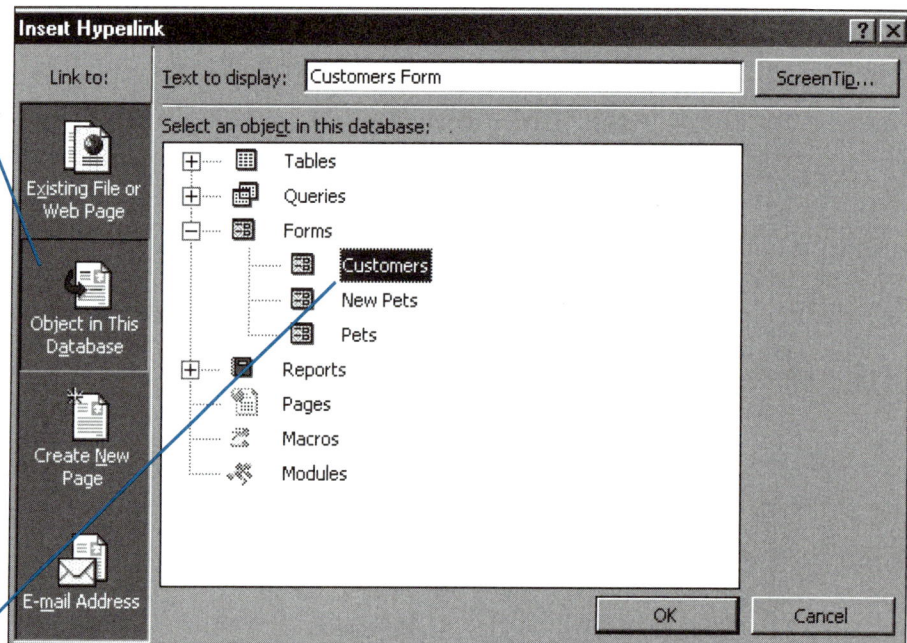

You can specify the specific Access object, Web page, or email address to which the hyperlink should point.

Hands-On 4.5 Insert a Hyperlink

In this exercise, you will switch to Design view and insert a hyperlink in the New Pets form. The hyperlink will be used to open the Customers form. This will allow you to open the Customers form directly from the New Pets form. The New Pets form should be open from the previous exercise.

1. Click the Design View ![icon] button on the left end of the Access toolbar.
   Access will display the form in Design view and a variety of dialog boxes and/or toolbars may appear.

2. Click the Insert Hyperlink ![icon] button on the Access toolbar.

3. Follow these steps to choose the Customers form as the desired hyperlink destination.

Ⓐ *Click the various* **Link to** *buttons, and notice that the method used to select the desired object varies with each object type.*

Ⓑ *Choose the* Object in This Database *option.*

Ⓒ *Click the plus sign (+) on the* Forms *object type, and choose the* Customers *form.*

Ⓓ *Add the word* **Form** *to the* **Text to display** *option. The text entered in this box will be displayed as the hyperlink text.*

Ⓔ *Click* OK *to insert the hyperlink at the top of the form. You will customize the form and hyperlink in the next exercise*

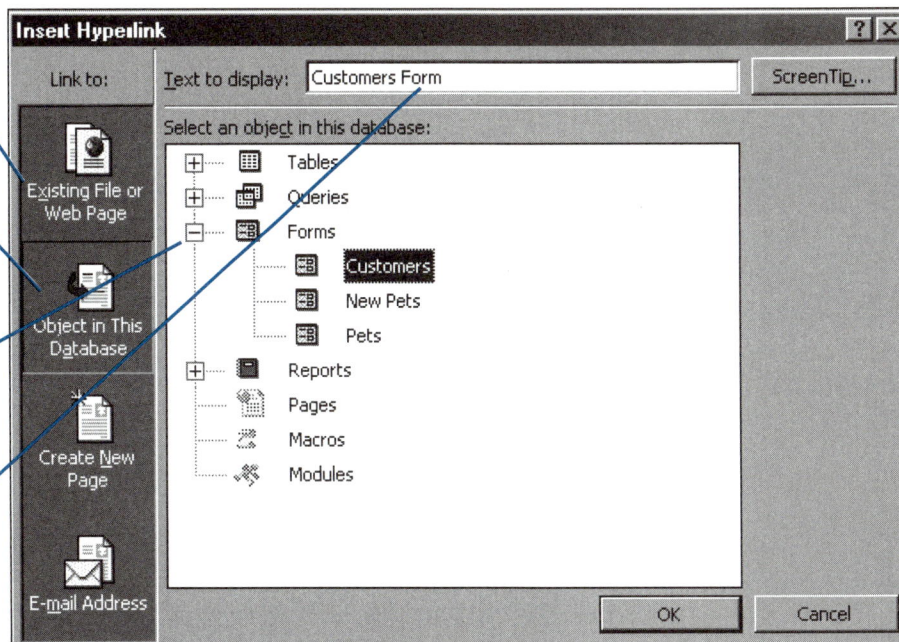

Insert Hyperlink

Link to:
- Existing File or Web Page
- Object in This Database
- Create New Page
- E-mail Address

Text to display: Customers Form   ScreenTip...

Select an object in this database:

- ⊞ Tables
- ⊞ Queries
- ⊟ Forms
  - Customers
  - New Pets
  - Pets
- ⊞ Reports
- Pages
- Macros
- Modules

OK   Cancel

Customizing Forms in Design View

Forms and other database objects can contain *controls*. For example, your New Pets form is currently displayed in Design view. You should be able to see a blue underlined hyperlink, text boxes for the Pet Name, Pet Type and other fields and descriptive labels to the left of the text boxes. All of these objects are types of controls. In Design view, you can add, delete, move, and modify controls. This gives you the ability to customize forms and other database objects.

Selecting and Moving Controls

In the next exercise, you will move the hyperlink to a different position on the form. You can move any control by selecting it and then dragging it to the desired location. You select a control by clicking anywhere on the control. You can also select a group of controls by pressing and holding the (SHIFT) key while clicking the desired controls. You move a control or group of selected controls by pointing to an edge of a control and dragging the control(s) to the desired location. You can also move selected controls by pressing (CTRL) while tapping the arrow keys on the keyboard. This allows you to nudge controls to the desired location.

The Grid

The form Design view window displays a grid of lines and dots. The grid is used to align objects and thus helps you lay out a form in an organized manner. However, there are times that you may want to turn the grid off because it may clutter the view. You turn the grid on and off with the **View→Grid** command.

Move the Hyperlink

1. If necessary, choose **View→Grid** from the menu bar to turn off the grid.
   *If the grid had already been turned off, then you probably just turned it on. If this happened, then you will need to issue the **View→Grid** command again to turn off the grid.*

2. Follow these steps to explore the Design view window and to adjust the size of the window.

Ⓐ *Notice the **Form Header** and **Detail** bars at the top of the window and the **Form Footer** at the bottom of the window. A form is divided into these three sections. You can place controls in any of the three sections. Currently, your form only has controls in the **Detail** section. In this lesson, you will only work with the **Detail** section.*

Ⓑ *Notice that the hyperlink shown here is selected. A selected control has* sizing handles *that appear on the edges of the control. You can move and size a control once it has become selected.*

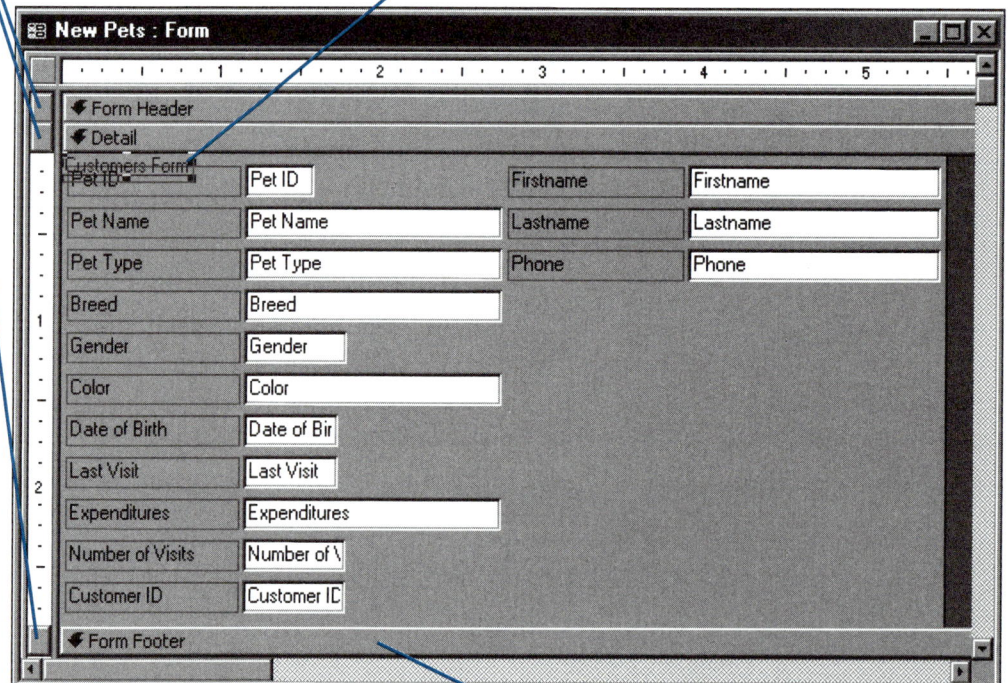

Ⓒ *Position the mouse pointer on a corner of the window and a double-headed arrow will appear.*

Ⓓ *If necessary, drag the corner until the **Form Footer** and all controls are visible, as shown here.*

3. Follow these steps to practice selecting controls.

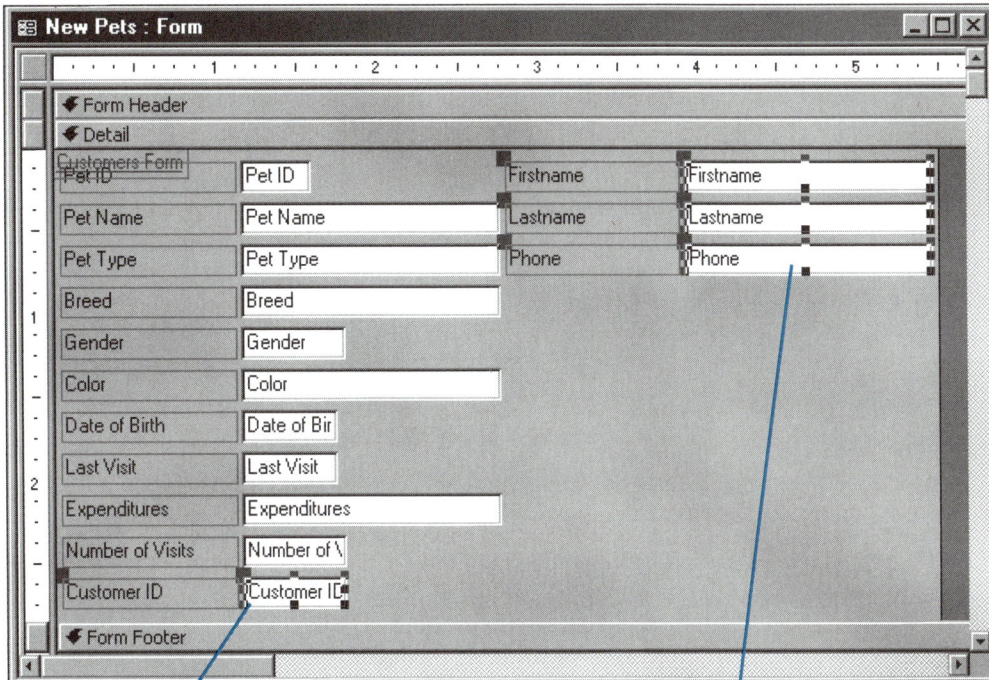

A *Click any control and sizing handles will appear. The control is now selected, and the hyperlink control should be deselected.*

B *Press* (SHIFT) *while you click other controls. Each control you click will become selected.*

4. Follow these steps to select and move the hyperlink control.

A *Release the* (SHIFT) *key, and click the hyperlink control.*

B *Position the mouse pointer on the bottom edge of the control, and a hand icon will appear.*

C *Drag the hyperlink to a position below the* **Phone** *control.*

(Continued on the next page)

Modify the Hyperlink Text

In the next few steps, you will modify the hyperlink text. The hyperlink will continue to point to the Customers form but it will have a more descriptive name.

5. Follow these steps to modify the hyperlink text.

Ⓐ *Make sure the hyperlink is selected and then click anywhere on the hyperlink text. The flashing insertion point will be positioned on the hyperlink text.*

Ⓑ *Use the left arrow key on the keyboard to position the insertion point at the beginning of the word Customers.*

Ⓒ *Type* **GoTo**, *tap the* (SPACE BAR), *and then click anywhere outside of the hyperlink to complete the editing process.*

6. Your completed form should match the example shown below. If necessary, move the other controls on the form until your form has the layout shown below.

Use the Hyperlink

7. Click the Form View 🖼 button on the left end of the Access toolbar.
   You must be in Form view to use a form.

8. Follow these steps to use the hyperlink.

A *Position the mouse pointer on the hyperlink, and it will have a "pointing finger" shape. The mouse pointer always has this shape when it is positioned on a hyperlink.*

B *Click the hyperlink, and the Customers form will appear. Notice that the **New Pets** form remains open.*

C *Feel free to browse through the records in the Customers form. Since both forms are open, you can easily move between them by clicking on the desired form.*

Insert a Hyperlink In the Customers Form

9. Make sure the Customers form is active.
   You can determine that a form is active because the title bar at the top of the form will have a blue color.

10. Click the Design view 🖼 button on the left end of the Access toolbar.

11. Click the Insert Hyperlink 🖼 button.

12. Choose New Pets from the list of forms and click **OK**.

(Continued on the next page)

13. Follow these steps to change the dimensions of the form and to move the hyperlink.

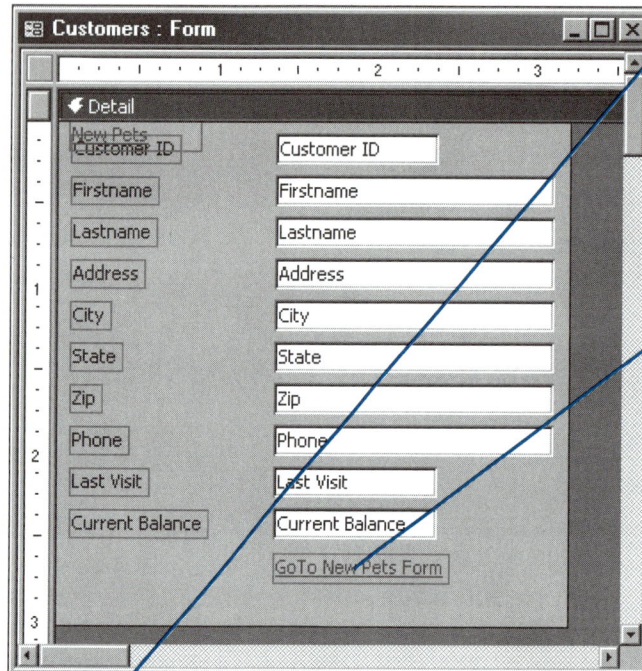

```
┌─ Customers : Form ─────────────────── _ □ × ─┐
│  · · · | · · · | · 1 · · · | · · · | · 2 · · · | · · · | · 3 · · · | · │
│ ┌─────────────────────────────────────────┐ │
│ │ ◆ Detail                                  │ │
│ │  New Pets                                 │ │
│ │  Customer ID      │ Customer ID       │   │ │
│ │  Firstname        │ Firstname         │   │ │
│ │  Lastname         │ Lastname          │   │ │
│ │  Address          │ Address           │   │ │
│ 1│  City             │ City              │   │ │
│ │  State            │ State             │   │ │
│ │  Zip              │ Zip               │   │ │
│ │  Phone            │ Phone             │   │ │
│ 2│  Last Visit       │ Last Visit        │   │ │
│ │  Current Balance  │ Current Balance   │   │ │
│ │                   │ GoTo New Pets Form│   │ │
│ 3│                                          │ │
│ └─────────────────────────────────────────┘ │
│ ◄ │                                       │ ► │
└──────────────────────────────────────────────┘
```

Ⓐ *Increase the size by dragging the bottom edge of the form down until there is about 1" of space between the **Current Balance** control and the scroll bar at the bottom of the form.*

Ⓑ *Drag the hyperlink to a position just below the **Current Balance** control. The light gray area on the form will expand to make room for the hyperlink.*

Ⓒ *Click on the hyperlink text, and change the name to* **GoTo New Pets Form**

Use the Hyperlink

14. Click the Form View 🔲 button on the left end of the Access toolbar.

15. Click the *GoTo New Pets Form* hyperlink.
The New Pets *form was already open, so it will simply move in front of the Customers form. If the form had been closed, then the hyperlink would have opened it.*

16. Notice that the hyperlink in the New Pets form now has a different color.
This is because the hyperlink has been used. Hyperlinks change color once they have been clicked to indicate that they have been used.

17. Now continue with the next topic where you will learn how to restrict data entry in controls.

Restricting Data Entry in Forms

The New Pets form contains controls that display data from fields in the Pets and Customers tables. This form will be used to enter and edit data in the Pets table. However, the customer information is displayed on the form for informational purposes only. In other words, you won't use this form to edit the customer name and telephone number. The customer data will be entered and edited using the Customers form. For this reason, you will prevent data entry from occurring in the customer information controls on the New Pets form. You will accomplish this by setting the *Enabled* property for the customer controls.

The Enabled and Locked Properties

The Properties 🖼 button on the Access toolbar displays the Properties box. The Data tab in the Properties box can be used to set the Enabled and Locked properties. The Enabled and Locked properties are described in the following table.

Property	Description
Enabled	The Enabled property determines whether or not a control can have the focus. Having the focus allows you to position the insertion point in the control. If the Enabled property is set to *No,* then the control appears dimmed on the form and you cannot position the insertion point in the control.
Locked	The Locked property determines whether or not data entry can occur in a control. If the Locked property is set to *No,* then data cannot be entered in the control.

Hands-On 4.7 Restrict Data Entry in Form Controls

1. Make sure the New Pets form is active and then click the Design view 🖼 button.

2. Follow these steps to select the customer information controls.

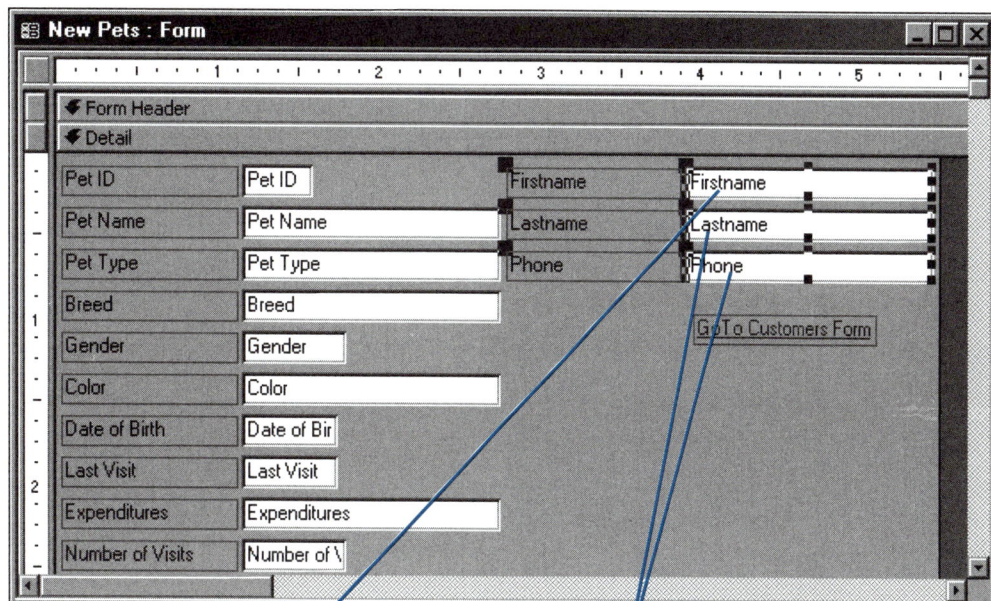

Ⓐ *Click the* **Firstname** *control, and it will become selected.*

Ⓑ *Press the* (SHIFT) *key while you click the* **Lastname** *and* **Phone** *controls. All three controls will become selected, as shown here.*

3. If necessary, click the Properties 🖼 button on the Access toolbar to display the Properties box. The Properties button will be recessed (pushed-in) when the box is displayed.

(Continued on the next page)

4. Follow these steps to set the Enabled property to No for the three controls.

Ⓐ *Click the* **Data** *tab.*

Ⓑ *Click in the* **Enabled** *box.*

Ⓒ *Click the drop-down button, and choose* No.

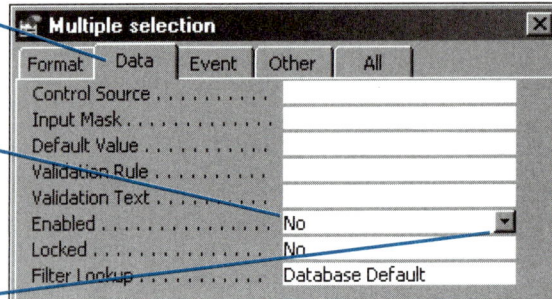

Multiple selection					✕
Format	Data	Event	Other	All	

Control Source . . . .
Input Mask . . . .
Default Value . . . .
Validation Rule . . . .
Validation Text . . . .
Enabled . . . . No ▼
Locked . . . . No
Filter Lookup . . . . Database Default

5. Close the Properties box.
Notice that the customer information controls now appear dimmed on the form.

6. Click the Form view 🖼 button on the left end of the toolbar.

7. Try clicking the dimmed customer information controls and notice that the insertion point cannot be positioned in the controls.
Setting the Enabled property to No prevents the controls from receiving the focus.

8. Browse through the records on the New Pets form and the correct customer information will continue to be displayed for each pet.

Close the Forms and Delete the Pets Form

9. Close both the New Pets and Customers forms by clicking the Close ✕ buttons at the top right corner of the forms. Choose **Yes** for both forms when Access asks if you want to save the changes.
The Access Database window should be displayed.

10. If necessary, click the Forms button on the Objects bar.

11. Choose the Pets (not New Pets) form and click the Delete ✕ button in the Access database window.

12. Click **Yes** to confirm the deletion.

Basing a Query On Multiple Tables

You can use a query to select data from multiple tables. However, it is important that a relationship be established between the tables so that the records remain synchronized. You can establish temporary relationships within the query window. However, these temporary relationships can only be used within the query. The best to way to create relationships is in the Relationships window. You used the Relationships window to create a relationship between the Customers and Pets tables earlier in this lesson. Relationships that are established within the Relationships window are then used in forms, queries, reports, and other objects that are dependent upon the relationship.

Hands-On 4.8 Create a Multiple Table Select Query

Al Smith wants a report that lists pets and the corresponding customer information based upon the last visit date of the pet. This way, his staff can contact customers if the pet has not visited the clinic recently. In this exercise, you will create a query that selects the appropriate data from the Pets and Customers tables. Later in this lesson, you will use the query as the basis for a report. The Pinnacle Pet Care database should still be open from the previous exercise.

1. Click the **Queries** button on the Objects bar.

2. Double-click the *Create query in Design view* option.
   The Design Grid will appear and the Show Table box will be displayed.

3. Add both the Customers and Pets tables to the query window and then close the Show Table box.

4. Maximize ▫ the Query window.

5. Follow these steps to size the window objects and to examine the relationship.

Ⓐ *Drag the border between the grid and field lists down to allocate more room to the field lists. Drag the bottom edges of the field lists down until all field names are visible.*

Ⓑ *Notice the join line between the field lists. The Customers table has a one-to-many relationship with the Pets table. You created this relationship in the Relationships window earlier in this lesson. The one-to-many relationship indicates that each customer can have many pets, but each pet can have just one owner.*

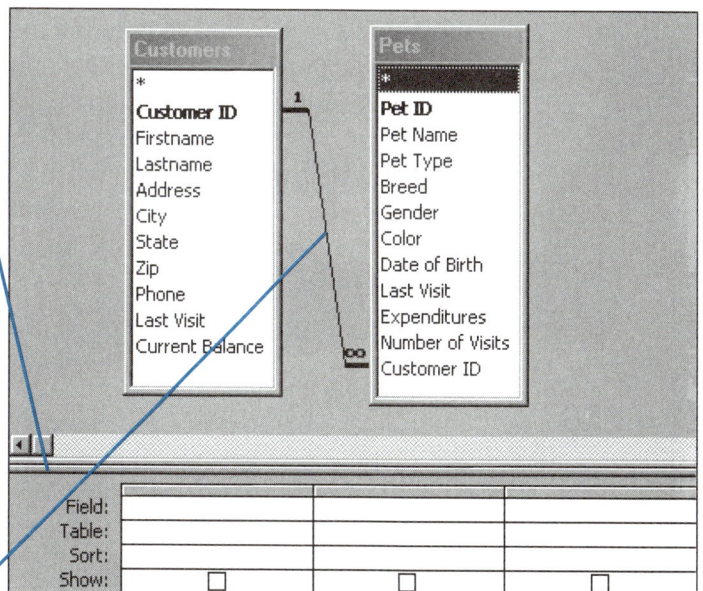

(Continued on the next page)

6. Double-click the Last Visit field on the Pets field list (not the Customers field list) to add that field to the design grid.

7. Now add the Pet Name and Pet Type fields from the Pets field list to the design grid.

8. Add the Firstname, Lastname, and Phone fields from the Customers field list to the design grid. The design grid should contain the field names shown below.

Field:	Last Visit	Pet Name	Pet Type	Firstname	Lastname	Phone
Table:	Pets	Pets	Pets	Customers	Customers	Customers
Sort:						
Show:	☑	☑	☑	☑	☑	☑
Criteria:						
or:						

9. Click the Run ![run] button to produce the query results shown to the right.

Notice that the query selects every record in the Pets table and displays the corresponding customer information. The relationship ensures that the correct customer information is associated with each pet.

Last Visit	Pet Name	Pet Type	Firstname	Lastname	Phone
7/7/99	Dillon	Dog	Mark	Roth	(510) 234-9090
7/7/99	Tony	Cat	Mark	Roth	(510) 234-9090
9/7/99	Bugs	Rabbit	Tony	Simpson	(510) 238-2233
9/7/99	Max	Cat	Tony	Simpson	(510) 238-2233
7/15/99	Wolfy	Dog	Jason	Jones	(415) 312-2312
7/15/99	Stripes	Cat	Jason	Jones	(415) 312-2312
9/10/99	Fetch	Dog	Jason	Jones	(415) 312-2312
10/8/99	Ben	Dog	Jacob	Samuels	(404) 367-8002
10/8/99	Spike	Dog	Jacob	Samuels	(404) 367-8002

10. Click the Design View ![design view] button on the Access toolbar.

In the next exercise, you will add a pop-up box to the query. The pop-up box will prompt you to enter a date.

Prompting for User Input

You can add a special type of criterion to a query that displays a pop-up dialog box when the query is run. The pop-up box lets you enter information, which is then used by the query to select records. For example, in the following exercise, you will add a criterion to the Last Visit field in the query that you just created. The criterion will display a pop-up box prompting you to enter a date. The only records that will be selected when you run the query are those with a Last Visit date that is prior to the date you entered. This technique can be quite useful because the pop-up box is also displayed when reports that are based upon the query are run.

Syntax for Pop-up Box Criteria

The following illustration shows the criterion that you will enter into the Last Visit field and the pop-up box that will appear. Take a few moments to study the criterion syntax.

The brackets [ ] instruct the query to display a pop-up box that prompts the user for input.

<[Before which date?]

The less than < sign instructs the query to only select dates that are prior to the date the user enters in the pop-up box.

Enter Parameter Value

Before which date?

[   ]

OK   Cancel

All text between the brackets is displayed as a prompt in the pop-up box.

Hands-On 4.9 Add Pop-Up Box Criteria to the Query

The query design grid should be displayed from the previous exercise.

1. Follow this step to enter the criteria.

A *Click in the Criteria box for the Last Visit field, and enter the criteria shown. Begin with a less than < sign, and enclose the text in square [ ] brackets.*

Field:	Last Visit	Pet Name	Pet Type
Table:	Pets	Pets	Pets
Sort:			
Show:	☑	☑	☑
Criteria:	<[Before which date?]		
or:			

2. Run [!] the query and the pop up box will appear.

3. Type **9/1/99** in the box and click **OK.**

    The query results shown to the right should appear although the sort order may be different than shown here.

Last Visit	Pet Name	Pet Type	Firstname	Lastname	Phone
7/15/99	Wolfy	Dog	Jason	Jones	(415) 312-2312
7/7/99	Dillon	Dog	Mark	Roth	(510) 234-9090
7/15/99	Stripes	Cat	Jason	Jones	(415) 312-2312
7/7/99	Tony	Cat	Mark	Roth	(510) 234-9090

   Only pets whose last visit was prior to 9/1/99 were selected by the query.

4. Choose **File→Close** to close the query window.

5. Click **Yes** when Access asks if you want to save the query.

6. Enter the name **Overdue for Visit** in the Save As box and click **OK.**

Basing Reports on Queries

You can use a query as the basis for a report. This can be useful if you want the report to display data from multiple tables, or if you want the report to display only certain records from the tables. You can use the Report Wizard to create a report that is based upon a query. The first screen in the Report Wizard lets you choose a table or query as the basis for the report.

Hands-On 4.10 Create a Report That is Based Upon a Query

1. Click the **Reports** button on the Objects bar in the database window.

2. Double-click the *Create report by using wizard* option.

3. Follow these steps to choose the desired query and fields for the report.

Ⓐ *Choose the* Overdue for Visit *query from the* **Tables/Queries** *list.*

Report Wizard

Which fields do you want on your report?

You can choose from more than one table or query.

Tables/Queries

Query: Overdue for Visit

Available Fields:

Selected Fields:

Last Visit
Pet Name
Pet Type
Firstname
Lastname
Phone

Ⓑ *Click the* **Add All Fields** *button to choose all fields.*

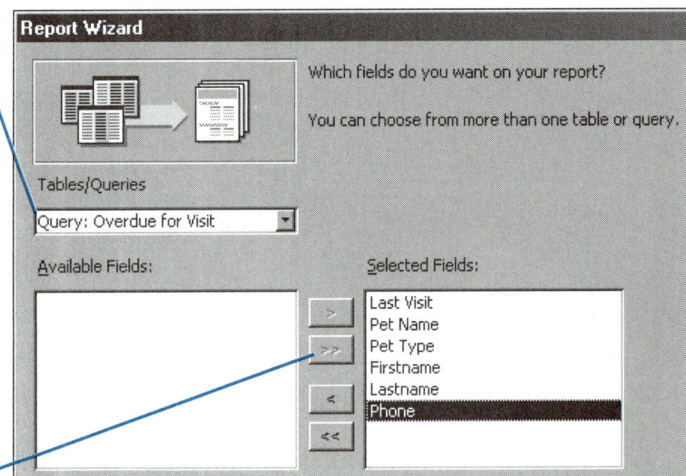

4. Click the **Next** button.

5. Make sure the *by Pets* option is chosen in the second Wizard screen and click **Next.**
   The by Pets option will base the report upon the records in the Pets table. The corresponding customer information will be displayed along with the pet information.

6. Click **Next** two more times and the Layout and Orientation options will appear.

7. Make sure the layout is set to Tabular and set the orientation to Landscape.
   Landscape orientation will cause the report to display horizontally on the page.

8. Click **Next** and choose the Corporate report style.

9. Click **Next** and type the report name **Overdue for Visit** in the last Wizard screen.

10. Click the **Finish** button.
    Access will display the pop-up box prompting you to enter a date. The pop-up box appears because the report is based upon the Overdue for Visit query, which contains the pop-up box criterion.

11. Enter the date **9/1/99** and click **OK**.

The report shown below should be generated. Notice that the data is left aligned in all controls except for the Last Visit control, where the dates are right aligned. Notice also that the Last Visit control is positioned close to the Pet Name control. In the next exercise, you will modify the report by left-aligning the date and adjusting the position of the Pet Name control.

Overdue For Visit

Last Visit	Pet Name	Pet Type	Firstname	Lastname	Phone
7/15/99	Wolfy	Dog	Jason	Jones	(415) 312-2312
7/7/99	Dillon	Dog	Mark	Roth	(510) 234-9090
7/15/99	Stripes	Cat	Jason	Jones	(415) 312-2312
7/7/99	Tony	Cat	Mark	Roth	(510) 234-9090

Moving and Resizing Report Controls

Design view can be used to customize reports. Like a form, a report has various sections and controls. You can change the position, size, and properties of report controls using the same techniques that are used with form controls.

Hands-On 4.11 Move and Size Report Controls

1. Click the Design View [icon] button on the left end of the Print Preview toolbar.
In the next few steps, you will adjust the alignment of the Last Visit label and the Last Visit control. A label in a report or form is simply a box with descriptive text. A control, on the other hand, reflects data from a table field. In your report, the blue Last Visit box in the Page Header section is a label. The Last Visit box in the Detail section is a control.

2. Follow these steps to explore the report in Design view and to adjust the alignment of the Last Visit label and control.

Ⓐ *Notice that the report has various sections. You will learn more about the sections in a later lesson.*

Ⓑ *Click the* Last Visit *label in the **Page Header** section and then press the* (SHIFT) *key while you click the* Last Visit *control in the **Detail section**. Both objects should be selected.*

Ⓒ *Click the Align Left [icon] button on the Access toolbar. You won't notice a change in the alignment until you preview the report later in this exercise.*

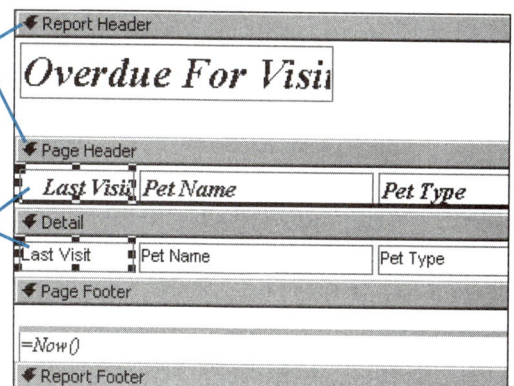

(Continued on the next page)

3. Follow these steps to adjust the width of the label and control.

Ⓐ *Click the* Pet Name *label in the* **Page Header** *section, and then press the* (SHIFT) *key while you click the* Pet Name *control in the* **Detail** *section. Both objects should be selected.*

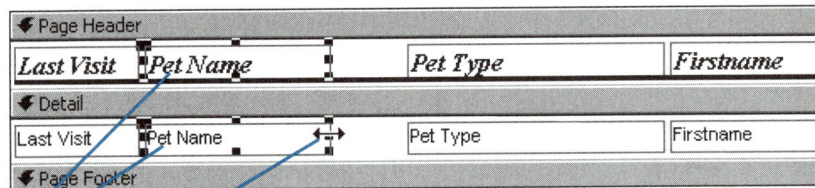

Ⓑ *Position the mouse pointer on a right side-sizing handle of either object, and a double-headed arrow will appear.*

Ⓒ *Drag the right border about ½" to the left to reduce the width of both controls.*

4. Now press the (CTRL) key while you repeatedly tap the right arrow key on the keyboard. This will move the selected controls slightly to the right. Continue to move the selected controls until they are centered between the Last Visit and Pet Type controls, as shown here.

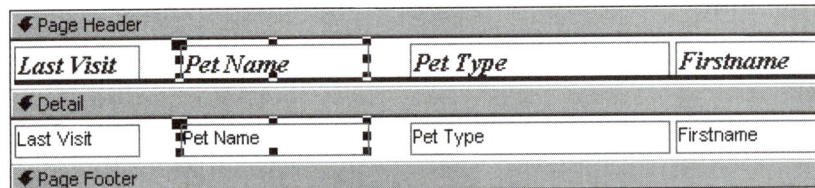

5. Click the Print Preview 🔍 button on the left end of the Access toolbar.

6. Type the date **9/1/99** in the pop-up box and click **OK**.
   The dates in the Last Visit column should now be right aligned and there should be additional space between the Last Visit and Pet Name columns.

7. Choose **File→Close** and choose **Yes** when Access asks if you want to save the changes.

Insert a Hyperlink to the Report

In the remainder of this exercise, you will insert a new hyperlink in the New Pets form. The hyperlink will open the Overdue for Visit report whenever it is clicked.

8. Click the **Forms** button on the Objects bar in the database window.

9. Choose the **New Pets** form and click the 🖉 Design button.

10. Click the Insert Hyperlink 📑 button.

11. Click the plus sign (+) next to the Reports object category to display the various reports.

12. Choose the **Overdue For Visit** report and click **OK**.

13. Drag the hyperlink until it is positioned below the GoTo Customers Form hyperlink.

14. Click the Form View 📑 button on the left end of the Access toolbar.

15. Click the **Overdue For Visit** hyperlink and the pop up box will appear.

16. Type the date **10/1/99** and click **OK**.
    The report will display seven records. As you can see, hyperlinks let you link database objects.

17. Close both the report and the form with the **File→Close** command. Click **Yes** when Access asks if you want to save the changes to the form.

18. Close the Pinnacle Pet Care database with the **File→Close** command.

Concepts Review

True/False Questions

1. Access lets you enforce referential integrity when creating relationships. TRUE FALSE

2. Forms can only display data from one table. TRUE FALSE

3. Reports can only display data from one table. TRUE FALSE

4. Filters are normally saved for later use. TRUE FALSE

5. The Filter by Selection ⬚ button displays a dialog box where you type the desired value that you want the filter to use. TRUE FALSE

6. The Enabled property for a control determines whether the control can receive the focus. TRUE FALSE

7. Queries can select data from multiple tables. TRUE FALSE

8. Pop-up boxes that prompt the user for input are created by placing criteria in the query design grid. TRUE FALSE

Multiple Choice Questions

1. Which button is used to display the Relationships window?
   a. ⬚
   b. ⬚
   c. ⬚
   d. ⬚

2. Which button is used to insert hyperlinks?
   a. ⬚
   b. ⬚
   c. ⬚
   d. ⬚

3. Which keystroke combination is used to move selected controls in Design view?
   a. CTRL+Arrow keys
   b. SHIFT+Arrow keys
   c. SHIFT+CTRL
   d. ALT+Arrow keys

4. Which pair of symbols should surround the desired phrase that you want displayed in a pop-up dialog box?
   a. ( )
   b. [ ]
   c. < >
   d. { }

Skill Builders

Skill Builder 4.1

In this exercise, you will establish a relationship between the Customers and Trips tables in the Tropical Getaways database.

1. Open the Tropical Getaways database on your exercise diskette.

2. Click the Relationships ⊞ button on the Access toolbar.

3. Choose **Customers in the Show Table** box and click the **Add** button.
   The Customers table will be added to the Relationships window.

4. Add the Trips table to the Relationships window and **close** the Show Table box.

5. If necessary, drag the bottom edges of the Customers and Trips field lists down until all field names are visible.

6. Follow these steps to establish a relationship between the Customer ID fields.

   Ⓐ *Drag the Customer ID field from the **Customers** table to the Customer ID field in the **Trips** table. A rectangular icon will be visible, as shown here.*

   Ⓑ *Release the mouse button, and the **Edit Relationships** box will appear.*

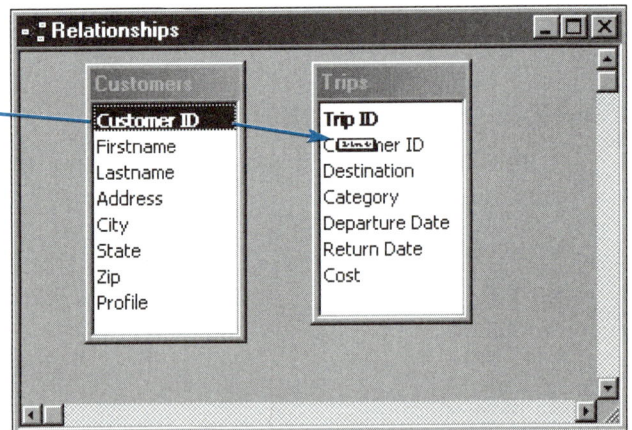

   Relationships

Customers	Trips
Customer ID	Trip ID
Firstname	Customer ID
Lastname	Destination
Address	Category
City	Departure Date
State	Return Date
Zip	Cost
Profile	

7. Follow these steps to enforce referential integrity.
   Referential integrity will require that every record in the Trips table has a corresponding Customer ID in the Customers table.

   Ⓐ *Check all three boxes to enforce referential integrity and to allow cascade updating and deleting.*

   Edit Relationships

   Table/Query: Related Table/Query: Create
   Customers   Trips   Cancel
   Customer ID   Customer ID   Join Type..
                                             Create New..
   ☑ Enforce Referential Integrity
   ☑ Cascade Update Related Fields
   ☑ Cascade Delete Related Records

   Relationship Type: One-To-Many

   Ⓑ *Click the **Create** button.*

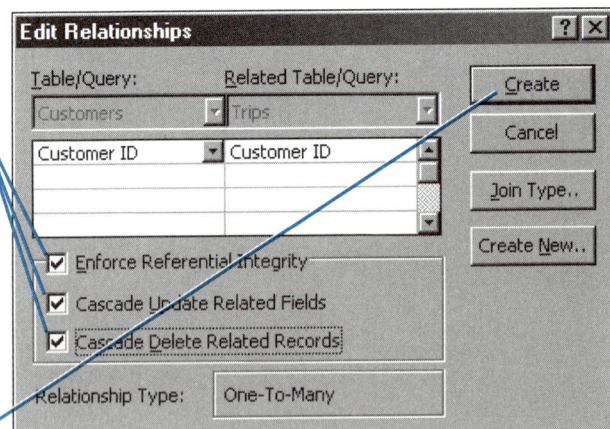

8. Click the Close ⊠ button at the top-right corner of the Relationships window.

9. Click **Yes** when Access asks if you want to save the changes to the Relationship.
The relationship is now established and it can be used to help you develop queries, forms, and reports.

Skill Builder 4.2

In this exercise, you will use the Form Wizard to create a new form. The form will use fields from both the Customers and Trips tables.

1. Click the Forms button on the Objects bar in the database window.

2. Double-click the *Create form by using Wizard* option.

3. Follow these steps to add the fields from the Trips table.

Ⓐ *Choose the* Trips *table from the* ***Tables/Queries*** *list.*

Ⓑ *Click the* **Add all fields** *button to move all fields to the* **Selected Fields** *list.*

Form Wizard

Which fields do you want on your form?

You can choose from more than one table or

Tables/Queries

Table: Trips

Available Fields:

Selected Fields:

Trip ID
Customer ID
Destination
Category
Departure Date
Return Date
Cost

(Continued on the next page)

4. Follow these steps to add five fields from the Customers table.

A *Choose the* Customers *table from the* **Tables/Queries** *list.*

Form Wizard

Which fields do you want on your form?

You can choose from more than one table or q

Tables/Queries

Table: Customers

Available Fields:

Customer ID
Address
Zip

Selected Fields:

Departure Date
Return Date
Cost
Firstname
Lastname
Profile
City
State

B *Use the* **Add field** *button to add the* Firstname, Lastname, Profile, City, *and* State *fields one field at a time.*

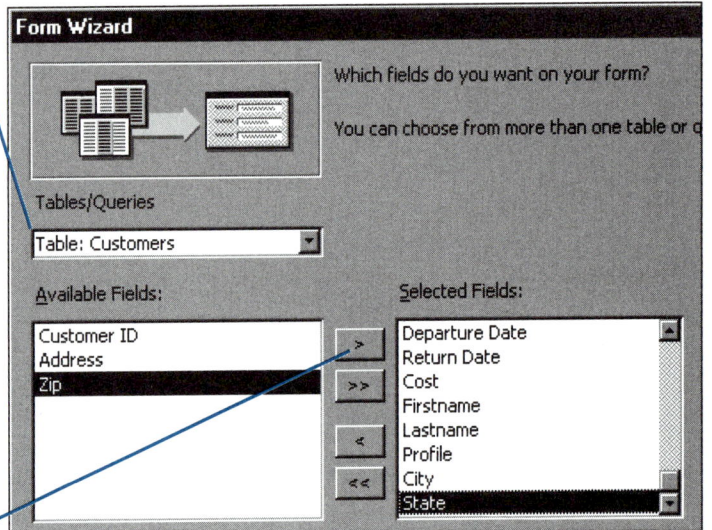

5. Click the **Next** button to display the next wizard screen.

6. Make sure the options are set to *by Trips* and *Single form* and click the **Next** button.

7. Make sure the Columnar option is chosen and click the **Next** button.

8. Choose Standard as the style and click the **Next** button.

9. Type the name **New Trips** as the title and click the **Finish** button.

Access will create the form shown to the right; however, your form may have a slightly different layout. The relationship that you set up in the previous exercise synchronizes the records in the Trips and Customers tables. For example, the Kenyan Safari trip was taken by Debbie Thomas. Access displays Debbie's information because the Customer ID field in the Trips table is set to 1 for this trip. Customer ID 1 belongs to Debbie Thomas, thus her name, profile, city, and state are displayed from the Customers table.

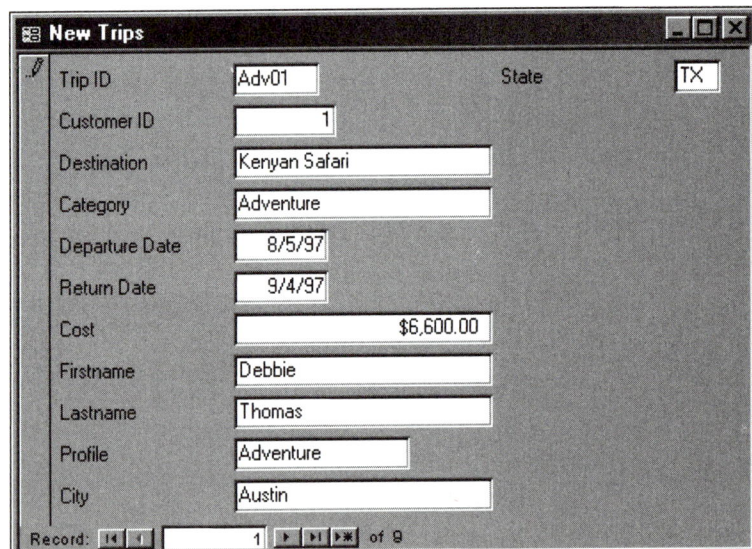

New Trips

Trip ID	Adv01
Customer ID	1
Destination	Kenyan Safari
Category	Adventure
Departure Date	8/5/97
Return Date	9/4/97
Cost	$6,600.00
Firstname	Debbie
Lastname	Thomas
Profile	Adventure
City	Austin

State: TX

Record: 1 of 9

10. Leave the form open as you will continue to use it in the next exercise.

Skill Builder 4.3

In this exercise, you will insert hyperlinks in the New Trips and Customers forms. You will also modify the Forms in Design view.

1. Click the Design View [icon] button on the Access toolbar.

2. Click the Insert Hyperlink [icon] button.

3. Make sure the *Objects in This Database* button is chosen on the left side of the dialog box.

4. Choose Customers from the Forms list and click **OK** to insert the hyperlink at the top of the form.

5. Follow these guidelines to modify the appearance of the form.

   ■ If necessary, increase the size of the form until it is large enough for the control arrangement shown below. You can accomplish this by dragging a corner-sizing handle. Also, the next bullet in this guideline list instructs you to rearrange the controls. Notice that all of the controls currently reside on a light gray area of the form. If you move controls out of the light gray area, then the light gray area will automatically expand to accommodate the new positions of the controls.

   ■ Rearrange the controls and the hyperlink until your form matches the example shown below. Keep in mind that you can select multiple controls by pressing the (CTRL) key while clicking the desired controls.

   ■ Modify the hyperlink text by clicking the hyperlink and typing the text shown below.

6. Click the Form View [icon] button on the left end of the Access toolbar.

7. Click the hyperlink to open the Customers form.

(Continued on the next page)

8. Click the Design view ![Design view button] button to display the Customers form in Design view.

9. Insert a hyperlink in the Customers form that opens the New Trips form when it is clicked. Adjust the size of the form, the position of the hyperlink, and change the hyperlink text to match the example shown to the right.

10. Click the Form View ![Form View button] button and then click the hyperlink.
The New Trips form should become active.

11. Switch to Design ![Design view button] view.

12. Select the Firstname, Lastname, Profile, City, and State controls. You can accomplish this by pressing the (SHIFT) key while clicking the controls.

13. If necessary, click the Properties ![Properties button] button on the Access toolbar to display the Properties dialog box.

14. Click the Data tab.

15. Set the Enabled property to **No** and the Locked property to **Yes.**

16. Click the Form view ![Form view button] button on the toolbar.
The Firstname, Lastname, Profile, City, and State controls will appear to be active. However, you will not be able to click in the controls because of the Enabled and Locked settings.

17. Feel free to browse through the records on the New Trips form and modify the form if desired.

18. Close both the New Trips and Customers forms and save any changes.
The Database window should be displayed. You will continue to modify the database in the following exercises.

Skill Builder 4.4

In this exercise, you will set up a new query in the Tropical Getaways database. The query will select data from both the Customers and Trips tables.

1. Click the Queries button on the Objects bar in the database window.

2. Double-click the Create query in Design view option.

3. Add both the Customers and Trips tables to the query window and close the Show Table box.

4. Maximize ⬚ the Query window and adjust the size of the window objects until all field names in the Customers and Trips field lists are visible.

5. Add the Firstname and Lastname fields from the Customers field list to the design grid.

6. Add the Destination, Category, Departure Date, Return Date, and Cost fields from the Trips field list to the grid.

   At this point, the design grid should contain the fields shown below.

Field:	Firstname	Lastname	Destination	Category	Departure Date	Return Date	Cost
Table:	Customers	Customers	Trips	Trips	Trips	Trips	Trips
Sort:							
Show:	☑	☑	☑	☑	☑	☑	☑
Criteria:							

7. Click the Run ⚡ button and the query results shown below should appear.

   Notice that the query selects every record in the Trips table and displays the corresponding customer information.

Firstname	Lastname	Destination	Category	Departure Date	Return Date	Cost
Debbie	Thomas	Kenyan Safari	Adventure	8/5/97	9/4/97	$6,600.00
Debbie	Thomas	Amazon Jungle Trek	Adventure	8/7/98	9/14/98	$7,765.00
Debbie	Thomas	Swiss Alps	Adventure	10/10/98	11/5/98	$3,500.00
Wilma	Boyd	Caribbean Cruise	Leisure	9/19/98	9/28/98	$2,390.00
Alice	Simpson	Orlando	Family	3/4/99	3/10/99	$3,400.00
Victor	Thomas	Rocky Mountains	Adventure	5/6/99	5/22/99	$2,190.00
Victor	Thomas	Baja California	Adventure	8/8/99	8/18/99	$2,900.00
Lisa	Simms	Hawaii	Leisure	2/5/99	2/15/99	$4,500.00
Ted	Carter	Hawaii	Family	3/7/99	3/15/99	$5,300.00

8. Click the Design View ◨ button to return to Design view.

   In the next step, you will enter a criterion in the Category criteria box. The criterion will display a pop-up box that prompts the user to enter a category. The query will only select trips with the same category type that is entered in the pop-up box.

(Continued on the next page)

9. Type the criterion **[Enter a category]** into the Category criteria box as shown below.
When you run the query, the square brackets surrounding the Enter a category phrase will instruct Access to display a pop-up box. Access will only select records where the Category is the same as the category you enter in the box.

Field:	Firstname	Lastname	Destination	Category
Table:	Customers	Customers	Trips	Trips
Sort:				
Show:	☑	☑	☑	☑
Criteria:				[Enter a category]
or:				

10. Run ⬛ the query and the pop-up box will appear.

11. Type **Adventure** in the box and click **OK.**
The query results shown below will appear. Notice that only trips with a category of Adventure have been selected.

Firstname	Lastname	Destination	Category	Departure Date	Return Date	Cost
Debbie	Thomas	Kenyan Safari	Adventure	8/5/97	9/4/97	$6,600.00
Debbie	Thomas	Amazon Jungle Trek	Adventure	8/7/98	9/14/98	$7,765.00
Debbie	Thomas	Swiss Alps	Adventure	10/10/98	11/5/98	$3,500.00
Victor	Thomas	Rocky Mountains	Adventure	5/6/99	5/22/99	$2,190.00
Victor	Thomas	Baja California	Adventure	8/8/99	8/18/99	$2,900.00

12. Choose **File→Close** from the menu bar to close the query window.

13. Click **Yes** when Access asks if you want to save the query.

14. Type the name **Trips-Specific Category** in the Save As box and click **OK.**
In the next exercise, you will use the query as the basis for a report.

Skill Builder 4.5

In this exercise, you will create a report that displays trip information. You will use the Trips-Specific Category query as the basis for the report.

1. Click the Reports button on the Objects bar in the database window.

2. Double-click the *Create report by using Wizard* option.

3. Follow these steps in the first Wizard screen.

Ⓐ *Choose* Query: Trips-Specific Category *from the* **Tables/Queries** *list.*

Ⓑ *Click the* **Add All Fields** *button.*

Ⓒ *Click* Next *to go to the next Wizard screen.*

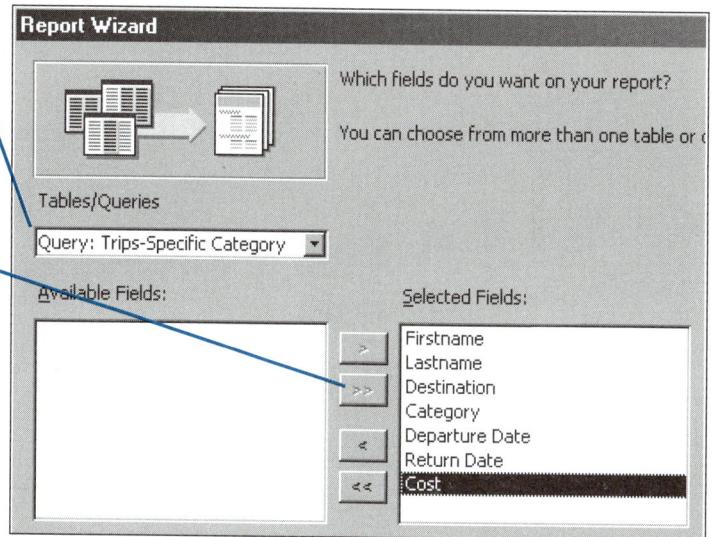

Report Wizard

Which fields do you want on your report?

You can choose from more than one table or (

Tables/Queries

Query: Trips-Specific Category

Available Fields:

Selected Fields:
Firstname
Lastname
Destination
Category
Departure Date
Return Date
Cost

4. Choose the *by Trips* option in the second Wizard screen and click the **Next** button.
   The table you choose determines how Access will group the data in the report. The Trips table is on the many side of the one-to-many relationship that exists between the Customers and Trips tables. Choosing the by Trips *option instructs Access to not group the data. Access will simply display all records from the Trips table that match the criteria in the underlying query.*

5. Click the **Next** button twice to bypass the next two screens.
   The Layout and Orientation options screen will appear.

6. Make sure the layout is set to Tabular and set the orientation to Landscape.

7. Click **Next** and choose the Soft Gray report style.

8. Click **Next** and enter the title `Trips-Specific Category` in the title box.

9. Click the **Finish** button.
   The Wizard will build the report and the pop-up box prompting you to enter a category will appear. The pop-up box appears because the report is based upon the Trips-Specific Category query, which contains the pop-up box criterion.

(Continued on the next page)

10. Type **Adventure** and click **OK**.

The report shown below should be generated. You will customize the report in the next exercise. The customization will correct the alignment problem with the Departure Date and Return Date headings.

Trips-Specific Category

Firstname	Lastname	Destination	Category	Departure Date	Return Date	Cost
Debbie	Thomas	Kenyan Safari	Adventure	8/5/97	9/4/97	$6,600.00
Debbie	Thomas	Amazon Jungle Trek	Adventure	8/7/98	9/14/98	$7,765.00
Debbie	Thomas	Swiss Alps	Adventure	10/10/98	11/5/98	$3,500.00
Victor	Thomas	Rocky Mountains	Adventure	5/6/99	5/22/99	$2,190.00
Victor	Thomas	Baja California	Adventure	8/8/99	8/18/99	$2,900.00

11. Continue with the next exercise, where you will customize the report.

Skill Builder 4.6

In this exercise, you will change control widths, control alignments, and move controls.

1. Click the Design View ![button] button on the left end of the Print Preview toolbar.

2. Follow these steps to adjust the width of the Category label and control.

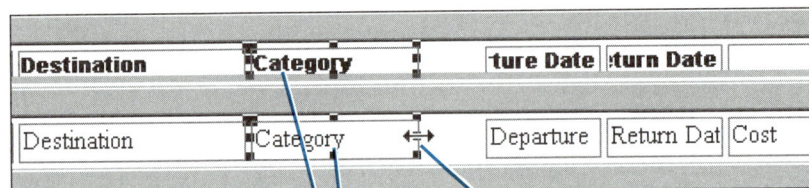

Ⓐ Click the Category *label in the* **Page Header** *section, and then press the* (SHIFT) *key while you click the* Category *control in the* **Detail** *section.*

Ⓑ Position the mouse *pointer on a side-sizing handle, and a double-headed arrow will appear.*

Ⓒ Drag the right borders *of the label and control about 1/2" to the* **left**.

3. Click the Departure Date label.
The Departure Date label will be selected and the Category label and control will be deselected.

4. Press the (SHIFT) key while you click the Departure Date control.
Both the label and control should be selected.

5. Increase the width of the label and control until the entire phrase *Departure Date* is visible in the label. You can accomplish this by dragging the left edge of the Departure Date label to the left. If necessary, reduce the width of the Category label and control to provide more room for the Departure Date label and control.

6. Click the Align Left 🔲 button on the Access toolbar.

This will align the date on the left side of the Departure Date control (although this setting may not be visible in Design view). At this point, your report should have the appearance shown below.

Report Header						
Trips-Specific Categor						
Page Header						
Firstname	**Lastname**	**Destination**	**Category**	**Departure Date**	**turn Date**	**Cost**
Detail						
Firstname	Lastname	Destination	Category	Departure Date	Return Dat	Cost
Page Footer						
=Now()			▪			="Page " & [Page] & " of " & [Pages]
Report Footer						

7. Click the Cost label and then press (SHIFT) while you click the Cost control.

8. Reduce the width of the label and control by about 1/2″.

9. Click the Align Right 🔲 button.

10. Now select the Return Date label and Return Date control.

11. Increase the width of the label and control about 1/2″ by dragging the right sizing handle.

12. Click the Align Left 🔲 button.

13. Click the Print Preview 🔲 button on the left end of the Access toolbar.

14. Type the category **Adventure** in the pop up box and click **OK.**

Your completed report should have the appearance shown below.

Trips-Specific Category

Firstname	Lastname	Destination	Category	Departure Date	Return Date	Cost
Debbie	Thomas	Kenyan Safari	Adventure	8/5/97	9/4/97	$6,600.00
Debbie	Thomas	Amazon Jungle Trek	Adventure	8/7/98	9/14/98	$7,765.00
Debbie	Thomas	Swiss Alps	Adventure	10/10/98	11/5/98	$3,500.00
Victor	Thomas	Rocky Mountains	Adventure	5/6/99	5/22/99	$2,190.00
Victor	Thomas	Baja California	Adventure	8/8/99	8/18/99	$2,900.00

15. Choose **File→Close** from the menu bar and choose **Yes** when Access asks if you want to save the changes.

Skill Builder 4.7

In this exercise, you will insert a hyperlink to the Trips-Specific Category report on the New Trips form. The report will open whenever the hyperlink is clicked.

1. Click the Forms button on the Objects bar in the database window.

2. Choose the New Trips form and click the [Design] button.

3. Click the Insert Hyperlink button.

4. Choose the Trips-Specific Category report from the Reports section and click **OK.**

5. Drag the hyperlink until it is located below the GoTo Customers Form hyperlink.

6. Modify the hyperlink text to read **Report Trips-Specific Category**.

7. Click the Form View button on the left end of the Access toolbar and the form should have the appearance shown below.

New Trips			
Trip ID	Adv01	Firstname	Debbie
Customer ID	1	Lastname	Thomas
Destination	Kenyan Safari	Profile	Adventure
Category	Adventure	City	Austin
Departure Date	9/4/97	State	TX
Return Date			GoTo Customers Form
Cost	$6,600.00		Report Trips-Specific Category

Record: 1 of 9

8. Click the *Report Trips—Specific Category* hyperlink and the pop up box will appear.

9. Type the category **family** and click **OK.**
   The report will display just two records.

10. Use the **File→Close** command to close both the report and the form. Choose **Yes** when Access asks if you want to save the changes to the form.

Skill Builder 4.8

In this exercise, you will make a copy of the Trips-Specific Category query. You will modify the new query and then create a new report that is based upon the query.

1. Click the **Queries** button on the Objects bar in the database window.

2. Choose the *Trips—Specific Category* query and then click the Copy 📋 button on the Access toolbar.

3. Click the Paste 📋 button and the Paste As box will appear.

4. Type the name **Trips—Cost Greater Than** and click **OK**.

5. Choose the *Trips—Cost Greater Than* query and click the 🖋 Design button.

6. Select the Criterion **[Enter a category]** in the Category criteria box and tap the (DELETE) key to remove it.

7. Enter the criterion **>[Cost Greater Than]** in the criteria box of the **Cost** field, as shown below.

   When the query is run, this criterion will display a pop-up box that prompts you to enter a cost. Only records where the cost is greater than the cost you enter will be selected by the query.

Field:	Firstname	Lastname	Destination	Category	Departure Date	Return Date	Cost
Table:	Customers	Customers	Trips	Trips	Trips	Trips	Trips
Sort:							
Show:	☑	☑	☑	☑	☑	☑	☑
Criteria:							>[Cost Greater Than]
or:							

8. Run ⊞ the query and the pop-up box will appear.

9. Type **4000** in the box and click **OK**.

   The query results shown below will appear. Notice that only trips with a cost that is greater than 4000 have been selected.

Firstname	Lastname	Destination	Category	Departure Date	Return Date	Cost
Debbie	Thomas	Kenyan Safari	Adventure	8/5/97	9/4/97	$6,600.00
Debbie	Thomas	Amazon Jungle Trek	Adventure	8/7/98	9/14/98	$7,765.00
Lisa	Simms	Hawaii	Leisure	2/5/99	2/15/99	$4,500.00
Ted	Carter	Hawaii	Family	3/7/99	3/15/99	$5,300.00

10. Choose **File→Close** from the menu bar and choose **Yes** to save the query changes.

(Continued on the next page)

11. Now use the Report Wizard and the following guidelines to create the report shown below.

  - Base the report upon the *Trips—Cost Greater Than* query.

  - Choose the By Trips option when Access asks how you want to view the data in the second wizard screen.

  - Use Landscape orientation.

  - Use the Soft Gray report style.

  - Name the report **Trips-Cost Greater Than**.

  - Modify the report in Design view until it matches the example shown below.

Trips-Cost Greater Than

Firstname	Lastname	Destination	Category	Departure Date	Return Date	Cost
Debbie	Thomas	Kenyan Safari	Adventure	8/5/97	9/4/97	$6,600.00
Debbie	Thomas	Amazon Jungle Trek	Adventure	8/7/98	9/14/98	$7,765.00
Lisa	Simms	Hawaii	Leisure	2/5/99	2/15/99	$4,500.00
Ted	Carter	Hawaii	Family	3/7/99	3/15/99	$5,300.00

12. Close the report when you have finished, and save any changes.

13. Now insert a hyperlink to the Trips—Cost Greater Than report on the New Trips form as shown below. The hyperlink should open the Trips—Cost Greater Than report when it is clicked.

New Trips

Trip ID: Adv01	Firstname: Debbie
Customer ID: 1	Lastname: Thomas
Destination: Kenyan Safari	Profile: Adventure
Category: Adventure	City: Austin
Departure Date: 8/5/97	State: TX
Return Date: 9/4/97	GoTo Customers Form
Cost: $6,600.00	Report Trips-Specific Category
	Report Trips-Cost Greater Than

Record: ◄◄ ◄ 1 ► ►► ►* of 9

14. Close the form when you have finished and save the changes.

15. Finally, close the Tropical Getaways database and continue with the Assessment exercise on the following pages.

Assessments

Assessment 4.1

1. Open the Classic Cars database.

2. Create a one-to-many relationship between the Collector ID fields in the Collectors and Cars tables as shown to the right. Enforce referential integrity and activate cascade updating of related fields and cascade deleting of related records.

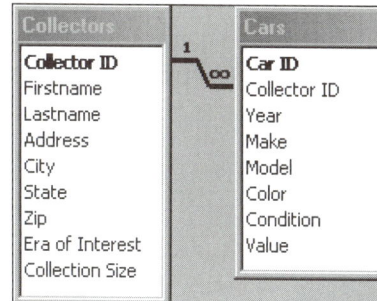

Collectors	Cars
Collector ID	**Car ID**
Firstname	Collector ID
Lastname	Year
Address	Make
City	Model
State	Color
Zip	Condition
Era of Interest	Value
Collection Size	

3. Follow these steps to create the form shown below.

   ■ Use the Form Wizard to set up the form using fields from both the Collectors and Cars tables. Use the Standard style for the form and assign the name **New Cars** to the form.

   ■ Use Design view to arrange the controls as shown.

   ■ Set the Enabled property to **No** and the Locked property to **Yes** for the Firstname, Lastname, and Collection Size controls. These settings will prevent data from being entered into these controls.

New Cars

Car ID	CJ01
Collector ID	1
Year	58
Make	Chevrolet
Model	Corvette
Color	Red and white
Condition	Mint
Value	$65,000.00

Firstname	Cindy
Lastname	Johnson
Collection Size	42

Record: |◄ ◄ | 1 | ► ►| ►*| of 7

(Continued on the next page)

4. Create a query that extracts data from the Cars and Collectors tables as shown below. The query should display a pop-up box that requests the user to enter a Model. Once a model is entered, the query should only select records containing the model the user enters. The pop-up box should display the phrase *Enter a Model*. The example below assumes that the model name Corvette has been entered into the pop-up box. Assign the name **Specific Model** to the query.

Year	Make	Model	Color	Condition	Value	Firstname	Lastname
58	Chevrolet	Corvette	Red and white	Mint	$65,000.00	Cindy	Johnson
62	Chevrolet	Corvette	Blue	Excellent	$30,000.00	Tammy	Olson
58	Chevrolet	Corvette	Black	Excellent	$35,000.00	Bob	Barker
57	Chevrolet	Corvette	Red	Excellent	$42,000.00	Bob	Barker

5. Create a report that is based upon the Specific Model query and that produces the results shown below. The report should display the data in Landscape mode. Use the Compact report style. You will need to customize the report by left aligning the Value label and control. Assign the name **Specific Model** to the report.

Specific Model

Year	Make	Model	Color	Condition	Value	Firstname	Lastname
58	Chevrolet	Corvette	Red and white	Mint	$65,000.00	Cindy	Johnson
62	Chevrolet	Corvette	Blue	Excellent	$30,000.00	Tammy	Olson
58	Chevrolet	Corvette	Black	Excellent	$35,000.00	Bob	Barker
57	Chevrolet	Corvette	Red	Excellent	$42,000.00	Bob	Barker

6. Insert hyperlinks on the New Cars and Collectors forms as shown below. The hyperlinks on the New Cars form should display the Collectors form and open the Specific Model report. The hyperlink on the Collectors form should display the New Cars form. You will need to modify the hyperlink text and reposition the hyperlinks as shown. Save the changes to the forms when you have finished.

7. Save and close all objects when you have finished, then close the Classic Cars database.

Form Customization and Advanced Controls

Forms are an important part of any Access database. Forms are the primary objects through which users interact with a database. The Forms Wizard can be used to set up forms that display data from more than one table. In addition, Access' form design view allows you to customize forms to meet your needs. Access provides a variety of form controls to assist users with data entry. These controls include Yes/No check boxes, combo boxes, and memo boxes. In this lesson, you will customize a form by adding new controls and enhancing the appearance of the form.

In This Lesson

Case Study

Al Smith wants a form to track pet visits to Pinnacle Pet Care. The form needs to display data from two tables—the Pets table and a Visits table that you will set up. Al wants the form to be easy to use and he wants the form designed to prevent data entry errors. In this lesson, you will set up the form requested by Al. The form will contain new types of controls including check boxes, combo boxes, and a memo field. You will use a header to enhance the appearance of the form. The header will contain formatted text and a picture. The form that you will create is shown below. The illustration also shows several of the controls that you will set up.

Combo boxes let you enter data by choosing options from drop-down lists.

Yes/No fields let you turn options on and off by clicking check boxes.

Memo fields let you type notes and other long text entries.

Additional Data Types

Thus far, you have used the Number, Text, Currency, and Date/Time data types in tables. Access provides additional data types, including the Memo and Yes/No data types.

Memo Data Type

The Memo data type creates fields in which you can enter up to 64,000 characters. You typically use the Memo data type when a large amount of text or notes will be entered into a field. Although a Memo field can hold up to 64,000 characters, only the characters that are entered into a record occupy storage space in the database file.

Yes/No Data Type

You use a Yes/No data type for fields requiring either yes or no values. The value of a Yes/No data field is often set by using a check box on a form. You can check or uncheck a box to set the value in the underlying field to Yes or No. The Yes/No data type is chosen when a table is set up. The corresponding check box is created when a form that is based upon the table is set up.

Hands-On 5.1 Set Up the Visits Table

In this exercise, you will set up a new table in the Pinnacle Pet Care database. The new table will record pet visits to the clinic. The table will contain various fields that record visit information. Later in this lesson, you will create a form that combines fields from the Visits tables and Pets tables.

1. Start Access and open the Pinnacle Pet Care database.

2. Click the **Tables** button on the Objects bar and double-click the *Create table in Design* view option.

3. Follow these steps to set up the Visits table.

   Ⓐ *Type the field names shown here, and choose the data types shown for each field name. Make sure you spell the field names correctly.*

   Ⓑ *Click in the Pet ID row, and set the Field Size to **6** in the Field Properties section at the bottom of the dialog box.*

   Ⓒ *Set the Appointment Type Field Size to 25.*

   Ⓓ *Click in the Visit ID row, and then click the **Primary Key** button on the Access toolbar. A key icon will appear indicating that Visit ID is the primary key. The primary key uniquely identifies each record in the table.*

Field Name	Data Type
Visit ID	AutoNumber
Visit Date	Date/Time
Pet ID	Text
Visit Notes	Memo
Appointment Type	Text
Next Visit Scheduled	Yes/No

   Ⓔ *Click in the Visit Date row, and then set the Format option in the Field Properties section at the bottom of the dialog box to Short Date.*

4. Make sure your table is set up properly and then choose **File→Close** from the menu bar.

5. Click **Yes,** type the name **Visits** in the Save As box and click **OK.**
   You will use the table throughout this lesson.

Designing the Visits Form

In the next few exercises, you will create a form that tracks pet visits to the Pinnacle Pet Care clinic. The form will include fields from both the Pets and Visits tables. In the previous lesson, you learned how to base a form upon multiple tables. You learned that a relationship must be created between tables if those tables are used in the same form. In the following exercise, you will use the Relationships window to create a one-to-many relationship between the Pets table and the Visits table. Each pet will be allowed to have many visits to the clinic but each visit will be associated with just one pet. You will use the Pet ID field to establish this one-to-many relationship between the tables.

Hands-On 5.2 Establish a Relationship and Set Up the Visits Form

Establish a Relationship

1. Click the Relationships 🔲 button on the Access toolbar to display the Relationships window.

2. If necessary, click the Show Table 🔲 button on the Access toolbar to display the Show Table box.

3. Choose Visits in the Show Table box and click the **Add** button.
   The Visits table will be added to the Relationships window.

4. Close the Show Table box.

5. If necessary, drag the bottom edge of the Visits field list down until all field names are visible.

6. Follow these steps to establish a relationship between the Pet ID fields.

   A *Drag the* Pet ID *field from the* **Pets** *table to the* Pet ID *field in the* **Visits** *table.*

   B *Release the mouse button, and the Edit Relationships box will appear.*

   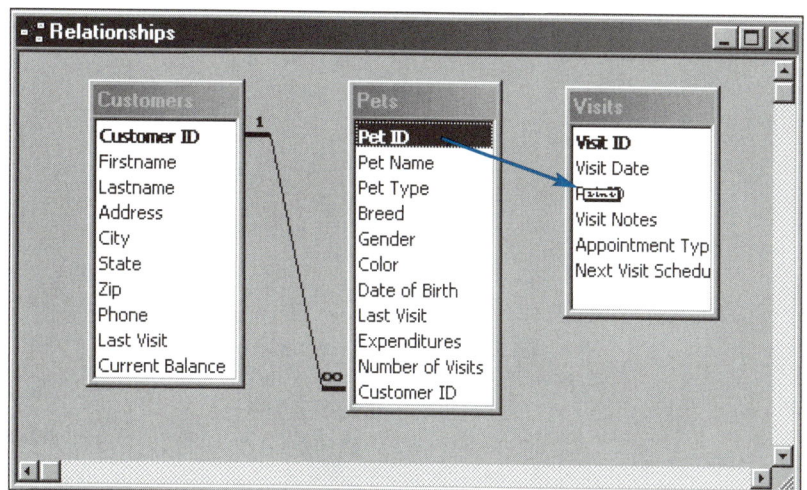

In the previous lesson, you learned that the Edit Relationships box lets you choose the desired relationship type and enforce referential integrity.

7. Check the *Enforce Referential Integrity* box and click the **Create** button. There is no need to check the Cascade Update and Cascade Delete boxes for this relationship.
   Referential integrity will require that each record in the Visits table has a corresponding Pet ID in the Pets table.

8. Close the Relationships window and choose **Yes** when Access asks if you want to save the changes to the Relationships.

(Continued on the next page)

Set Up the Visits Form

9. Click the **Forms** button on the Objects bar.

10. Double-click the *Create form by using Wizard* option.
    In the next few steps, you will choose the fields that will be displayed on the form. It is important that you choose the fields in the order specified in this exercise. This will make it easy for you to modify the form later in this lesson.

11. Follow these steps to add the fields from the Visits table.

    Ⓐ *Choose the* Visits *table from the* **Tables/Queries** *list. You can base a form on one or more tables, or even on a query.*

    Ⓑ *Click the* **Add all fields** *button to move all fields to the Selected Fields list.*

12. Follow these steps to add five fields from the Pets table.

    Ⓐ *Choose the* Pets *table from the* **Tables/Queries** *list.*

    Ⓑ *Use the* **Add Single Field** *button to add the* Pet Name, Pet Type, Breed, Gender, *and* Date of Birth *fields to the Selected Fields list. The fields will appear at the bottom of the Selected Fields list as shown here.*

13. Click the **Next** button to display the next wizard screen.

14. Make sure the view your data option is set to *by Visits* and click **Next**.
The *by* Visits *option instructs Access to base the form on the Visits table. The pet data for a particular pet is then displayed on the form along with the visit data.*

15. Make sure the Columnar option is chosen in the next screen and click **Next**.

16. Choose Standard as the style and click **Next**.

17. Choose the *Modify the form's design* option in the last wizard screen and click the **Finish** button.
Access will create the form and display it in Design view as shown below; however, your form may have a different layout. Notice that the form contains a check box for the Next Visit Scheduled field. If you create a form with the Form Wizard, Access creates a check box for fields that have a Yes/No data type. A Yes/No field in the underlying table is set to Yes when a box is checked and No when the box is unchecked. Also notice the large field for Visit Notes. Access creates a large block for fields that have a Memo data type. This way, you can type large amounts of text in the field. In the previous lesson, you used Design view to make simple modifications to a form. You will make extensive modifications to the Visits form as you progress through this lesson.

Form Sections

A form is composed of a header, detail section, and footer. Typically, controls that display data are positioned in the detail section of a form. The displayed data in the detail section changes as different records are displayed in the form. The header and footer sections typically contain labels, pictures, command buttons, and other objects that do not display data. This way, the header and footer remain the same regardless of the data displayed on the form. When you first create a form, the header area is not exposed. To expose the header area, you simply drag the Detail bar down slightly while working in Design view. Once the header is exposed, you can insert objects in it. The footer area is already exposed when a form is first created.

Hands-On 5.3 Expose the Header and Expand the Detail Section

The Visits form should already be displayed in Design view.

1. Click the Maximize ⬜ button at the top-right corner of the Visits form window.
   Maximizing the window will give you more room to work.

2. Follow these steps to expose the header area.

Ⓐ *Position the mouse pointer on the top edge of the **Detail** bar so that a double-headed arrow appears.*

Ⓑ *Drag the **Detail** bar down until the header area is approximately 2.0" high.*

Ⓒ *Drag the **Form Footer** bar down until it nearly touches the bottom of the window. This will expand the Detail area. Expanding the Detail area will give you more room to rearrange controls in the next exercise.*

3. Take a moment to examine the form.
   Notice that the form window has a light gray area and a dark gray area. The light area automatically expands when controls and other objects are positioned over the dark area. The appearance of the window is a bit deceiving. Both the light and dark areas appear in the same light gray color when the form is displayed in Form view.

Working with Controls

Thus far, you have entered data into controls and used various techniques to move and manipulate controls in Design view. Controls are objects that display data, initiate events, or enhance the appearance of a form or report. Controls can be categorized as either bound or unbound. **Bound controls** are linked to a field in an underlying table. Bound controls are most often used for entering and editing data. For example, all controls with a white background on the Visits form are bound controls that are linked to fields in either the Visits or Pets tables. **Unbound controls,** on the other hand, have no data source in the underlying table. Examples of unbound controls include labels, pictures, lines, and rectangles.

Aligning Controls

There are certain design techniques that you can use to improve the appearance of forms. One important technique is to align controls and other objects in vertical columns or horizontal rows. Your forms will have a clean and organized appearance if the controls are aligned properly. Access lets you align selected controls with the **Format→Align** command. You can align selected controls on the left, right, top, and bottom.

Adjusting the Size of Controls

The forms in the Pinnacle Pet Care database contain a variety of controls. You can adjust the width of any control by selecting the control and dragging one of the sizing handles that appears. The size of the control only affects the appearance of the control on the form. The underlying fields in a table are not affected when controls are resized.

Hands-On 5.4 Rearrange, Size, and Align Controls

1. Follow these steps to reposition the Gender and Date of Birth controls.
   These controls are part of the pet information, so they should be grouped together with the Pet Name, Pet Type, and Breed controls.

Ⓐ *Press the* (SHIFT) *key while you click the Gender and Date of Birth controls. Make sure you click the controls and not the labels to the left of the controls.*

Ⓑ *Drag either of the selected controls to a position below the Breed control.*

Ⓒ *If necessary, fine-tune the position of the controls by pressing the* (CTRL) *key while you tap the arrow keys on the keyboard.*

(Continued on the next page)

2. Follow these steps to adjust the size of the Visit Notes control.

Ⓐ *Click the Visit Notes control, and it will become selected.*

Ⓑ *Drag the middle sizing handle to the left until the control has the approximate width shown here.*

3. Follow these steps to reposition the Visit Date and Visit Notes controls and to select the controls.

Ⓐ *Drag the* Visit Date *control to the right of the* Visit ID *control as shown here. The* Visit Date *label will move with the control.*

Ⓑ *Now drag the* Visit Notes *control to the right of the* Visit Date *control.*

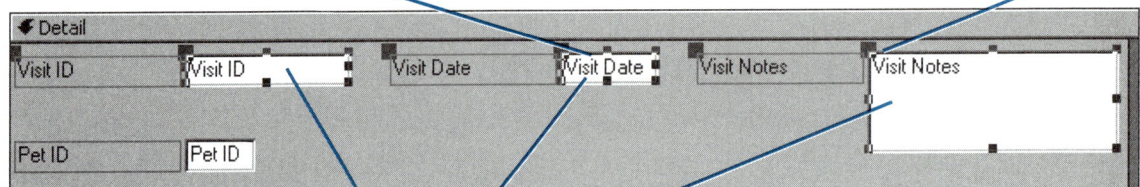

Ⓒ *Select the* Visit ID, Visit Date, *and* Visit Notes *controls by pressing* (SHIFT) *and clicking them.*

Ⓓ *Choose* **Format→Align→Top** *to align the controls vertically.*

Access will move two of the controls up until they are aligned with the highest of the three selected controls. However, notice that Access does not move the labels to the left of the selected controls. The labels behave as separate objects. In the next step, you will include the labels in the selection, thus aligning the labels and the controls at the same time.

4. Press (SHIFT) while you click the labels to the left of the Visit ID, Visit Date, and Visit Notes controls. The labels and controls should be selected.

5. Choose **Format→Align→Top** to align the labels and controls vertically.

6. Follow these steps to reposition the Appointment Type and Next Visit Scheduled controls.

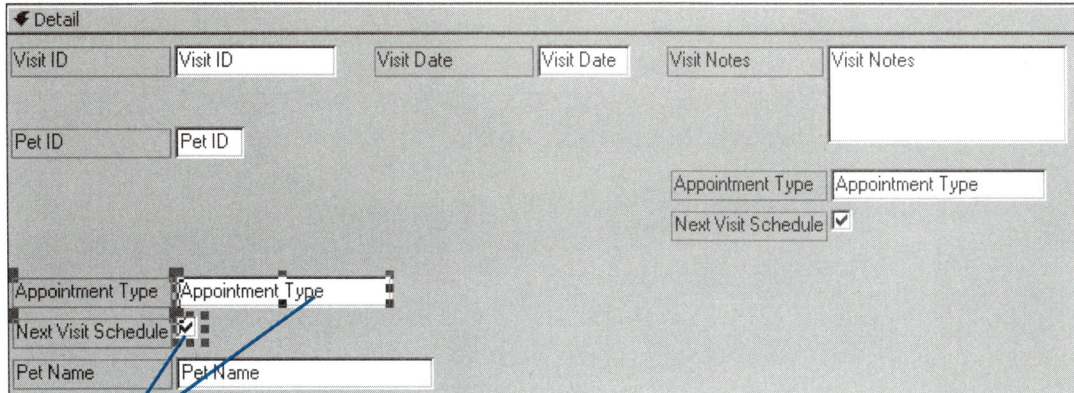

Ⓐ *Click the* Appointment Type *control, press* (SHIFT), *and then click the* **Next Visit Scheduled** *check box.*

Ⓑ *Drag the controls below the* Visit Notes *control. If necessary, use the* (CTRL)*-plus-arrow-keys technique to fine-tune the position of the controls.*

7. Follow these steps to move the Pet ID control down.

Ⓐ *Select the* Pet ID *control by clicking it.*

Ⓑ *Press* (CTRL)+↓ *until the control is positioned above the* Pet Name *control.*

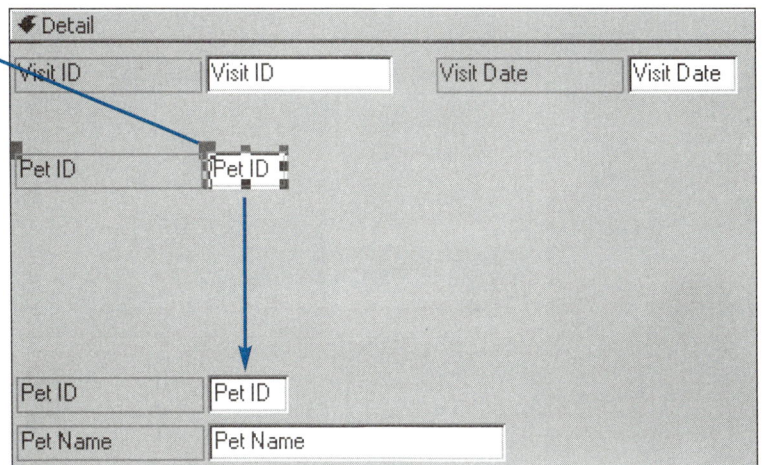

8. Use the (SHIFT) key technique to select the Pet ID, Pet Name, Pet Type, Breed, Gender, and Date of Birth controls.

9. Use the (CTRL)+↑ keystroke combination to move the controls up until they are positioned just below the Visit ID control, as shown below.

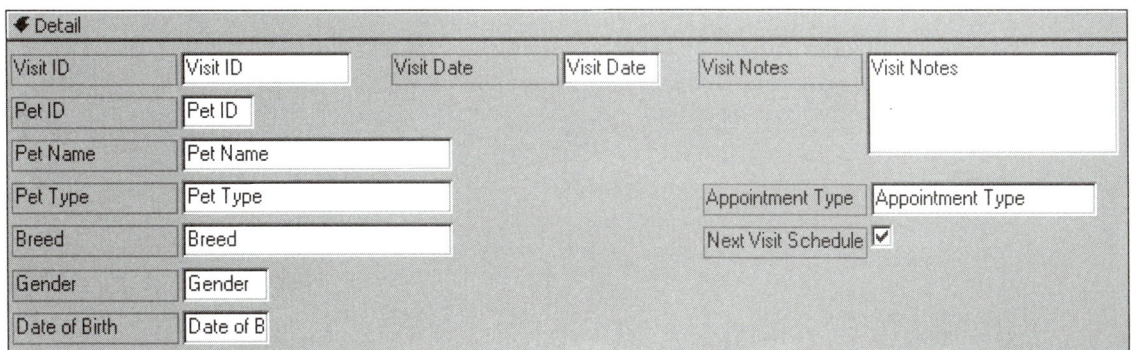

(Continued on the next page)

10. Now choose **Edit→Select All** to select all objects on the form.

11. Tap CTRL+↓ 15 times to move all of the objects down slightly.
Your completed form should closely match the example shown below.

12. Click the Save 🖫 button to save the changes to your form.
You will continue to enhance the form in the next exercise.

The Toolbox

You use the toolbox in form Design view to add new controls to a form. Access usually provides Wizards and other guidance when you attempt to add controls to a form. You can display or hide the toolbox with the **View→Toolbox** command. The toolbox is shown below with descriptions of several frequently used buttons. You will use these buttons to add controls to the Visits form. The toolbox may also be visible on your screen in form Design view.

Add descriptive text labels.

Text boxes are bound to fields in tables. Most of the controls on the Visits form are text box controls.

Combo boxes display drop-down lists of options from which you can choose.

Use an unbound object frame to add pictures and other unbound objects to forms and reports.

Draw lines and rectangles.

Adding Pictures to Forms

The Unbound Object Frame tool lets you position pictures and other objects in forms. Access displays the Insert Object dialog box when you click in a form after clicking the Unbound Object Frame button. The Insert Object box lets you choose the object type that you wish to insert. You can choose the Microsoft Clip Gallery option to insert clips from the Office 2000 Clip Gallery. Once a picture is inserted, you can display the Properties box for the picture and set the Size Mode setting to Stretch. You can adjust the size of the picture once the Size Mode setting is set to Stretch.

1. If necessary, choose **View→Toolbox** to display the toolbox.
   The toolbox will be displayed as a floating palett or a toolbar.

2. Click anywhere in the header area to highlight the Form Header bar.

3. Click the Unbound Object Frame [icon] button on the toolbox.

4. Follow this step to specify the picture location.

   A *Click in the top-left corner of the header area. Access will display the Insert Object box.*

   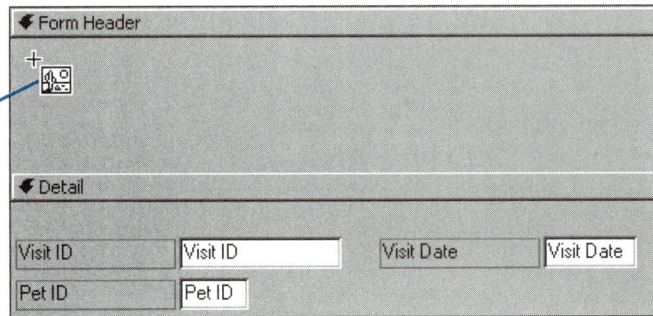

5. Choose Microsoft Clip Gallery and click **OK.**

6. Choose the Animals category in the clip gallery.

7. Choose the "veterinarian with the dog" picture as shown to the right (or some other picture if it is not available) and click the **Insert Clip** button (first button on the pop up toolbar).
   Notice that the inserted picture is quite large. In the next few steps, you will correct this by changing the Size Mode property setting.

8. Make sure the picture is selected, with sizing handles surrounding it.

9. If necessary, click the Properties [icon] button on the Access toolbar to display the Unbound Object Frame Properties box.

10. If necessary, click the Format tab in the Properties box and set the Size Mode option (the first option in the box) to Stretch.

11. Reduce the size of the picture by dragging a corner-sizing handle until it is approximately 1.0" high by 1.0" wide.

12. Follow these steps to reposition the picture and reduce the height of the header area.

Ⓐ *If necessary, drag the picture to the top-left corner of the header area.* Ⓑ *Drag the top edge of the **Detail** bar up until the header has the height shown here.*

Adding Labels to Forms

You can use the Label [Aa] button on the toolbox to easily add descriptive text labels to forms. Text labels can be placed in headers, footers, and detail sections. Text labels are not bound to fields in tables. They simply allow you to place text anywhere on a form. You insert labels by clicking the Label button, clicking at the desired location in the form, and then typing the label text.

Formatting Labels and Other Controls

You can format labels and other controls using formatting buttons on the Access toolbar or by setting format properties in the Format tab of the Properties box. You can specify the font, font size, color, and other properties. The formats you apply affect all text in a label.

Formatting Section Backgrounds

The Fill/Back Color [icon] button appears on the Access toolbar whenever a form section is selected. The Fill/Back Color button can be used to change the background color of a section. You can select the header, footer, or detail sections by clicking the header bar at the top of the section.

Hands-On 5.6 Insert and Format a Label

Insert the Label

1. Click the Label [Aa] button on the toolbox.

2. Follow these steps to insert the label.

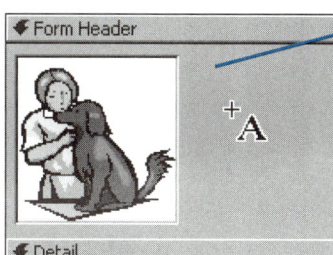

Ⓐ *Click just to the right of the picture, as shown here. A thin box with the flashing insertion point will appear.*

Ⓑ *Type **Pinnacle Pet Care - Visits**.*

3. Click anywhere outside of the label.

(Continued on the next page)

Format the Label

4. Click anywhere on the label and it will become selected (sizing handles will surround the label).
   If you have trouble selecting the label, then click outside of it and try clicking it again.

5. Use the Formatting toolbar to set the font size to 18 and to apply Bold **B** formatting.
   The text will be too large for the box and will be hidden from view.

6. Follow these steps to adjust the label box size.

Ⓐ *Drag the corner sizing handle until all of the text is visible.*

Ⓑ *If necessary, use the* (CTRL)+*ArrowKey(s) keystroke combinations to adjust the position of the box as shown here.*

7. Make sure the label is still selected, then follow these steps to change the text color.

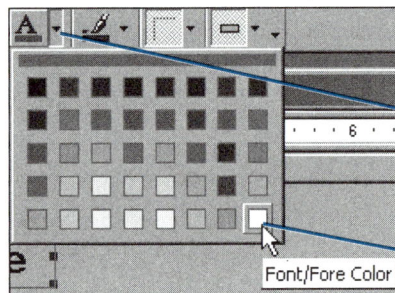

Ⓐ *Click the Font Color drop-down button on the Access toolbar. The color palette shown here will appear.*

Ⓑ *Choose white to format the text with a white color.*

Format the Header Background

8. Follow this step to select the header section.

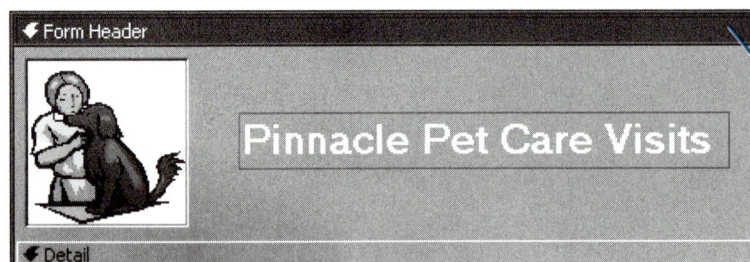

Ⓐ *Click the **Form Header** bar, and it will become selected as shown here. Any changes made to the background color will only impact the selected section.*

9. Follow these steps to change the background color.

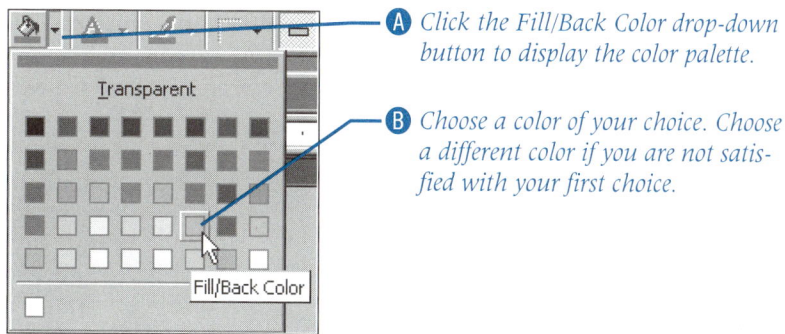

A Click the Fill/Back Color drop-down button to display the color palette.

B Choose a color of your choice. Choose a different color if you are not satisfied with your first choice.

10. Click the Form View ⊞ button on the left end of the Formatting toolbar.
    Your form should match the one shown below. Notice that the form is maximized and thus occupies the entire window. You will continue to enhance and develop the form while it is maximized. Maximizing the form gives you a larger working area and makes it easier to rearrange objects and modify the layout.

11. Click the Design view ⬚ button to return to Design view.

12. Click the Save 🖫 button and continue with the next topic.

Using Controls to Ensure Data Integrity

Keeping data reliable is one of the biggest challenges facing database designers. Thus far, you have learned that Access uses referential integrity to help ensure data integrity. Access provides a variety of other features that also help ensure data integrity. In particular, Access provides various types of controls that are specifically designed to restrict data entry in fields.

Combo Boxes

Perhaps the most useful type of control for restricting data entry is the combo box. A combo box is bound to a table field and contains a drop-down button. A list of values is displayed when a user clicks the drop-down button. Only values that are on the drop-down list can be chosen and entered into the bound field. Thus, a combo box ensures data integrity by forcing users to only choose data from the combo box drop-down list. The following illustration shows one of the combo boxes that you will add to the Visits form in the following exercises.

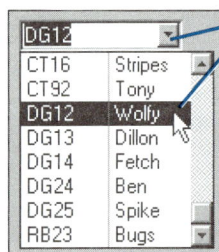

A list of values is displayed when you click the drop-down button on a combo box. A value is entered into a field in the underlying table when you choose a row from the list. In this combo box, the Pet ID in the first column is entered into the Pet ID field in the Visits table.

Lookup Tables and Other Combo Box Data Sources

The list of values that a combo box displays can come from either of two sources. You can specify the values for the list when you create a combo box; however, this approach is restrictive since the list is only available in that combo box, and adding and deleting values to/from the list is cumbersome. A better approach is to create a lookup table and to use that lookup table as the data source for the combo box. A lookup table typically contains just one field. The values in that field are used as the data source for the combo box. The following illustration shows a combo box and the associated lookup table that you will create in the Pinnacle Pet Care database.

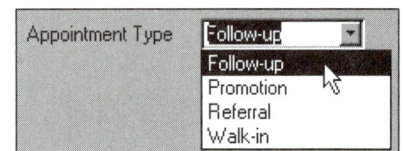

*The values from the **Appointment Type** lookup table are displayed on the combo box list when the drop-down button is clicked.*

Setting Up Combo Boxes

The Combo Box ⬚ button on the toolbox initiates the Combo Box Wizard. The Combo Box Wizard guides you through the process of setting up a combo box. The Wizard prompts you to specify the field that the combo box will be bound to (the field that data will be entered into), the number of columns that you want displayed in the combo box, and the lookup table or other data source for the combo box list. The wizard is initiated when you click in the form after clicking the Combo Box button.

In this exercise, you will remove the Pet ID control from the Visits form. You will replace the control with a combo box. The combo box will be bound to the Pet ID field in the Visits table. The Pet ID field in the Pets table will be used as the data source for the combo box. This way, you will choose Pet ID's from the Pets table where the Pet ID is the primary key. The Pet ID you choose will be entered into the Visits table. This will ensure that each Pet ID in the Visits table has a matching Pet ID in the Pets table.

Create the Combo Box

1. Follow these steps to delete the Pet ID control from the form.

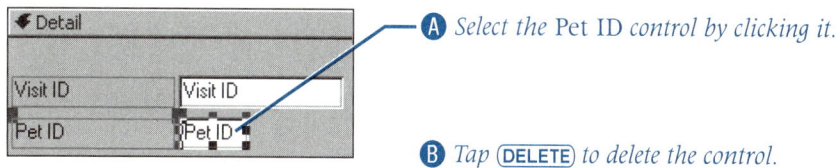

A Select the Pet ID *control by clicking it.*

B *Tap* (DELETE) *to delete the control.*

2. Click the Combo Box ▦ button on the toolbox.

3. Follow this step to specify the combo box position on the form.

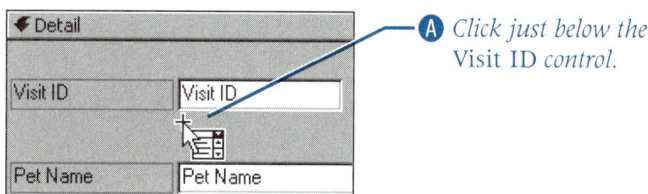

A *Click just below the* Visit ID *control.*

The first Wizard screen will ask where the combo box will get its values. Your combo box will get its values from the Pet ID and Pet Name fields in the Pets table.

4. Make sure the *I want the combo box to look up the values in a table or query* option is chosen and click **Next.**
    The next screen will ask which table or query should provide the values for the combo box.

5. Choose the Pets table and click **Next.**
    The next screen will ask which fields you want included in the combo box.

6. Use the Add Field ⊐ > ⊏ button to add the Pet ID and Pet Name fields to the Selected Fields list.
    When the drop-down button is clicked on the combo box, the data in these fields will be displayed as columns in the combo box.

(Continued on the next page)

7. Click **Next** and follow these steps to display the Pet ID column, and to adjust the column widths.

> ☐ Hide key column (recommended)
>
> | | Pet ID | Pet Name |
> |---|---|---|
> | ▶ | DG12 | Wolfy |
> | | DG13 | Dillon |
> | | RB23 | Bugs |
> | | CT02 | Max |
> | | CT16 | Stripes |
> | | CT92 | Tony |
> | | DG14 | Fetch |

A *Remove the check from the **Hide key column** box. The **Pet ID** column will be displayed.*

B *Position the mouse pointer on the right edge of the **Pet ID** column, and drag the column to the left slightly to reduce the width.*

C *Reduce the width of the **Pet Name** column slightly.*

8. Click **Next** and the Wizard will ask you to choose a field that uniquely identifies the row.
   In the next step, you will choose the Pet ID field. This will instruct the Wizard to choose the Pet ID field from the Pets table when you enter data into the database and choose a row from the combo box. Notice that you could specify either the Pet ID field or the Pet Name field. The Wizard requires you to choose one field because data from only one of the fields will be stored in the Pet ID field of the Visits table. In this combo box, the Pet Name field is used just for display purposes to help the user choose the correct Pet ID.

9. Choose Pet ID and click **Next.**

10. Follow these steps to instruct the Wizard to store the value that is chosen from the combo box in the Pet ID field of the Visits table.

A *Click this option button.*

B *Click the drop-down button, and notice that the field names are taken from both the Pets and Visits tables. These field names are available because you chose these fields when you based the Visits form upon the Pets and Visits tables earlier in this lesson.*

> ○ Remember the value for later use.
> ⊙ Store that value in this field: Pet ID ▾

C *Choose Pet ID from the drop-down list. This is the Pet ID field in the Visits table.*

The settings that you have made will create a combo box that displays a list of Pet IDs and Pet Names for each pet in the Pets table. When you choose a pet from the combo box, Access will take the Pet ID from the Pets table and enter it into the Pet ID field in the Visits table. Thus, each record in the Visits table will have a Pet ID that also exists in the Pets table. Earlier in this lesson, you established a one-to-many relationship between the Pet ID fields in the Pets and Visits tables. This relationship will ensure that the Visits form always displays the proper pet information for each visit.

11. Click **Next** to display the final Wizard screen.

12. Type the name **Pet ID** in the label box and click the **Finish** button.
    You will adjust the position and alignment of the combo box in a moment.

Use the Combo Box to Enter Data

13. Click the Form view [⊞] button on the Access toolbar.

14. Tap the (TAB) key, and the insertion point will move from the Visit ID field to the Visit Date field.

15. Follow these steps to enter data into the form.

A *Type the visit date shown here, then tap the* (TAB) *key to move to the* **Visit Notes** *control.*

B *Type the text shown here into the* **Visit Notes** *memo field. A scroll box on the memo control will allow you to scroll up or down if necessary.*

C *Click the drop-down button on the Pet ID combo box, and choose Wolfy. Access will display all information for the Wolfy record in the* **Pet Name, Pet Type, Breed, Gender,** *and* **Date of Birth** *fields. The relationship between the Pet ID fields in the Pets and Visits tables allows Access to synchronize the tables on the form. In other words, all information for Wolfy will appear on the form whenever the Visit ID 1 record is displayed.*

D *Click the* **Next Visit Scheduled** *box and a check will appear. This field is now set to Yes in the underlying Visits table. Leave the* **Appointment Type** *field empty.*

(Continued on the next page)

16. Take a moment to examine the following illustration. It describes the relationships between the tables, fields, controls, and the Visits form.

*Visit ID, the primary key field in the Visits table, controls the form. Each visit has a unique Visit ID that is assigned by the AutoNumber data type of the **Visit ID** field.*

*The **Visit Date, Visit Notes, Appointment Type**, and **Next Visit Scheduled** fields are in the Visits table. The data below is stored in Record 1 of the Visits table.*

*This **Pet ID** is also stored in the Visits table. It was copied to the Visits table from the Pet ID field in the Pets table when you chose Wolfy from the combo box. Access displays Wolfy's information from the Pets table because there is a relationship between the Pet ID fields in the two tables. The relationship ensures that Wolfy's information will always be displayed along with the Visit information for visit number 1.*

*The **Pet Name, Pet Type, Breed, Gender**, and **Date of Birth** controls are displaying data from the Pets table.*

Using Lookup Tables With Combo Boxes

Lookup tables can be used as data sources for combo boxes. Lookup tables are like any other Access table, though they usually contain just one or two fields. Lookup tables are beneficial because you can easily add or remove data to or from lookup tables. Combo boxes will then reflect the most recent changes made in the lookup tables. The Combo Box Wizard gives you the option of using a lookup table as a data source.

Hands-On 5.8 Use a Lookup Table With a Combo Box

Create the Lookup Table

1. Close the Visits form and save any changes that have been made.

2. Click the **Tables** button on the Objects bar in the Access database window.

3. Double-click the *Create table in Design view* option.

4. Add a field named **Appointment Type** to the table.

5. Leave the Data Type set to Text but change the Field Size to 25, as shown to the right.

   It is important to have the data type set to Text and the field size set to 25 because these settings are also used for the Appointment Type field in the Visits table. The combo box that you will create will copy data from this lookup table into the Appointment Type field in the Visits table.

Table1 : Table	
Field Name	Data Type
Appointment Type	Text

   General | Lookup
   Field Size   25
   Format

6. Click on the phrase *Appointment Type,* then click the Primary Key 🔑 button to make Appointment Type a primary key.

7. Click the Datasheet View 🗔 button on the Access toolbar, choose **Yes,** and save the table as **Appointment Type**.

Appointment Type
Promotion
Referral
Walk-in

8. Enter the three records shown to the right into the table.

9. **Close** the table.

Create the Combo Box

10. Click the **Forms** button on the Objects bar in the database window.

11. Choose the Visits form and click the 🗔 Design button.

12. Click the Appointment Type control and tap the (DELETE) key to remove the control and the label to the left of the control.

13. Click the Combo Box 🗔 button on the toolbox.

14. Click just above the Next Visit Scheduled check box to specify the position of the combo box.

15. Click the **Next** button on the first Wizard screen.

16. Choose *Appointment Type* from the list of tables and click **Next.**

17. Add the Appointment Type field to the Selected Fields list and click **Next.**

18. Adjust the column width until the Appointment Type heading is completely visible, then click **Next.**

19. Choose Appointment Type from the *Store that value in this field* box and click **Next.**

20. Type the name **Appointment Type** in the final Wizard screen and click **Finish.**
    Access will create the Appointment Type combo box.

(Continued on the next page)

Adjust the Size and Position of Labels

21. Follow these steps to adjust the size of the label attached to the Appointment Type combo box.

Ⓐ *Select the label by clicking it.*

Ⓑ *Drag this sizing handle to the right until the entire phrase Appointment Type is visible.*

22. Follow this step to select the labels for the Visit Notes, Appointment Type, and Next Visit Scheduled fields.

Ⓐ *Press the (SHIFT) key while you click the labels. Make sure you click the labels and not the controls to the right of the labels. The labels will become selected, as shown here.*

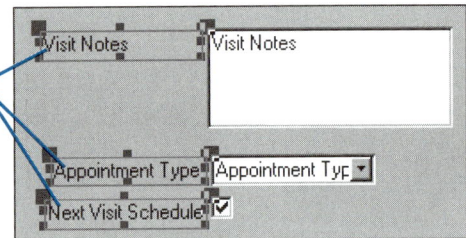

23. Choose **Format→Align→Left** from the menu bar.
Access will align the labels with the leftmost of the three labels.

24. Release the (SHIFT) key, and click the **Pet ID** label.

25. Press (SHIFT) and click the **Visit ID** label.

26. Choose **Format→Align→Left** to align the Pet ID label with the Visit ID label.

27. Make any other adjustments to your form until it has the appearance show below.

28. Save 🖫 the changes to the form.

Enter Data

29. Click the Form view 🔲 button.

30. Click the drop-down button on the Appointment Type combo box.
    Wolfy is actually visiting the clinic as a follow-up appointment, but there is no follow-up appointment type on the list. Fortunately, this combo box gets its values from the Appointment Type lookup table. In the next few steps, you will add the follow-up appointment type to the lookup table. Then, you will use the combo box to choose the follow-up appointment type.

31. Click outside of the Appointment Type combo box to close it without choosing an entry.

32. **Close** the Visits form and, if necessary, save any changes.

33. Click the **Tables** button on the objects bar and double-click the Appointment Type table to open it.
    You can always open tables in datasheet view by double-clicking them.

34. Add the entry **Follow-up** to the fourth table row.

35. **Close** the table and then click the **Forms** button on the Objects bar.

36. **Open** the Visits form by double-clicking it.

37. Click the Appointment Type drop-down button notice that Follow-up is at the top of the list.
    Access sorts the rows in the list alphabetically so that they are easy to locate in long lists.

38. Choose **Follow-up** from the list to complete the record.

39. Click the New Record 🔲 button on the navigation bar at the bottom of the form.

40. Enter 10 new visit records using the following data. You will need to type data in some fields and enter data in other fields by choosing the desired data from combo boxes. Notice that there are no instructions for entering the Pet Name, Pet Type, Breed, Gender, and Date of Birth data. This data will simply be reflected from the Pets table when you choose the indicated Pet IDs. Also, you should check the Next Visit Scheduled box to set that field to Yes and leave the box unchecked to set that field to No. Finally, you don't need to enter the Visit IDs since the Visit IDs Autonumber data type will automatically number the records as you enter data in the other fields.

Visit ID	Pet ID	Visit Date	Visit Notes	Appointment Type	Next Visit Scheduled
2	DG13	10/9/99	Dillon's owner stopped in to schedule his advanced obedience training.	Walk-in	Yes
3	RB23	10/10/99	Bugs came by for the free grooming promotion.	Promotion	No
4	CT02	10/10/99	Max came by for the free grooming promotion.	Promotion	No
5	CT16	10/11/99	Stripes was suffering from a virus.	Walk-in	Yes
6	DG12	10/12/99		Promotion	No
7	CT16	10/12/99	Stripes viral infection seems to have been cured.	Follow-up	No
8	DG13	10/15/99	First day of obedience training.	Follow-up	Yes
9	DG24	10/15/99	First day of obedience training	Follow-up	Yes
10	DG25	10/15/99	First day of obedience training.	Follow-up	Yes
11	CT92	10/16/99		Walk-in	No

41. Leave the Visits form open and continue with the next topic when you have finished.

Lines and Rectangles

The Line ⬉, Rectangle ⬜, and Line/Border Color 🖊 buttons on the toolbox can be used to enhance the appearance of forms. You draw a line or rectangle by clicking the desired button and dragging on the form in Design view. The Line/Border Color tool can be used to change the color of selected lines or rectangles.

Hands-On 5.9 Add a Line, Rectangle, and Finishing Touches

Add a Line and Rectangle

1. Click the Design view 🖊 button.

2. Click the Rectangle ⬜ tool on the toolbox.

3. Follow these steps to draw a rectangle and line.

Detail

Visit ID | Visit ID | Visit Date | Visit Date | Visit Notes | Visit Notes

Pet ID | Pet ID

Pet Name | Pet Name

Pet Type | Pet Type

Breed | Breed

Gender | Gender

Date of Birth | Date of B

Appointment Type | Appointment Typ

Next Visit Schedule ☑

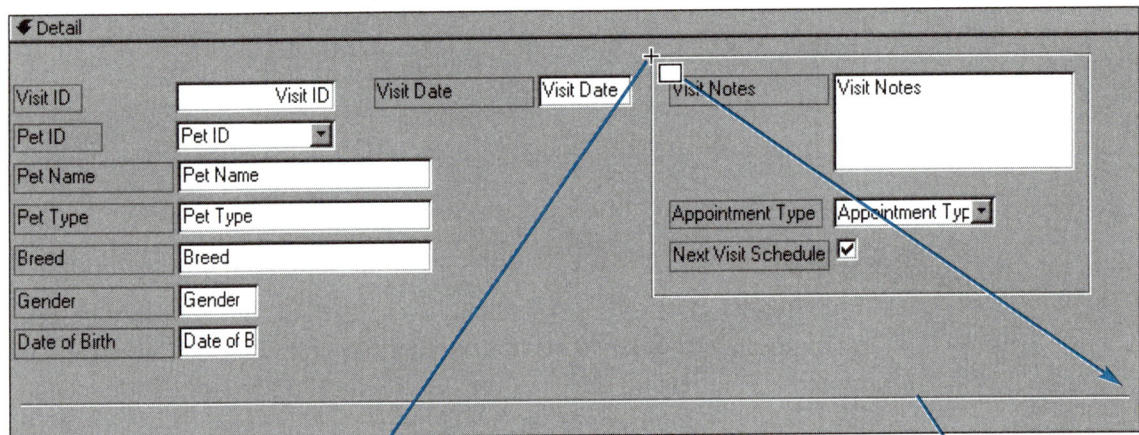

Ⓐ *Position the mouse pointer just above and to the left of the* Visit Notes *label.*

Ⓑ *Drag down and right to draw this rectangle.*

Ⓒ *Click the* **Line** ⬉ *button on the toolbox.*

Ⓓ *Draw this horizontal line.*

4. Feel free to change the color of the line or rectangle with the Line/Border Color 🖊 button. You will need to select the line or rectangle before using the button.

Add Finishing Touches

5. Follow these steps to right-align the Visit Date label.
   Right-aligning the label will position it closer to the control.

Ⓐ *Select the* Visit Date *label by clicking it.*

Ⓑ *Click the Align Right* 🔳 *button on the Access toolbar.*

⟵Visit Date |Visit Date|

Ⓒ *Reduce the label width by dragging the left-middle sizing handle until the label is just wide enough to hold the text.*

6. Increase the width of the Next Visit Scheduled label slightly until the entire label is visible. You can accomplish this by clicking the label and dragging the left-middle sizing handle.

7. Follow these steps to drag the Appointment Type label slightly to the left without moving the Appointment Type control.

   Ⓐ *Select the* Appointment Type *label by clicking it.*

   Ⓑ *Position the mouse pointer on the square box at the top-left corner of the selected label, and a pointing finger icon will appear.*

   Ⓒ *Drag the label slightly to the left, and it will move independent of the* Appointment Type *control. You can always use this technique to move a label without moving the associated control.*

8. If necessary, continue to adjust the position of the Appointment Type label until it is aligned with the Next Visit Scheduled label. You can also align the labels by selecting both of them and issuing the **Format→Align→Left** command.

9. Adjust the position of the Visit Notes label until it is aligned with the Appointment Type and Next Visit Scheduled labels.

10. Switch to Form view to view your completed form.
    Your form should closely match the following example.

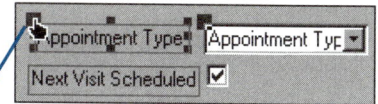

11. **Close** the form when you have finished and save the changes.

12. **Close** the Pinnacle Pet Care database and continue with the end-of-lesson questions and exercises.

Concepts Review

True/False Questions

1. A control can be sized by dragging sizing handles on the edges of the control.   TRUE   FALSE

2. A form header can be exposed by dragging down the Form Header bar.   TRUE   FALSE

3. Bound controls are linked to fields in underlying tables.   TRUE   FALSE

4. Pictures can be inserted using the Unbound Object Frame [icon] button on the toolbox.   TRUE   FALSE

5. Lookup tables typically contain three or more fields.   TRUE   FALSE

6. Controls can be used to help ensure data integrity.   TRUE   FALSE

7. Combo boxes always use lookup tables as their data sources.   TRUE   FALSE

8. The Rectangle Wizard is used to draw rectangles.   TRUE   FALSE

Multiple Choice Questions

1. What is the maximum number of characters that a memo field can contain?
   a. 256
   b. 2,400
   c. 32,000
   d. 64,000

2. Which command is used to align controls?
   a. Format→Align
   b. Edit→Align
   c. Click the Align button on the toolbox.
   d. Controls cannot be aligned.

3. Which of the following sections are part of forms?
   a. Header
   b. Detail
   c. Footer
   d. All of these

4. Which of the following buttons initiates the Combo Box Wizard?
   a. [icon]
   b. [icon]
   c. [icon]
   d. [icon]

Skill Builders

Skill Builder 5.1 Set Up a New Table

In this exercise, you will set up a new table in the Tropical Getaways database. The managers at Tropical Getaways need a form and table for the new Custom Travel Packages program. The table will record important information about the packages. In a later exercise, you will create a form that displays information from both the Customers table and the Custom Packages table.

1. Open the Tropical Getaways database.

2. Click the **Tables** button on the Objects bar.

3. Double-click the *Create table in Design view* option.

4. Follow these steps to set up the Custom Packages table.

Ⓐ *Type the field names shown in the* Field Name *column, and choose the data types shown in the* **Data Type** *column. Make sure you spell the field names correctly.*

Ⓑ *Click in the* Package Category *row, and set the Field Size to 30.*

Field Name	Data Type
Package ID	AutoNumber
Customer ID	Number
Order Date	Date/Time
Package Notes	Memo
Package Category	Text
Destination	Text
Paid	Yes/No

Ⓒ *Click in the* Package ID *row, and make the Package ID field the primary key.*

Ⓓ *Click in the* Order Date *row, and set the format at the bottom of the dialog box to Short Date.*

5. **Close** the table and save it as **Custom Packages**.

Skill Builder 5.2 Establish a Relationship

1. Click the Relationships 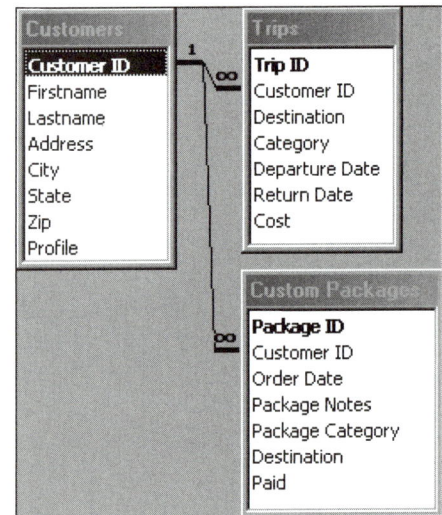 button on the toolbar.

2. If necessary, click the Show Table button on the toolbar.

3. Choose **Custom Packages** in the Show Table box and click the **Add** button.

4. **Close** the Show Table box.

5. Create a one-to-many relationship between the Customer ID fields in the Customers and Custom Packages tables as shown to the right. You can reposition the Custom Packages field list by dragging its blue title bar to the desired position. Enforce referential integrity and activate cascade updating of related fields and cascade deleting of related records.

6. **Close** the Relationships window when you have finished, and save the changes.

Skill Builder 5.3 Set Up a Form

In this exercise, you will use the Form Wizard to set up a form that displays fields from both the Customers and Custom Packages tables.

1. Click the **Forms** button on the Objects bar.

2. Double-click the *Create form by using wizard* option.

3. Add all fields from the Custom Packages table to the Selected Fields list as shown to the right.

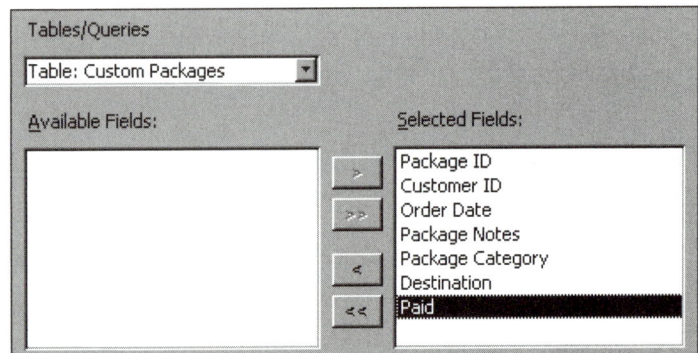

4. Add the Firstname, Lastname, Address, City, State, Zip, and Profile fields from the Customers table. The fields will appear at the bottom of the Selected Fields list.

5. Click the **Next** button to display the next Wizard screen.

6. Make sure the options are set to *by Custom Packages* and *Single form*.

7. Click the **Next** button.

8. Make sure the Columnar option is chosen and click the **Next** button.

9. Choose **Standard** as the style and click the **Next** button.
Access should propose the name Custom Packages *in the title box.*

10. Choose *Modify the form's design* in the last Wizard screen and click the **Finish** button.

11. Continue with the next exercise, where you will customize the form.

Skill Builder 5.4 Customize the Form Appearance

1. Maximize ▣ the Custom Packages form window.

2. Follow this step to drag the Form Footer bar down and enlarge the working area.

Ⓐ *Position the mouse pointer on the top edge of the* **Form Footer** *bar, then drag the bar down.*

(Continued on the next page)

3. Follow these guidelines to reorganize the form as shown below.

- ■ Reduce the width of the Package Notes control.

- ■ Rearrange the controls.

- ■ Right-align the text in the Order Date label.

- ■ Widen the Package Category label until all text is visible in the label.

- ■ Use the **Format**→**Align**→**Left** command to align the Package Notes, Package Category, Destination, and Paid labels.

- ■ Drag the Form Footer bar up until it is about 1.0″ below the controls.

4. Click the Save 💾 button to save the changes to the form.

Skill Builder 5.5 Set Up a Form Header

1. Follow these steps to expose the header area.

> **A** *Position the mouse pointer on the top edge of the Detail bar, then drag the bar down as shown here.*

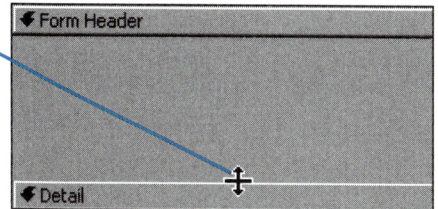

2. Click anywhere in the header area and the header section bar will become highlighted.

3. Click the Unbound Object Frame [icon] button on the toolbox.

4. Follow this step to specify the picture placement.

> **A** *Click in the top-left corner of the header area as shown here, and the Insert Object dialog box will appear.*

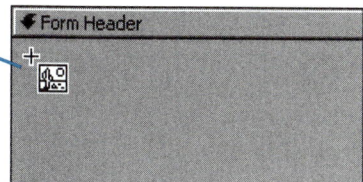

5. Choose *Microsoft Clip Gallery* from the dialog box and click **OK.**

6. Choose a clip category and insert the clip of your choice. The Skill Builders throughout this lesson use the tropical bird picture found in the Animals category.

7. Make sure that the picture is selected with sizing handles surrounding it.

8. If necessary, click the Properties [icon] button on the Access toolbar to display the Properties box.

9. If necessary, click the **Format** tab in the Properties box and set the Size Mode option (the first option in the box) to Stretch.

10. Adjust the size of the picture until it fits within the header area.

11. If necessary, reposition the picture and reduce the height of the header area until the picture is located in the top-left corner, as shown to the right.

12. Click the Label [icon] button on the toolbox.

13. Click just to the right of the picture to place the label at that location.

14. Type the phrase **Tropical Getaways - Custom Packages** in the label box.

15. Click anywhere outside of the label, then click the label to select it.

(Continued on the next page)

16. Use the Formatting toolbar to set the font size to 14 and click the Bold **B** button.

17. Increase the size of the label until the text is visible.

18. Feel free to use the Font Color **A** button on the toolbar to add color to the label.

19. Feel free to use the Fill/Back Color button to change the color of the header section.

20. Click the Form view button to view the completed form in Form view.

21. Click the Restore button at the top-right corner of the form.

22. Adjust the size of the form by dragging the edges of the form window until your form has the approximate dimensions shown below.

23. Click the Design view button to return to Design view.

24. Click the Save button and continue with the next exercise.

Skill Builder 5.6 Set Up a Combo Box

1. Follow this step to delete the Customer ID control from the form.

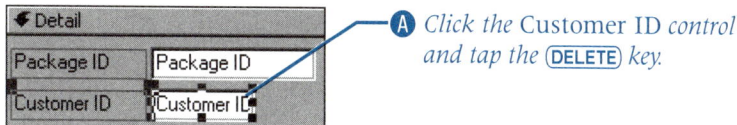

Ⓐ *Click the* Customer ID *control and tap the* (DELETE) *key.*

2. Click the Combo Box ▦ button on the toolbox.

3. Click just below the **Package ID** control to specify the position of the combo box.
   The first Wizard screen will ask where the combo box will get its values. Your combo box will get its values from the Customer ID, Firstname, and Lastname fields in the Customers table.

4. Make sure the *I want the combo box to look up the values in a table or query* option is chosen and click **Next.**
   The next screen will ask which table or query should provide the values for the combo box.

5. Choose the *Customers* table and click **Next.**
   The next screen will ask which fields you want included in the combo box.

6. Use the Add Field ⟩ button to add the Customer ID, Firstname, and Lastname fields to the Selected Fields list.
   When the drop-down button is clicked on the combo box, the data in these fields will appear as columns in the combo box.

7. Click **Next,** and remove the check from the *Hide key column (recommended)* box.
   The Customer ID column will appear along with the Firstname and Lastname columns.

8. Click **Next,** and the Wizard will ask you to choose a field that uniquely identifies the row.

9. Choose *Customer ID* and click **Next.**

10. Choose the *Store that vlaue in this field* option and choose *Customer ID* from the drop-down list.
    These settings will store the Customer ID that is chosen from the combo box in the Customer ID field of the Custom Packages table. The Customer ID that is chosen in the combo box will be taken from the Customers table. Thus, choosing a Customer ID will copy the Customer ID from the Customers table to the Custom Packages table.

11. Click **Next** and the final Wizard screen will appear.

12. Type the name **Customer ID** in the label box and click the **Finish** button.

13. Increase the width of the Customer ID label and adjust the position of the label and combo box control until your combo box is aligned as shown to the right.

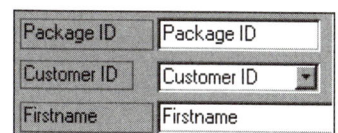

14. Save 💾 the changes to your form and continue with the next exercise.

Skill Builder 5.7 Use Lookup Tables

In this exercise, you will create two lookup tables. In the next exercise, you will use the lookup tables as data sources for two new combo boxes.

1. Close the Custom Packages form.

2. Click the **Tables** button on the Objects bar in the Access database window.

3. Double-click the **Create table in Design view** option.

4. Add a single field named **Package Category** to the table.

5. Leave the Data Type set to Text but change the Field Size to **30**.
   It is important to have the data type set to Text and the field size set to 30 because these settings are also used for the Package Category field in the Custom Packages table. The combo box that you will create will copy data from this lookup table into the Package Category field in the Custom Packages table.

6. Make Package Category a Primary Key 🔑 field.

7. Click the Datasheet View 📇 button and save the table with the name **Package Category.**

8. Enter the four records shown to the right into the table.

9. Close the table.

Package Category
Adventure
Family
Leisure
Singles

10. Set up a new lookup table with a single field named **Destination.** Leave the Data Type set to Text and the field size set to 50.

11. Make the Destination field a primary key.

12. Switch to Datasheet View 📇 and save the table as **Destination**.

13. Add the records shown to the right to the table.

14. Close the table when you have finished.

Destination
Kenyan Safari
Amazon Jungle Trek
Swiss Alps
Rocky Mountains
Baja California
Orlando
Hawaii
Caribbean Cruise

Skill Builder 5.8 Set Up Combo Boxes

In this exercise, you will create two new combo boxes on the Custom Packages form. The lookup tables that you created in the previous exercise will be used as data sources for the combo boxes.

1. Open the Custom Packages form in Design view.

2. Delete the Package Category and Destination controls and their associated labels.

3. Follow these guidelines to set up a combo box to replace the Package Category control. Your combo box should be positioned just below the Package Notes control.

   - Use the Combo Box Wizard. The combo box should look up values in the Package Category lookup table, and store the values in the Package Category field of the Custom Packages table.

   - Assign the name **Package Category** to the combo box.

   - Adjust the width of the label after the box is created so that the name Package Category is completely visible.

   - Your combo box should display the list shown to the right when the drop-down button is clicked.

4. Follow these guidelines to set up another combo box to replace the Destination control. The combo box should be positioned below the Package Category combo box that you just set up.

   - Use the Combo Box Wizard.

   - The combo box should look up values in the Destination lookup table and store the values in the Destination field of the Custom Packages table.

   - Assign the name **Destination** to the combo box.

   - Adjust the width of the label after the box is created so that the name Destination is visible.

   - Your combo box should display the following list when the drop-down button is clicked.

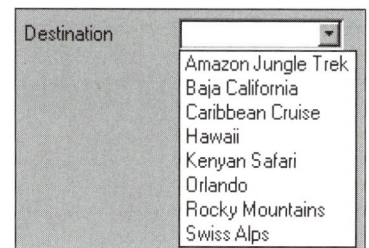

(Continued on the next page)

5. Adjust the position of the combo boxes and other controls until the form has the layout shown below (in Form view).

6. Save 🖫 the changes to your form and continue with the next exercise.

Skill Builder 5.9 Enter Data

In this exercise, you will enter data using the Custom Packages form.

1. If necessary, display the Custom Packages form in Form view 🖼.

2. Enter 10 records using the following data. You will need to type data in some fields and enter data in other fields by choosing the desired data from combo boxes. Notice that there are no instructions for entering the Firstname, Lastname, Address, City, State, Zip, and Profile data. This data will be reflected from the Customers table when you choose the indicated Customer IDs. Also, you should check the Paid box to set that field to Yes and leave the box unchecked to set that field to No. You won't need to enter the Package IDs because that field has an Autonumber data type.

Package ID	Customer ID	Order Date	Package Notes	Package Category	Destination	Paid
1	4	7/8/99	Need to secure non-smoking rooms prior to departure.	Family	Orlando	Yes
2	1	9/9/99	Debbie needs to get her new passport prior to departure.	Adventure	Baja California	No
3	5	9/10/99		Adventure	Rocky Mountains	No
4	6	10/8/99		Leisure	Caribbean Cruise	Yes
5	2	10/8/99	Need to book Wilma's room in the same section as Lisa Simms.	Leisure	Caribbean Cruise	Yes
6	4	12/11/99		Family	Hawaii	Yes
7	3	12/20/99		Adventure	Kenyan Safari	No
8	6	1/5/00	Request vegetarian meals.	Leisure	Hawaii	No
9	1	1/7/00		Adventure	Swiss Alps	Yes
10	5	1/10/00		Adventure	Baja California	Yes

3. When you have finished, carefully check all of your data to make sure it is accurate.

4. Close the database and continue with the Assessment exercises.

Assessments

Assessment 5.1 Customize the Events Form

1. Open the Classic Cars database.

2. Follow these guidelines to set up a new table with the structure shown below.

   - Leave the field lengths of the Event Title, Sponsor, and Location fields set to 50.

   - Set the number of decimal places for the Entrance Fee field to 2. You can do this in the Decimal Places box at the bottom of the dialog box after setting the Data Type to Currency.

Field Name	Data Type
Event ID	AutoNumber
Collector ID	Number
Event Title	Text
Sponsor	Text
Event Date	Date/Time
Location	Text
Entrance Fee	Currency
Mailing Sent	Yes/No
Notes	Memo

   - Make the Event ID field a primary key.

   - Assign the name **Events** to the table.

3. Create a one-to-many relationship between the Collector ID fields in the Collectors and Events tables as shown to the right. Enforce referential integrity and activate cascade updating of related fields and cascade deleting of related records.

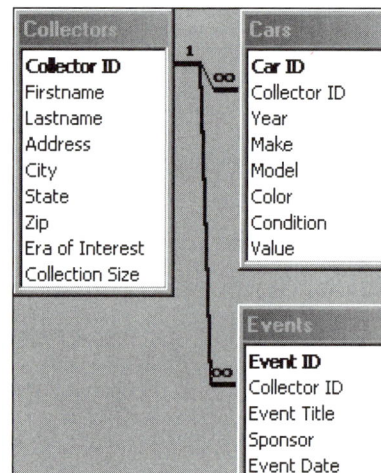

   Collectors
   - Collector ID
   - Firstname
   - Lastname
   - Address
   - City
   - State
   - Zip
   - Era of Interest
   - Collection Size

   Cars
   - Car ID
   - Collector ID
   - Year
   - Make
   - Model
   - Color
   - Condition
   - Value

   Events
   - Event ID
   - Collector ID
   - Event Title
   - Sponsor
   - Event Date

4. Create the lookup table shown to the right. The lookup table should have just one field named Sponsor. Make the Sponsor field a primary key. Set the data type of the Sponsor field to Text and leave the size set to 50. Enter the data shown to the right into the lookup table. Close the table when you have finished and assign the name **Sponsors** to the table.

Sponsor
American Collector's Association
Arizona Auto Enthusiasts
California Auto Collectors
Classic Automobiles Magazine
Classic Cars
Classic Cars - Bay Chapter
Paramount Auto Parts

5. Follow these guidelines to create the completed form shown on the next page.

■ Use the Form Wizard to set up the form using fields from both the Collectors and Events tables. All fields should be taken from the Events table except for the Firstname and Lastname fields, which should be taken from the Collectors table. Assign the name **Events** to the form.

■ Create and format the form header as shown. Use the classic car picture, or another picture if the classic car is not available on your system. The classic car can be found in the Transportation category of the Clip Gallery. Format the header background with the color of your choice. Format the Classic Cars - Scheduled Events label by increasing the size of the text and adding color to the label.

■ Use Design view to arrange the controls as shown. You will also need to adjust the size of several controls.

■ Delete the Collector ID control that the Wizard set up and create a Collector ID combo box to display the drop-down list shown to the right. The Collector ID, Firstname, and Lastname fields from the Collectors table should be used as the data source for the combo box. When a row is chosen from the combo box, the Collector ID should be copied from the Collectors table to the Collector ID field in the Events table. This field identifies a Collector as the person who is coordinating the event. The Firstname and Lastname fields on the form should simply be reflected from the Collectors table.

(Continued on the next page)

■ Set up the Sponsor combo box to display the drop-down list shown to the right. The Sponsors lookup table should be used as the data source for the combo box. When a row is chosen from the combo box, a Sponsor should be copied from the Sponsors lookup table to the Sponsor field in the Events table. This field identifies the sponsor that is supporting the event.

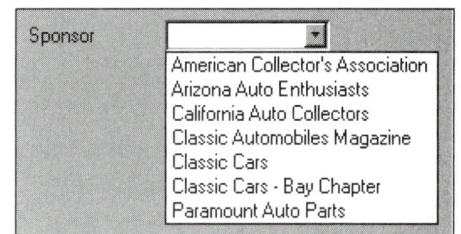

Sponsor	
American Collector's Association	
Arizona Auto Enthusiasts	
California Auto Collectors	
Classic Automobiles Magazine	
Classic Cars	
Classic Cars - Bay Chapter	
Paramount Auto Parts	

Events

Classic Cars - Scheduled Events

Event ID	(AutoNumber)	Event Title	
Collector ID		Event Date	
Firstname		Sponsor	
Lastname		Location	
		Entrance Fee	
		Mailing Sent	

Notes

Record: |◄ ◄ 1 ► ►| ►* of 1

6. Enter six records using the following data. You will need to type data in some fields and enter data in other fields by choosing the desired data from combo boxes. Notice that there are no instructions for entering the Firstname and Lastname data. This data will be reflected from the Collectors table when you choose the indicated Collector ID. Also, you should check the *Mailing sent* box to set that field to Yes and leave the box unchecked to set that field to No.

Event ID	Collector ID	Event Title	Event Date	Sponsor	Location	Entrance Fee	Mailing sent	Notes
1	4	1950s Classic Chevys	9/1/99	Classic Cars - Bay Chapter	San Francisco	$50	Yes	
2	3	Early American Automobiles	10/18/99	American Collector's Association	Columbus	$25	Yes	
3	2	Classic Cars - Annual Auto Show	2/1/00	Classic Cars	Los Angeles	$10	Yes	
4	1	Chicago Classic Auto Show	4/8/0	Classic Automobiles Magazine	Chicago	$45	No	The location is being decided.
5	5	Early American Auto Show	6/14/00	American Collector's Association	Detroit	$15	No	
6	2	Classic Corvette Show	7/11/00	California Auto Collectors	Sacramento	$35	No	This date is tentative.

7. When you have finished, carefully check all of your data to make sure it is accurate.

8. Close the Classic Cars database when you have finished

Subforms and Calculated Controls

Access databases are often used for entering order information. In a typical order entry database, order information is stored in an orders table while order details are stored in an order details table. Order data may include the customer's name, address, telephone number, credit card number, etc. The order details include the individual transaction items, such as the products ordered, price, quantity, etc. Subforms are useful in order entry systems for displaying order details on a main order form. Access also lets you use calculated controls on forms to calculate order totals, sales tax, freight charges, and other calculations. In this lesson, you will use Access' Subform Wizard to easily set up an order entry system.

In This Lesson

Case Study

Al Smith has decided to integrate order entry into his Access database system. He realizes that Access is a powerful database system that can automate the order-taking process. Al decides that the best place to display order information is on the Visits form in the Pinnacle Pet Care database. A Visit Details subform is added to the Visits form to record service and product information, calculate subtotals, totals, and sales tax.

Study the form below. In the first Hands-On exercise of this lesson you will begin to set up the Visits Details subform displayed here.

*—This is the **Visit Details** subform. This subform allows Al to enter product and pricing information. The **Extended Price** field automatically calculates the Extended Price by multiplying the **Unit Price** by the **Quantity.***

*—The **Subtotal, Sales Tax,** and **Total** controls are calculated controls. These controls will automatically calculate the Subtotal, Sales Tax, and Total for each order.*

Subforms

A subform is a form within a form. Subforms are often used to display detailed order information. For example, in this lesson, you will create a subform within the Visits form. The subform will display the services and products purchased during the visit.

Hands-On 6.1 Set Up the Visit Details table

In this exercise, you will set up a table to record visit details in the Pinnacle Pet Care database. The visit detail records will be displayed in the subform.

1. Start Access and open the Pinnacle Pet Care database.

2. Click the **Tables** button on the Objects bar.

3. Double-click the *Create table in Design view* option.

4. Follow these steps to set up the Visit Details table.

    Ⓐ *Type these field names, and choose the data types shown for each. Make sure you spell the field names correctly.*

    Ⓑ *Leave the field size for the **Service/Product** field set to 50. Set the number of decimal places for the **Unit Price** field to 2.*

Field Name	Data Type
Visit ID	Number
Service/Product	Text
Unit Price	Currency
Quantity	Number

5. Do not set a primary key for this table.
    You will learn why a primary key is unnecessary (and undesirable) as you work through this lesson.

6. Close the table and click **Yes** when Access asks if you want to save the table.

7. Type the name **Visit Details** in the Save As box, and click **OK.**
    Access will display a warning box indicating that a primary key has not been defined.

8. Click **No** to save the table without defining a primary key.
    Once again, you will learn why a primary key is unnecessary as you work through this lesson.

Basing Subforms On Queries

Subforms can be based upon tables or queries. When you run a query, Access displays the query results in a **recordset.** If you change data in the recordset, then the data in the underlying table(s) that the query is based upon may be changed as well. Access has a rather complex set of rules that determine when a query can be used to update underlying tables. Basically, if a query is based upon a single table, then the data in the underlying table is updateable. In other words, if you change data in the query recordset, then the data in the underlying table is changed as well. This is also true for a form that is based upon a query. If a form is based upon a query and you enter or change data in the form, then the data in the underlying table that the query is based upon is updated as well. This allows you to use queries as the basis for subforms. Another benefit of using queries as the basis for subforms is that queries can contain calculated fields. Calculated fields are often used to calculate extended prices, and for other types of calculations on order entry forms.

Hands-On 6.2 Set Up the Visit Details Query

In this exercise, you will set up a query that is based upon the Visit Details table. The query will contain a calculated field named Extended Price. The Extended Price field will multiply the Unit Price of each item by the Quantity ordered.

1. Click the **Queries** button on the Objects bar.

2. Double-click the *Create query in Design view* option.

3. Choose Visit Details in the Show Table box and click the **Add** button.

4. Close the Show Table box.

5. Add all fields to the design grid by double-clicking them on the Visit Details field list.

6. Follow these steps to display the Zoom dialog box.
   In the next few steps, you will enter a calculated field into the Zoom dialog box.

Ⓐ *Click in the empty field cell to the right of* Quantity.

Ⓑ Right-click, *and the menu shown here will pop up.*

Ⓒ *Choose* **Zoom** *from the menu.*

Field:	Visit ID	Service/Product	Unit Price	Quantity		
Table:	Visit Details	Visit Details	Visit Details	Visit Details		Σ Totals
Sort:						Table Names
Show:	☑	☑	☑	☑		
Criteria:						Cut
or:						Copy
						Paste
						Build...
						Zoom...
						Properties...

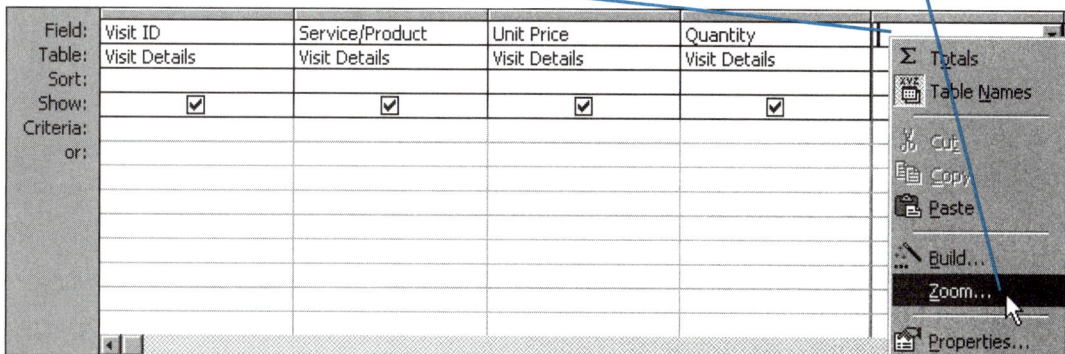

(Continued on the next page)

7. Enter the expression shown below into the Zoom box. Make sure you enter the expression exactly as shown. In particular, make sure you use a colon : (not a semicolon ;), correctly spell the field names, and use the correct open and closed brackets [ ] as shown.

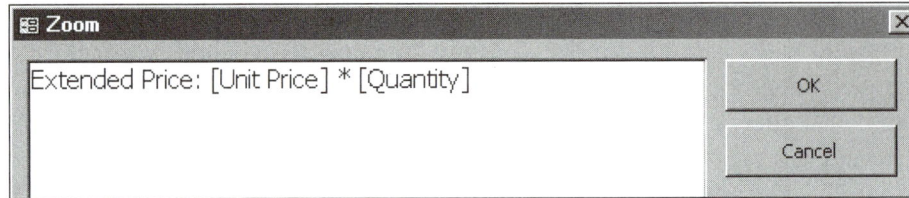

```
┌─ Zoom ──────────────────────────────────────────────────────────────[X]─┐
│                                                                           │
│ Extended Price: [Unit Price] * [Quantity]              ┌──────────────┐   │
│                                                        │      OK      │   │
│                                                        └──────────────┘   │
│                                                        ┌──────────────┐   │
│                                                        │    Cancel    │   │
│                                                        └──────────────┘   │
│                                                                           │
└───────────────────────────────────────────────────────────────────────┘
```

8. Click **OK** to insert the expression into the field.
   When you create the subform in a later exercise, this expression will calculate the extended price for each row in the subform.

9. Use the arrow keys on your keyboard to scroll through the expression within the cell. Make sure the syntax is correct. If necessary, you can edit the expression within the cell or redisplay the Zoom dialog box and make any necessary changes.

10. Click the Show check box for the Extended Price field and the box will become checked, as shown below.
    Checking the box is necessary to make the Extended Price field appear in the query recordset and the subform.

Field:	Visit ID	Service/Product	Unit Price	Quantity	Extended Price: [Uni
Table:	Visit Details	Visit Details	Visit Details	Visit Details	
Sort:					
Show:	☑	☑	☑	☑	☑
Criteria:					

11. Close the query and save it as **Query - Visit Details**.
    You cannot give the query the name Visit Details because the Visit Details table already has that name. In Access, you cannot give a table and query the same name.

12. Continue with the next topic, where you will create the subform.

The Subform Wizard

The Subform Wizard is initiated by clicking the Subform ▦ button on the toolbox while working in Form Design view. The Subform Wizard makes it easy to set up subforms within an existing main form. Prior to using the Subform Wizard, you must set up the table or query that the subform will be based upon. The Subform Wizard automatically synchronizes the subform with the main form, provided that you have set up the underlying table and/or query properly. Synchronization ensures that the appropriate records are displayed in the subform for each record in the main form.

Synchronizing a Main Form and Subform

The Subform Wizard automatically synchronizes a main form and subform, provided that a relationship has been established between the tables or queries that the forms are based upon. Synchronization also occurs automatically if the subform and main form have a field with the same name defined as a primary key in the main form. The matching field name technique will be used to synchronize the Visit Details subform with the Visits form in the Pinnacle Pet Care database. The following illustration discusses the structure of the Visits and Visit Details tables, and the synchronization that will occur between the tables.

The Visit ID *field is a primary key in the Visits table and a non-primary key field in the Visit Details table. The Subform Wizard will automatically use the* Visit ID *field to synchronize the subform with the main form. Synchronization will ensure that the correct visit detail records are displayed in the subform for each visit displayed in the main form.*

Field Name	Data Type
Visit ID	AutoNumber
Visit Date	Date/Time
Pet ID	Text
Visit Notes	Memo
Appointment Type	Text
Next Visit Scheduled	Yes/No

Field Name	Data Type
Visit ID	Number
Service/Product	Text
Unit Price	Currency
Quantity	Number

Hands-On 6.3 Set Up the Subform

1. Click the **Forms** button on the Objects bar.

2. Choose the Visits form and click the ⬓ Design button.
   A subform is set up while the main form is open in Design view.

3. If necessary, click the Maximize ▫ button to maximize the form.

4. If necessary, use the **View→Toolbox** command to display the toolbox.

(Continued on the next page)

5. Follow these steps to make room for the subform and to specify the subform location.

A *If necessary, drag the Form Footer bar down to make room for the subform.*

B *Click the Subform button on the toolbox.*

C *Click here to specify the subform location. The first Wizard screen will appear.*

The first screen will ask if you would like to build a new subform using an existing table or query.

6. Click the **Next** button to choose the *Use existing Tables and Queries* option.

7. Follow these steps to choose options in the second Wizard screen.

A *Choose the Query - Visit Details query from the **Tables/Queries** list. You will need to scroll to the bottom of the list.*

B *Click the Add all fields button to move all fields to the **Selected Fields** list.*

Tables/Queries

Query: Query - Visit Details

Available Fields:

Selected Fields:
Visit ID
Service/Product
Unit Price
Quantity
Extended Price

8. Click the **Next** button.

9. Leave the option in the third Wizard screen set to *Choose from a list.*
The Wizard will automatically create a link between the Visit ID fields in the two tables when this option is chosen. This link will keep the main form and subform synchronized.

10. Click the **Next** button.

11. Type the name **Visit Details** in the last Wizard screen and click the **Finish** button.

12. Maximize ⬜ the Visits form window again and a placeholder box for the subform will appear.
Subforms appear as a large placeholder box when the main form is displayed in Design view.

13. Click the Form view 🖼 button on the Access toolbar.

14. Examine the following illustration to understand the relationship between the main form and subform.

Ⓐ *Notice that Access automatically inserts 4 in the **Visit ID** field of the subform. This is because the Visit ID field is set to 4 in the main form. As you enter data in the subform, Access will automatically assign the Visit ID that is currently displayed in the main form to the subform records. This keeps the main form record synchronized with the sub-form records.*

Ⓑ *Notice that the subform displays the fields from the underlying Query - Visit Details query, on which the subform is based. When you enter data in these fields, the data will be stored in the underlying Visit Details table, which the query is based upon. However, data will not be stored in the Extended Price field because this is a calculated field. In fact, the Extended Price field does not even exist in the Visit Details table. The Extended Price will simply be calculated by the query then displayed on the form.*

(Continued on the next page)

15. Make sure the flashing insertion point is positioned in the Visit ID field at the top of the form.

16. Click the Sort Ascending ![Sort Ascending button] button on the toolbar.
This will ensure that the records in the main form are sorted on the Visit ID field. The "Wolfy the dog" record should be displayed because it has Visit ID 1.

17. Click the Design view ![Design view button] button on the Access toolbar to return to Design view.
In the next exercise, you will increase the size of the subform placeholder box in Design view. This will allocate more space to the subform. The subform will then be able to display multiple rows so that all five columns are fully visible in the subform.

Adjusting the Size of a Subform

You can change the overall size of a subform within a main form by first displaying the main form in Design view. The size of the subform placeholder box can then be increased by clicking on the box and dragging the sizing handles. You can also specify a precise size for the subform by first clicking the subform to select it and then setting the Width and Height properties in the Properties dialog box.

Adjusting Subform Column Widths

To adjust the individual column widths of a subform, you must first open the subform in Form view. The column widths can then be adjusted by dragging the column headings or by clicking on the column headings and using the **Format→Column Width** command to specify precise widths. You can also double-click the border between two column headings to AutoFit a column.

Hands-On 6.4 Adjust the Size of the Subform

Adjust the Overall Size of the Subform

1. Follow these steps to adjust the size of the subform placeholder box.

Ⓐ *If necessary, click on the subform box and it will become selected with sizing handles.*

Ⓑ *Drag a corner-sizing handle until the subform has the approximate size shown here. You can also drag the bottom or side sizing handles as necessary.*

Ⓒ *If necessary, use the* (CTRL)*+ArrowKey keystrokes to position the subform box as shown here.*

2. Make sure the subform is selected and, if necessary, click the Properties ![icon] button to display the Properties box.
   In Step 4, you will specify a precise height and width for the subform. You can use either the dragging technique shown in Step 1 or the precise technique shown in Step 4 to specify the overall size of a subform within a main form.

3. If necessary, click the Format tab on the Properties box.

4. Set the Width property to **6.9″** and the Height property to **1.1″**.

5. Click the Form view ![icon] button and the subform should have the same dimensions in Form view that it had in Design view.
   At this point, the subform column widths won't fill the subform. You will widen the columns in the following steps.

6. Close the Visits form and save the changes.

Adjust Subform Column Widths

7. If necessary, click the **Forms** button on the Objects bar in the database window.
   Notice the Visit Details form. The Subform Wizard created the Visit Details form.

8. Double-click the Visit Details form to open it in Form view.

9. Follow these steps to adjust the subform column widths.
   These steps will adjust the column widths to fill the space on the subform, provided that you used the correct field names in the Visit Details table.

   Ⓐ Double-click *the border between the* **Visit ID** *and* **Service/Product** *column headings. This will AutoFit the Visit ID column.*

   Ⓑ Click the **Service/Product** *column heading, choose* **Format→Column Width,** *and set the width to 58.*

Visit ID	Service/Product	Unit Price	Quantity	Extended Price
▶ 0		$0.00	0	

   Ⓒ *AutoFit the* **Unit Price, Quantity,** *and* **Extended Price** *columns by* double-clicking *the column heading borders.*

10. Close the Visit Details subform and Access should automatically save the changes.

(Continued on the next page)

11. Double-click the Visits form to open it in Form view. Your completed main form and subform should closely match the following example. If necessary, make adjustments to the subform column widths and/or the overall size of the subform. You will need to make adjustments to the subform column widths by opening the Visit Details subform in Form view. Adjustments to the overall subform size can be made by displaying the Visits form in Design view.

Entering Data with Subforms

You can enter data into a subform just as you enter data into a main form. If the subform is set up properly, then Access will automatically keep the main form and subform synchronized by entering the appropriate record identifiers into the subform records. For example, Access will automatically enter the appropriate Visit ID in the Visit ID field of your subform records.

Hands-On 6.5 Enter Data and Navigate Through Records

1. Follow these steps to enter two records into the subform.

A *Click in the Service/Product box in the subform and type Flea Bath.*

B *Tap the TAB key, and type 35 in the Unit Price field.*

C *Tap TAB and type 1 in the Quantity field. Access will automatically apply the Currency format to the Unit Price.*

Visit Details

	Visit ID	Service/Product	Unit Price	Quantity	Extended Price
	1	Flea Bath	$35.00	1	$35.00
	1	Flea Shampoo	$12.50	2	$25.00
▶	1		$0.00	0	

Record: |◄ ◄ | 3 | ► ►| ►* | of 3 ◄ ►

D *Click in the Service/Product field for the second record and Access will calculate the Extended Price for the first record. The Extended Price is automatically calculated by the query, on which the subform is based.*

E *Enter the Product, Unit Price, and Quantity for the second subform record, as shown. The query will calculate the Extended Price only after you click in the Extended Price field, or some other field.*

2. Follow these steps to understand the relationship between the record navigation bars on the forms, and to navigate to another Visit record.

Visit Details

	Visit ID	Service/Product	Unit Price	Quantity	Extended Price
	1	Flea Bath	$35.00	1	$35.00
	1	Flea Shampoo	$12.50	2	$25.00
▶	1		$0.00	0	

Record: |◄ ◄ | 3 | ► ►| ►* | of 3 ◄ ►

Record: |◄ ◄ | 1 | ► ►| ►* | of 11

A *This navigation bar is for navigating through the records on the subform. However, your subform only contains two records for the current record on the main form, so the navigation bar here has little use. This navigation bar becomes useful when there are many subform records for the current record in the main form.*

B *Click the Next Record button on this navigation bar to move to the next record in the main form. The "Dillon the dog" record should appear. At this point, there should be no data in the Dillon subform.*

(Continued on the next page)

3. Enter the following Visit Details data in the subform for "Dillon the dog."

	Visit ID	Service/Product	Unit Price	Quantity	Extended Price
	2	Advanced Obedience Training	$85.00	1	$85.00
▶	2	Leather Collar	$23.89	1	$23.89
	2	Deluxe Chain	$16.50	1	$16.50
✳	2		$0.00	0	

Record: |◀ ◀ 2 ▶ ▶| ▶✳ of 3

4. Click the Next Record ▶ button on the record navigation bar of the Visits form (not the Visit Details subform).

The "Bugs the rabbit" record should appear.

5. Enter the following Visit Details data in the subform for "Bugs the rabbit."

	Visit ID	Service/Product	Unit Price	Quantity	Extended Price
▶	3	Deluxe Grooming	$15.00	1	$15.00
	3	Pet Shampoo	$8.50	3	$25.50
✳	3		$0.00	0	

Record: |◀ ◀ 1 ▶ ▶| ▶✳ of 2

6. Close the Visits form and, if necessary, save any changes.

Calculated Controls in Forms

Subforms are often used in order entry systems to enter and display order detail records. The order detail records usually contain pricing information and other numeric data. For example, the Visit Details subform records service and product order information. Main forms often require subtotal, sales tax, freight, and total controls. **Calculated controls** can be placed on main forms to perform these and other calculations. Main form controls can also be used to display the results of calculated controls on subforms. Take a moment to review the following illustration. You will add the Subtotal, Sales Tax, and Total controls to the Visits form in the following exercises.

*The subtotal is calculated in the Visit Details subform and is then displayed in the **Subtotal** control on the Visits main form. The Sales Tax and Total calculations are performed within calculated controls on the main form.*

Calculating Subtotals in Subforms

You can subtotal the detail records in subforms by placing a text box control in the Footer section of the subform. The text box control contains a mathematical Sum function that adds the detail rows. The main form contains another text box control that simply reflects the subtotal that is calculated in the subform footer. The following illustration shows a subform calculated control that sums the detail records in the subform.

The footer section is expanded to make room for the subtotal control.

The Text Box **abl** *button is used to place a text box control in the footer section of the subform. The Properties box is displayed, and the expression =Sum([Extended Price]) is entered into the Control Source property box. When the Visits form (the main form) is displayed, the expression sums up the Extended Prices for all detail records displayed in the subform. This produces the subtotal, which is the intended result.*

Using Expressions in Text Box Controls

Earlier in this lesson, you created a calculated field within a query. You used the expression Extended Price: [Unit Price] * [Quantity] to calculate the extended price. Expressions can also be used within text box controls on forms and reports to perform calculations. For example, the expression =Sum([Extended Price]) is used within a subform to calculate subtotals. The following illustration discusses the process and syntax that are required to create calculated controls on a form.

First, the Text Box **abl** *button is used to add a text box control to the form. The control must be placed in the footer section if you are calculating a subtotal in a subform.*

Next, while the control is selected, an expression is entered into the Control Source field of the Properties box. In this example, the expression calculates the sum of the extended prices.

Finally, the control displays the expression that has been entered into the Control Source box. In this example, the Text10 label has also been changed to Subtotal.

Expression Syntax

You must use proper syntax when creating expressions. Otherwise, Access will either reject the expression or perform an incorrect calculation. Expression syntax is discussed in the following illustrations. You will use all four of the expressions shown in the illustrations when you add calculated controls to the Visits and Visit Details forms.

- **Example 1**—The expression =Sum([Extended Price]) will calculate the sum of the extended prices in the Visit Details subform. This expression will be placed in a text box control in the footer section of the subform.

Expressions that are used in controls begin with equal = signs.

This expression contains a Sum function. The function name is placed immediately after the equal sign.

=Sum([Extended Price])

Open and closed parentheses ( ) are always required when a function is used. The parentheses enclose the function arguments. In this example, the argument is simply a reference to the Extended Price [Extended Price].

Names of controls, forms and other objects are enclosed in square brackets [ ]. Sometimes Access will automatically insert the brackets for you. However, it is better that you insert them, so that your syntax will be accurate.

The following illustration shows the Subtotal, Sales Tax, and Total controls that you will add to the Visits form. The illustration also shows the expressions that you will assign to the controls. A detailed discussion of each expression follows the illustration.

Product	Unit Price	Quantity	Extended Price
	$35.00	1	$35.00
	$12.50	2	$25.00
	$0.00	0	

=[Visit Details].[Form]![Subtotal]

Subtotal	$60.00
Sales Tax	$4.95
Total	$64.95

=[Subtotal] * .0825

=[Subtotal] + [Sales Tax]

- **Example 2**—The expression =[Visit Details].[Form]![Subtotal] gets the subtotal from the Visit Details subform, and displays it in the Subtotal control of the Visits form.

The period (.) is used to separate the name of the object [Visit Details] from the object type [Form]. You must use this syntax when you are referring to a control that is outside of the current object.

The exclamation point (!) separates the object type [Form] from the control [Subtotal]. Also notice that all elements are enclosed in square brackets.

=[Visit Details].[Form]![Subtotal]

- **Example 3**—The expression =[Subtotal] * .0825 calculates the sales tax by multiplying the Subtotal by .0825 (8.25%). Notice that the control name Subtotal is surrounded by square brackets. Also, notice that the asterisk * is used to represent multiplication. Finally, spaces are used before and after the asterisk. Access is quite forgiving when it comes to blank spaces, so spaces are optional in this expression.

- **Example 4**—The expression =[Subtotal] + [Sales Tax] calculates the Total as the Subtotal plus Sales Tax. Once again, square brackets surround the control names and spaces are optional before and after the plus + sign.

Hands-On 6.6 Insert a Subtotal in the Visit Details Subform

Display the Footer Area

1. If necessary, click the **Forms** button on the Objects bar.

2. Choose the Visit Details subform and click the [Design] button.

3. If necessary, maximize ▣ the window.

Set Up the Calculated Control

4. Click the Text Box [ab] button on the toolbox.

5. Follow this step to specify the text box position.

Ⓐ *Click anywhere in this section of the footer area. The text box will be inserted, and the word* Unbound *will appear in the box.* Unbound *means that the control is not linked to a field in an underlying table and no expression has been assigned to the control. The position of this text box is not critical as long as it is in the footer area. This box will simply be used to perform the calculation.*

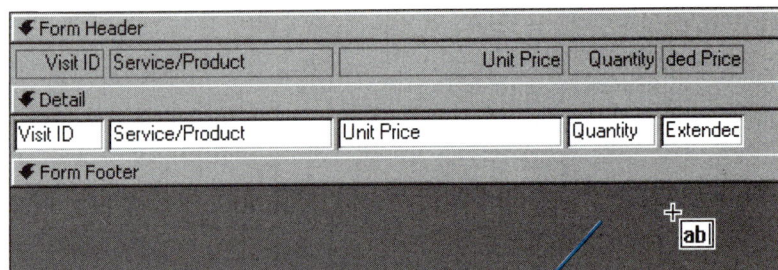

In the next few steps, you will assign the =Sum([Extended Price]) expression to the control. You will also assign the name Subtotal to the control.

6. If necessary, use the Properties [▤] button to display the Properties box.

7. Click the Data tab and enter the expression **=Sum([Extended Price])** in the Control Source box.

8. Follow these steps to assign a name to the control.

Ⓐ *Click the **Other** tab.*

Ⓑ *Change the **Name** to **Subtotal** as shown here. The Control now has the name Subtotal assigned to it. However, the label to the left of the control will still have the phrase Text#. The name of the control and the label text are entirely different things. The control name will be used whenever you wish to reference the control in an expression.*

Text Box: Subtotal

| Format | Data | Event | Other | All |

Name . . . . Subtotal
Status Bar Text . . . .
Enter Key Behavior . . . . Default
Allow AutoCorrect . . . . Yes

9. *Double-click* the label to the left of the control and change the label text to **Subtotal**. *The completed Visit Details form should have the appearance shown below.*

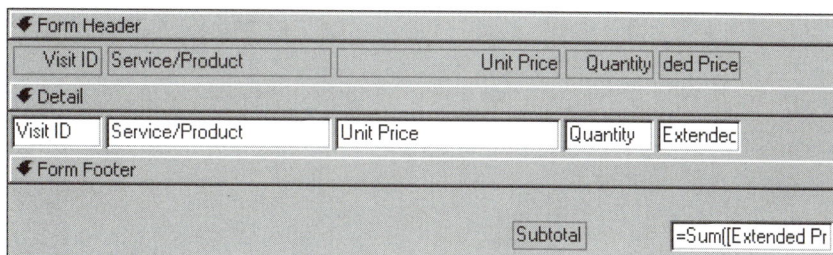

```
♦ Form Header
  Visit ID  Service/Product                    Unit Price  Quantity  ded Price
♦ Detail
  Visit ID  Service/Product      Unit Price            Quantity  Extendec
♦ Form Footer

                                        Subtotal        =Sum([Extended Pr
```

10. Close the Visit Details form and save the changes.

Place a Subtotal Control On the Visits Form

11. Open the Visits form in Design view.

12. If necessary, maximize ☐ the form.

13. Follow these steps to prepare the form for the Subtotal, Sales Tax, and Total controls.

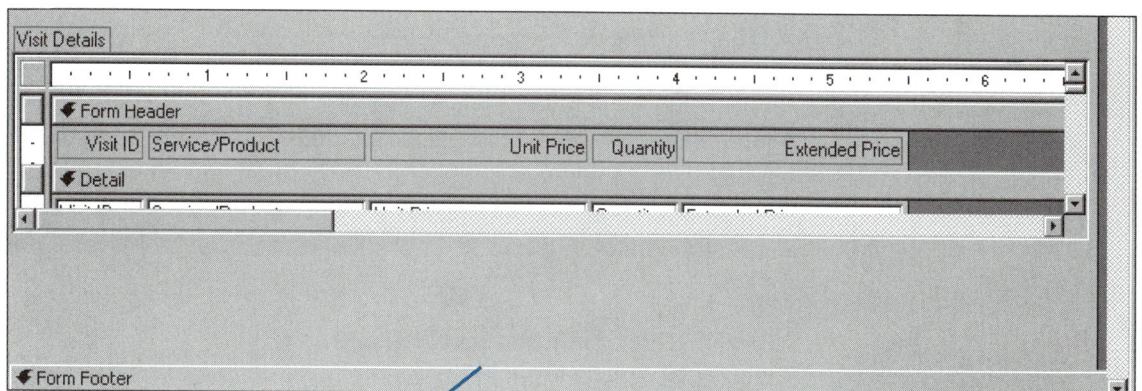

```
Visit Details
         . . . I . . . 1 . . . I . . . 2 . . . I . . . 3 . . . I . . . 4 . . . I . . . 5 . . . I . . . 6 . . .
  ♦ Form Header
    Visit ID  Service/Product              Unit Price  Quantity        Extended Price
  ♦ Detail




♦ Form Footer
```

Ⓐ *If necessary, scroll down until the **Form Footer** bar is visible.*

Ⓑ *If necessary, drag the **Form Footer** bar down until there is approximately 2" of light gray area below the **Visit Details** placeholder box.*

At this point, you may find that your form is too large to fit on the screen. If so, then there are two approaches that you can use to address this issue. First, you can ignore the problem and use the vertical scroll bar to scroll up and down through the form in both Design and Form views. The second approach is to modify the layout of the form by rearranging controls so that the form requires less vertical space. You can also decrease the height of the Visit Details placeholder box. However, if you do this, then you won't be able to see as many detail rows when you view the Visits form in Form view.

(Continued on the next page)

14. Click the Text Box ![ab] button on the toolbox.

15. Follow this step to specify the text box position.

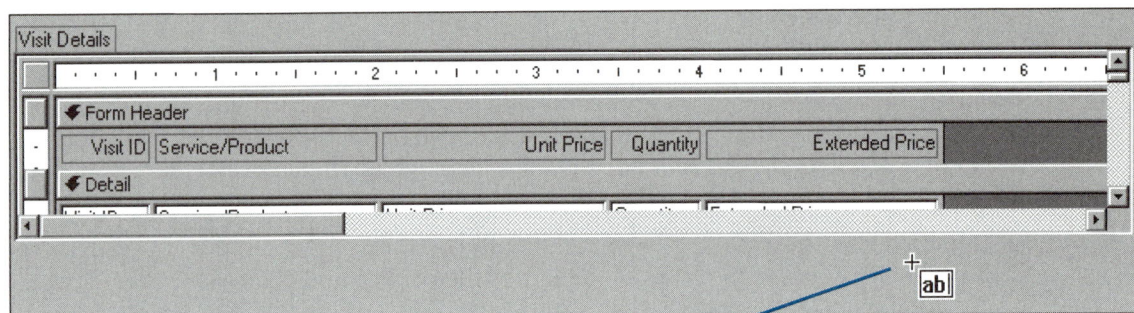

Ⓐ *Click just below the subform placeholder box.*

16. If necessary, display the Properties box and click the Data tab.

17. Enter the expression =**[Visit Details].[Form]![Subtotal]** in the Control Source box. Make sure you include the open and closed brackets [ ], the period, and the exclamation mark as shown.

18. Click the Other tab and enter the name **Subtotal** in the Name box.

19. Double-click the label to the left of the control on the form and change the label text to **Subtotal**.

The completed control should have the appearance shown below. Don't be concerned with the position of the control or the label. You will adjust the positions in a later exercise.

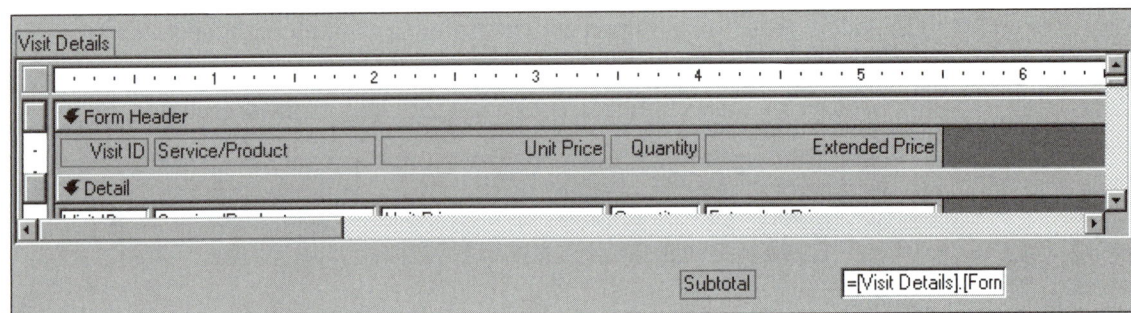

20. Click the Form view ![button] button on the toolbar.

Access should calculate the subtotal for the current record. In a later exercise, you will format the Subtotal and other calculated controls, so that the numbers are displayed with a Currency format.

21. Feel free to browse through the records on the Visits form by using the navigation bar at the bottom of the form.

Access will calculate the subtotal each time you go to a new record. However, at this point, only three records on the main form should have detail records. You will complete the data entry in a later exercise.

Place Sales Tax and Total Controls On the Visits Form

22. Switch to Design ⊡ view.

23. Follow these guidelines to add the Sales Tax and Total controls to the form as shown below.

- ■ Use the Text Box `ab` button to add the controls to the form.

- ■ Set the Control Source property for the Sales Tax control to `=[Subtotal] * .0825`. Change the name of the Sales Tax control to **Sales Tax**. You can accomplish this in the Other tab of the Properties dialog box. Change the label in front of the control to **Sales Tax**.

- ■ Set the Control Source property for the Total control to `=[Subtotal] + [Sales Tax]`. Change the name of the Total control to **Total**. You can accomplish this in the Other tab of the Properties dialog box. Change the label in front of the control to **Total**.

- ■ Don't be concerned with the alignment and position of the controls. You will change the alignment and position in the next exercise.

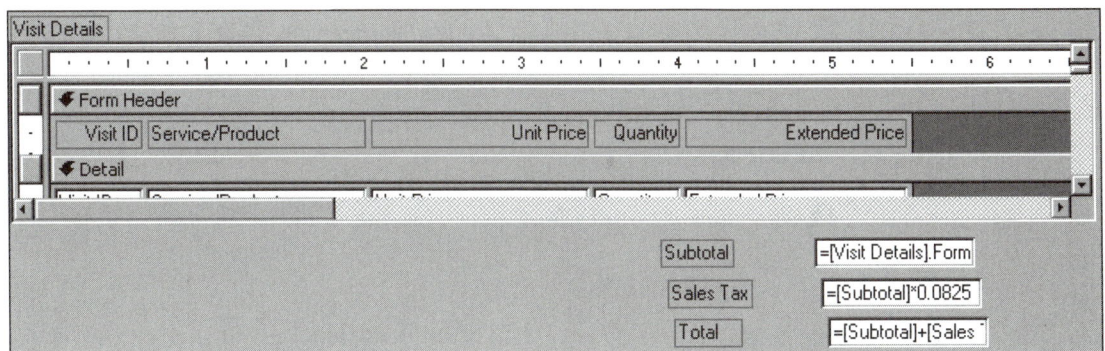

24. Click the Form view ⊞ button on the toolbar.
Access should calculate the Subtotal, Sales Tax, and Total for the current record. However, the numbers may have a large number of decimals and they may be aligned on the left side of the boxes. You will format and align the numbers in a moment.

25. Feel free to browse through the records on the Visits form by using the navigation bar at the bottom of the form.
Access will calculate the Subtotal, Sales Tax, and Total for each record.

26. Switch back to Design view ⊡ and continue with the next topic.

Formatting Controls with the Properties Box

The Format tab in the Properties box gives you complete control over the formatting of controls. For example, the Format tab lets you adjust the size of controls and the format of numbers. You will use the Properties box to format the numbers in the Subtotal, Sales Tax, and Total controls. You will also change the size of the controls, the font that is used in the controls, and their positions on the form.

Hands-On 6.7 Format and Position Controls

Set Number Properties

1. Click the Subtotal control, and then press (SHIFT) while you click the Sales Tax and Total controls. *Make sure you click the controls and not the labels to the left of the controls.*

2. Follow these steps to format the controls with a Currency format.

   Ⓐ *Click the* ***Format*** *tab in the Properties box.*

   Ⓑ *Click in the* ***Format*** *box, click the drop-down button, scroll down through the list, and choose* ***Currency.***

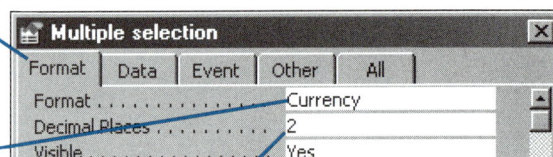

   Ⓒ *Click in the* ***Decimal Places*** *box and set the number of decimals to* **2.**

Set Text Format Properties

3. Now press the (SHIFT) key while you click the labels to the left of the selected controls. You will need to click each label. All three labels and all three controls should be selected.

4. Scroll through the list of properties on the Format tab and set the Font Size property to **10**.

5. Click in any other box on the Properties box and the new font size will take effect.
   You can set all text formats using either the buttons on the toolbar or the Properties box. Notice that the font size increased but that the height and width of the controls and labels remain the same. In the next step, you will increase the height of all selected objects by setting the Height property in the Properties box.

6. Scroll up through the Format properties until you locate the Height property.

7. Change the Height property setting to **.2** and tap (ENTER).
   The height of all six selected objects will increase.

8. Click in an empty part of the form to deselect the controls.

9. Use the (SHIFT) key technique to select only the Subtotal, Sales Tax, and Total labels that are to the left of the controls.

10. Click in the Width box (within the Properties box) and set the width to **.8**.

11. Make sure the labels are still selected and use the **Format→Align→Left** command to align the labels on the left.

12. Use the (SHIFT) key technique to select only the Subtotal, Sales Tax, and Total controls (not the labels to the left of the controls).

13. Use the **Format→Align→Left** command to align the controls on the left.

14. Use the (CTRL)+ArrowKey keystroke combinations to adjust the position of the controls as shown below. You may need to deselect the controls and move them one at a time to achieve the intended results.

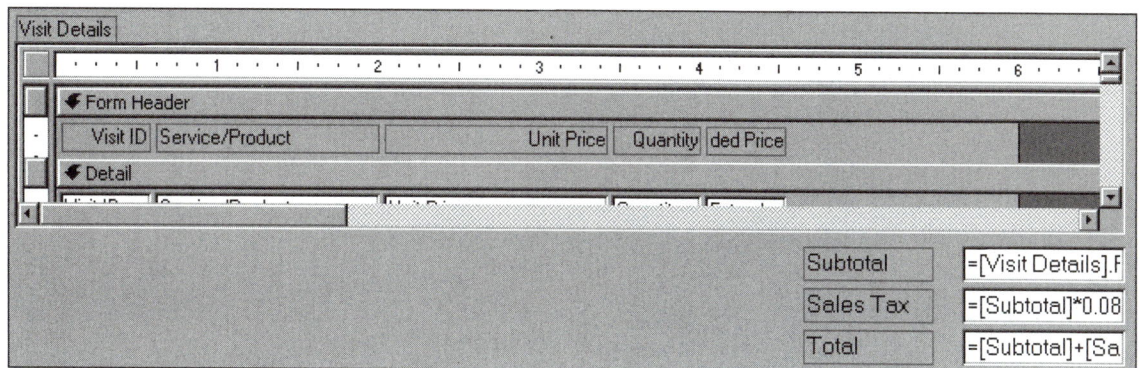

15. Use the (SHIFT) key technique to select only the Total label and the Total control.

16. Set the Font Weight format property to Bold.

17. Click in the Fore Color format property box and then click the Ellipses ⬛ button that appears in the box.
    Access will display a color palette.

18. Choose a dark blue color and click **OK.**
    A number will be displayed in the Font Color property. The number represents the color you chose.

(Continued on the next page)

Examine the Completed Form and Enter Data

19. Click the Form view [▥] button on the toolbar to view the completed form.
Your form should closely match the example shown below.

*The subtotal is calculated in the Visit Details subform and is then displayed in the **Subtotal** control on the Visits main form. The Sales Tax and Total calculations are performed within calculated controls on the main form.*

20. Use the navigation bar at the bottom of the Visits form to navigate to the record with Visit ID 4 (the "Max the cat" record).

21. Enter the following data into the "Max the cat" record.
As you enter the data, Access will automatically calculate the Subtotal, Sales Tax, and Total.

22. Enter the following data into the subform for Visit ID's 5–11. Notice that you will need to enter up to three detail records for each Visit ID.

Visit ID	Service/Product	Unit Price	Quantity
5	Standard Medical Checkup	85.00	1
	Antibiotics	50.00	1
6	Deluxe Grooming	15.00	1
	Pet Shampoo	8.50	3
7	Standard Medical Checkup	85.00	1
8	**Do not enter data for record 8**		
9	Advanced Obedience Training	85.00	1
10	Advanced Obedience Training	85.00	1
	Deluxe Chain	16.50	1
11	Standard Medical Checkup	85.00	1
	Flea Bath	35.00	1
	Flea Shampoo	12.50	5

23. If necessary, make any adjustments to your form until it matches the form on the previous page.

24. Close the form when you have finished and save the changes.

25. Close the Pinnacle Pet Care database and continue with the end-of-lesson questions and exercises.

Concepts Review

True/False Questions

1. A subform is a form within a form. TRUE FALSE

2. Subforms are not based upon tables or queries. TRUE FALSE

3. Synchronization between a main form and a subform occurs automatically only when a relationship has been established between the forms. TRUE FALSE

4. Calculated controls cannot be used in subforms. TRUE FALSE

5. A subtotal is calculated in a subform by placing a calculated control in the subform footer. TRUE FALSE

6. Calculated control expressions are placed in the Control Source box of the Properties box. TRUE FALSE

7. Expressions can contain functions, such as the Sum function. TRUE FALSE

8. The Data tab in the Properties box is used to set formatting options for controls. TRUE FALSE

Multiple Choice Questions

1. Which button initiates the Subform Wizard?
   a. [image]
   b. [image]
   c. [image]
   d. [image]

2. Which symbols are used to enclose function arguments in expressions?
   a. { }
   b. ( )
   c. [ ]
   d. < >

3. Which symbols are used to enclose the names of controls, forms, and other objects?
   a. { }
   b. ( )
   c. [ ]
   d. < >

4. Which symbol is used to separate the object type from the control?
   a. =
   b. -
   c. .
   d. !

Skill Builders

Skill Builder 6.1 Set Up a Package Details Table

In this exercise, you will set up a new table in the Tropical Getaways database. The table will be used to record package details for the Custom Packages program.

1. Open the Tropical Getaways database.

2. Click the **Tables** button on the Objects bar.

3. Double-click the *Create table in Design view* option.

4. Follow these steps to set up the Package Details table.

Ⓐ *Type the field names shown here, and choose the data types shown for each field name. Make sure you spell the field names correctly.*

Ⓑ *Leave the field size for the **Item** field set to **50**. Set the number of decimals for the **Unit Price** field to **2**.*

Field Name	Data Type
Package ID	Number
Item	Text
Unit Price	Currency
Quantity	Number

5. Do not set a primary key for this table.

6. Close the table and choose **Yes** when Access asks if you want to save the table.

7. Type the name **Package Details** in the Save As box and click **OK**.
   Access will display a warning box indicating that a primary key has not been defined.

8. Choose **No** to save the table without defining a primary key.

Skill Builder 6.2 Set Up a Query with a Calculated Field

In this exercise, you will create a query based upon the Package Details table. The query will contain an Extended Price field that will calculate the extended price.

1. Click the **Queries** button on the Objects bar.

2. Double-click the *Create query in Design view* option.

3. Choose Package Details in the Show Table box and click the **Add** button.

4. Close the Show Table box.

5. Add all fields to the design grid by double-clicking them on the Package Details field list.

6. Click in the empty field to the right of the Quantity field.

7. Click the right mouse button and choose Zoom from the pop up menu.

8. Enter the expression **Extended Price: [Unit Price] * [Quantity]** and click **OK**.

9. Check the Show box for the Extended Price field.
   Your completed query should match the following example.

Field:	Package ID	Item	Unit Price	Quantity	Extended Price: [Uni
Table:	Package Details	Package Details	Package Details	Package Details	
Sort:					
Show:	☑	☑	☑	☑	☑

10. Close the query and save it as **Query - Package Details**.

Skill Builder 6.3 Insert a Subform

In this exercise, you will use the Subform Wizard to insert a subform in the Custom Packages form. The Custom Packages form was created in the previous lesson. You will base the subform upon the Query - Package Details query.

Insert the Subform

1. Click the **Forms** button on the Objects bar.

2. Choose the Custom Packages form and click the [⬛ Design] button.

3. If necessary, click the Maximize [⬛] button to maximize the form.

4. Follow these steps to make room for the subform and to specify the subform location.

```
◀ Form Header
```

Tropical Getaways – Custom Packages

```
◀ Detail
```

Package ID	Package ID
Customer ID	Customer ID ▾
Firstname	Firstname
Lastname	Lastname
Address	Address
City	City
State	State
Zip	Zip
Profile	Profile

Order Date | Order Date

Package Notes | Package Notes

Package Category | Package Categc ▾

Destination | Destination ▾

Paid | ☑

```
◀ Form Footer
```

Ⓐ *If necessary, drag the **Form Footer** bar down to make room for the subform.*

Ⓑ *Click the **Subform** [⬛] button on the toolbox.*

Ⓒ *Click here to specify the subform location. The first Wizard screen will appear.*

(Continued on the next page)

5. Click the **Next** button to choose the *Use existing Tables and Queries* option in the first Wizard screen.

6. Choose the *Query - Package Details* query in the second screen and add all fields to the Selected Fields list.

7. Click the **Next** button.

8. Leave the option in the third Wizard screen set to *Choose from a list* and click **Next.**

9. Type the name **Package Details** in the last Wizard screen and click the **Finish** button.

10. Maximize 🔲 the Visits form window again and a placeholder box for the subform will appear.

Adjust the Overall Subform Size

11. Make sure the subform is selected and, if necessary, click the Properties 🖼 button to display the Properties box.

12. If necessary, click the Format tab on the Properties box.

13. Set the Width property to **6.6″** and the Height property to **1.1″**.

14. Close the Custom Packages form and save the changes.

Adjust Subform Column Widths

15. If necessary, click the **Forms** button on the Objects bar in the database window.
    Notice the Package Details form, created by the Subform Wizard.

16. Double-click the Package Details form to open it in Form view.

17. AutoFit the widths of the Package ID, Unit Price, Quantity, and Extended Price columns by double-clicking the right edge of their column headings.

18. Select the Item column by clicking the column heading.

19. Choose **Format→Column Width,** and set the width to **46**.

20. Close the Package Details subform and Access should automatically save the changes.

21. Double-click the Custom Packages form to open it in Form view. Your completed main form and subform should closely match the following example. If necessary, make adjustments to the subform column widths and/or the overall size of the subform. You will need to make adjustments to the subform column widths by opening the Package Details subform in Form view. Adjustments to the overall subform size can be made by displaying the Custom Packages form in Design view.

22. Close the Custom Packages form when you have finished.

Skill Builder 6.4 Insert a Calculated Control

In this exercise, you will create a Subtotal control in the Package Details form.

1. Open the Package Details form in Design view.

2. Maximize ▣ the form window.

3. Click the Text Box ▣ button on the toolbox.

4. Click below the Form Footer bar under the Extended Price control. The dark area of the footer will become light gray behind the text box control.

5. Make sure the text box control is selected and, if necessary, display the Properties box.

6. Click the Data tab in the Properties box, and enter the expression **=Sum([Extended Price])** in the Control Source property. Make sure you use the open and closed parenthesis ( ) and open and closed brackets [ ].

7. Click the Other tab and enter the name **Subtotal** in the Name box.

8. Click the label on the form to the left of the Subtotal control and change the label text to **Subtotal**.

9. Close the Package Details form and save the changes.

Skill Builder 6.5 Add Calculated Controls

In this exercise, you will add Subtotal, Sales Tax, and Total controls to the Custom Packages form.

1. Open the Custom Packages form in Design view and maximize ▣ the form.

2. Follow these guidelines to add the Subtotal, Sales Tax, and Total controls to the form as shown on the next page.

   ▪ If necessary, drag the Form Footer bar down to make room for the controls.

   ▪ Use the Text Box ▣ button to add the controls to the form.

   ▪ Set the Control Source property for the Subtotal control to the expression **=[Package Details].[Form]![Subtotal]**. Change the name of the Subtotal control to **Subtotal**. You can accomplish this in the Other tab of the Properties box. Change the label in front of the control to **Subtotal**, as shown on the next page.

   ▪ Set the Control Source property for the Sales Tax control to **=[Subtotal] * .075**. This expression assumes the sales tax rate is 7.5%. Change the name of the Sales Tax control to **Sales Tax**. Change the label in front of the control to **Sales Tax**, as shown on the next page.

■ Set the Control Source property for the Total control to **=[Subtotal] + [Sales Tax]**. Change the name of the Total control to **Total**. Change the label in front of the control to **Total**.

■ Don't be concerned with the layout of the controls. In a moment, you will format the controls and modify their positions.

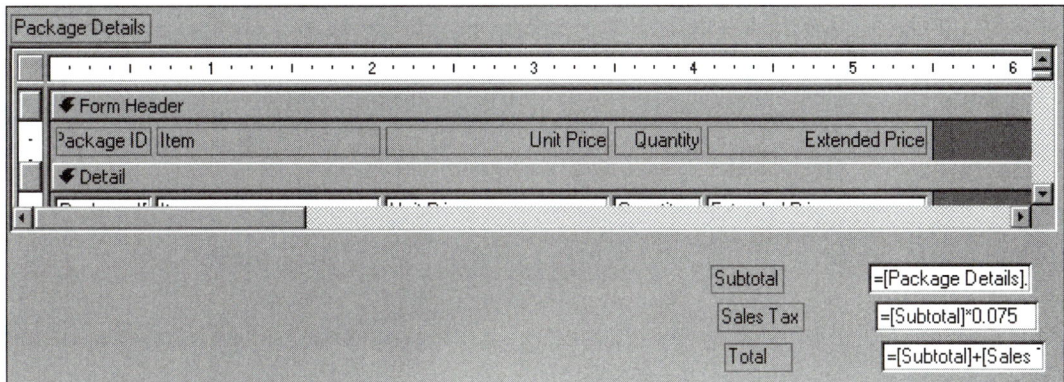

3. Use the (SHIFT) key technique to select all three of the controls and all three of the labels.

4. Click the Format tab in the Properties box.

5. Set the Font Size property to **10**.

6. Set the Height property to **.2**.

7. Click on a blank area of the form to deselect the controls.

8. Select only the three labels to the left of the controls.

9. Set the Width property to **.8**.

10. Use the **Format→Align→Left** command to align the selected labels.

11. Select only the Subtotal, Sales Tax, and Total controls.

12. Set the Format property to Currency and the Decimal Places property to **2**.

13. Use the **Format→Align→Left** command to align the selected controls.

14. Click on a blank area of the form to deselect the controls.

15. Select only the Total control and the Total label.

16. Use the Bold [B] button on the Formatting toolbar to apply bold formatting.
You can apply text formats using buttons on the Formatting toolbar or properties in the Properties box.

(Continued on the next page)

17. Use the Font Color ![A] button on the Formatting toolbar to apply the color of your choice to the Total label and the Total Control.

18. Use the (CTRL)+Arrow Keys technique to position the controls under the Visit Details subform as shown below.

Package Details

```
Form Header
Package ID | Item          Unit Price  Quantity         Extended Price
Detail

                                              Subtotal    =[Package Det
                                              Sales Tax   =[Subtotal]*0.07
                                              Total       =[Subtotal]+[$
```

19. Switch to Form ![icon] view and continue with the next exercise.

Skill Builder 6.6 Enter Data in the Subform

1. Make sure the flashing insertion point is positioned in the Package ID field at the top of the Custom Packages main form.

2. Click the Sort Ascending ![button] button on the Access toolbar.
The records in the main form should now be sorted by Package ID. The "Alice Simpson" record should appear first because it has Package ID 1.

3. Enter the four items shown below into the Package Details subform.
The Extended Price, Subtotal, Sales Tax, and Total should automatically be calculated as shown. If your controls to do not calculate correctly, you should switch to Design view and modify the calculated control expressions.

Package Details

	Package ID	Item	Unit Price	Quantity	Extended Price
▶	1	Airfare	$450.00	4	$1,800.00
	1	Hotel Rooms	$75.00	28	$2,100.00
	1	Rental car	$35.00	7	$245.00
	1	Disneyland Package	$125.00	4	$500.00

Record: ◀◀ ◀ 1 ▶ ▶◀ ▶* of 4

Subtotal	$4,645.00
Sales Tax	$348.38
Total	$4,993.38

4. Enter the following data into the subform for Package ID's 2-10.

Package ID	Item	Price Unit	Quantity
2	Airfare	$375.00	1
	Deep Sea fishing package	$500.00	1
	Snorkeling package	$450.00	1
3	Airfare	$175.00	1
	Rental car	$25.00	4
	Climbing package	$350.00	1
4	Airfare	$485.00	1
	All inclusive cruise package	$2,790.00	1
5	Airfare	$485.00	1
	All inclusive cruise package	$2,790.00	1
6	Airfare	$525.00	4
	Hotel rooms	$145.00	24
	Rental car	$28.50	7
	Golf and tennis package	$450.00	3
7	Airfare	$1,890.00	2
	All inclusive safari package	$3,450.00	2
8	Airfare	$300.00	1
	Hotel room	$85.00	6
	Rental car	$28.00	7
	Touring package	$235.00	1
9	Airfare	$1,560.00	1
	Climbing package	$2,750.00	1
10	Airfare	$375.00	1
	Deep sea fishing package	$500.00	1
	Snorkeling package	$450.00	1

5. Close the Custom Packages form when you have finished and save any changes.

6. Close the Tropical Getaways database and continue with the Assessment project on the following pages.

Assessments

Assessment 6.1

1. Open the Classic Cars database.

2. Follow these guidelines to set up a new table with the structure shown below.

   - Use the field names and data types shown below.

   - Leave the field length of the Item field set to 50.

   - Set the number of decimal places for the Daily Cost field to **2**.

   - Do not set a primary key.

   - Close the table and save it as **Event Details**.

Field Name	Data Type
Event ID	Number
Item	Text
Daily Cost	Currency
Number of Days	Number

3. Follow these guidelines to set up a query with the structure shown below.

   - Add all fields from the Event Details table to the query.

   - Create the calculated field named Total shown below. Enter the expression **Total: [Daily Cost] * [Number of Days]** to calculate the Total.

   - Check the Show box for the Total field as shown.

   - Close the query and save it as **Query - Event Details**.

Field:	Event ID	Item	Daily Cost	Number of Days	Total: [Daily Cost]*[
Table:	Event Details	Event Details	Event Details	Event Details	
Sort:					
Show:	☑	☑	☑	☑	☑
Criteria:					

4. Use the Subform Wizard and the following guidelines to insert a subform in the Events form as shown below.

■ Use the Query - Event Details query as the basis for the subform. Add all fields from the query to the subform.

■ Let the Wizard automatically synchronize the Events form with the Subform by choosing the *Choose from a list* option in the third Wizard screen.

■ Assign the name **Event Details** to the subform.

■ Adjust the size of the subform placeholder box and the column widths of the subform until it closely matches the following example.

(Continued on the next page)

5. Follow these guidelines to add a calculated control to the footer section of the Event Details subform as shown below. This control is similar to the Subtotal controls that you created in the Hands-On exercises and the Skill Builder exercises in this lesson.

- Use the expression shown below to sum the Total fields in the query.

- Assign the name **Grand Total** (in the Properties box) to the control.

- Change the label text in front of the control to **Grand Total**.

6. Open the Events form and sort the records in the Events form by Event ID.
The "Bob Barker" record should be visible since it has Event ID 1.

7. Follow these guidelines to add a Grand Total control to the Events form as shown on the following page.

- Use an expression that references the Grand Total control in the Event Details subform. The Grand Total from the subform should be reflected into this new control on the Events form.

- Assign the name **Grand Total** to the new control.

- Change the label text in front of the control to **Grand Total.**

- Change the font size of the control and the label in front of the control to **10**.

- Increase the height of the control and the label to **.2"**.

- Increase the width of the label until all text is visible in the label.

- Apply bold formatting and a color to both the control and the label.

- Set the Format property of the control to Currency and the Decimal Places property to **2**.

- The form below shows three records in the Event Details subform. Add the records shown below to the subform in your database. Your Grand Total should be calculated as shown below.

Event Details					
	Event ID	Item	Daily Cost	Number of Days	Total
▶	1	Location fee	$500.00	2	$1,000.00
	1	Utilities	$125.00	2	$250.00
	1	Security	$180.00	2	$360.00
✱	1		$0.00	0	

Record: ◄◄ ◄ 1 ► ►I ►✱ of 3

Grand Total $1,610.00

8. Enter the following data into the subform for Event ID's 2–6.

Event ID	Item	Daily Cost	Number of Days
2	Location fee	$850.00	4
	Set up fees	$3,000.00	1
	Utilities	$350.00	4
3	Location fee	$3,500.00	2
	Set up fees	$3,400.00	1
	Utilities	$235.00	2
4	Location fee	$5,600.00	3
	Set up fees	$8,500.00	1
	Utilities	$700.00	3
	Security	$400.00	3
5	Location fee	$8,500.00	2
	Set up fees	$6,500.00	1
	Utilities	$650.00	2
	Security	$475.00	2
6	Location fee	$1,200.00	1
	Utilities	$235.00	1

9. Close the Events form when you have finished and save any changes.

10. Close the Classic Cars database.

Importing Data and Customizing Reports

The database needs of many organizations evolve over time, requiring more and more sophisticated database systems. These organizations often begin by storing data in Excel worksheets, Word datasource files, or older databases such as Dbase. As their needs become more sophisticated, an organization will often need to use data stored in these formats within an Access database. Fortunately, Access lets you import data from these—and other—data sources. In this lesson, you will import an Excel worksheet, sort the records in the imported worksheet, and apply input masks to facilitate the entry of phone numbers and other data. In addition, you will learn how to customize reports to suit your needs. You will add calculated controls to reports, work with report sections and groups, and enhance the appearance of reports.

In This Lesson

Case Study

The staff at Pinnacle Pet Care has been storing employee information in an Excel worksheet. Al Smith has been so pleased with Pinnacle's Access database system that he wants to bring all data at Pinnacle Pet Care into the Access system. For this reason, he decides to import the employee worksheet into Access. Al also wants to make it easy for his staff to enter data, so he decides to apply input masks to two fields in the new employee table. The input masks make it easy for the staff to enter telephone numbers and zip codes. Al also needs a report that summarizes all of the visit information, including the services and products purchased. He wants the report to provide a total for each visit, a grand total, and an average for all visits made to the clinic. To accomplish this, Al must create a custom report that uses calculated controls to perform the desired calculations.

*The imported employee table has input masks applied to the **Zip** and **Telephone** fields. The input masks place hyphens in 9-digit zip codes and parenthesis, spaces, and hyphens in phone numbers.*

Firstname	Lastname	Title	Address	City	State	Zip	Telephone
Reggie	Williams	Veterinarian	1200 Palmer Court	El Sobrante	CA	94803-2323	(510) 223-4545
Samantha	Torres	Trainer	2450 Wilson Lane	El Sobrante	CA	94804-	(510) 222-3222
Carl	Adamson	Receptionist	2100 Valley View	El Sobrante	CA	98408-	(510) 222-4343

Visit ID	Service/Product	Unit Price	Quantity	Extended Price
11	Standard Medical Checkup	$85.00	1	$85.00
11	Flea Bath	$35.00	1	$35.00
			Visit Total	$182.50
			Grand Total	*$915.39*
			Average	*$45.77*

The Visit Details report uses calculated controls to calculate totals for each visit, a grand total, and an average for all visits.

Importing Data

Access can import data from other databases, text files, spreadsheets, and HTML documents. The database formats supported include dBASE, Paradox, and SQL. The supported spreadsheet formats include Lotus 1-2-3 and Excel. Data can be imported to a new table or appended to an existing table.

Initiating an Import

The **File→Get External Data** command is used to initiate the import process. This command also gives you the option of linking to an external file. Linking can be useful if you want to maintain the data outside of Access but access it from within Access. Once you initiate the File→Get External Data Command, Access displays an Import box. The Import box lets you choose the location and type of file you wish to import. Access then initiates Wizards or displays dialog boxes to guide you through the import process.

Importing Excel Worksheets

Perhaps the most common type of import is when an Excel worksheet is imported into Access as a new table. Excel and Access both store data in a table structure; this facilitates the import of Excel worksheets into Access. In addition, the Import Spreadsheet Wizard guides you step-by-step through the process of importing a worksheet.

Preparing to Import a Worksheet

If the first row in your worksheet contains column headings, then the Import Spreadsheet Wizard can use those headings as the field names in the new Access table. In addition, the Wizard will assign data types to the fields in the Access table depending upon the formats used in the worksheet. For example, a column of names will be assigned a text data type while a column of numbers formatted with the Currency format will be assigned a currency format. The wizard examines the first few rows in the worksheet to determine which data types to assign to the fields. You can include rows at the top of the worksheet with "dummy" data and the formats you desire to trick the wizard into assigning a desired data type.

In this exercise, you will import a worksheet containing employee data into the Pinnacle Pet Care database.

Examine the Worksheet

1. Start Excel 2000 and obtain the worksheet shown below using one of the following methods.

   ■ Type the data shown below into Excel, or

   ■ download the worksheet file from Labyrinth Publication's Off to Work Web site located at www.offtowork.com/access, or

   ■ ask your instructor to copy the worksheet file to your exercise diskette.

	A	B	C	D	E	F	G	H	I	J
1	Prefix	Firstname	Lastname	Title	Address	City	State	Zip	Telephone	Status
2	Dr.	Al	Smith	President	2300 Wilson Lane	Walnut Creek	CA	94432	9252345463	Partner
3	Dr.	Mary	Boyd	Chief Veterinarian	4350 Birch Lane	Pleasant Hill	CA	94523	9259456578	Salaried
4	Mr.	Alex	Larkson	Boarding Manager	2100 Maple Street	Berkeley	CA	94720	5106673232	Salaried
5	Ms.	Cindy	Marshall	Training Manager	3450 Pierce Avenue	Berkeley	CA	94721	5106478909	Salaried
6	Dr.	David	Sylvester	Veterinarian	1800 Lexington Avenue	El Cerrito	CA	94834	5102378990	Salaried
7	Dr.	Nancy	Carlin	Veterinarian	2345 Vermont Court	Oakland	CA	92345	5105532323	Salaried
8	Ms.	Cathy	Bollinger	Grooming Specialist	9089 Oakland Avenue	Berkeley	CA	94720	5106458756	Hourly
9	Mr.	Anthony	Robinson	Receptionist	3210 Washington Street	Oakland	CA	92345	5105543456	Hourly
10	Ms.	Wendy	Allison	Trainer	2345 San Pablo Avenue	Richmond	CA	94834	5102284567	Hourly
11	Ms.	Kimberly	Watson	Trainer	2134 Addison Lane	Richmond	CA	94823	5102123456	Hourly
12	Mrs.	Maria	Vasquez	Accountant	2390 Crestview Drive	Berkeley	CA	94724	5106545656	Salaried
13	Mrs.	Theresa	Chin	Office Manager	3456 Ridge Court	Pleasant Hill	CA	94523	9259443456	Partner
14	Mr.	Carlos	Martinez	Partner	3456 Forest Lane	Bandon	OR	97411	5413474567	Partner
15	Mr.	Richard	Sample	Partner	4567 Carlton Avenue	Albuquerque	NM	87103	5057689090	Salaried

2. Once you enter the worksheet data or obtain the worksheet file, make sure it is open in Excel and saved to your exercise diskette as **Pinnacle Employee Data**.

3. Notice that the first row of the worksheet contains headings.
   The Import Spreadsheet Wizard will use these headings as the field names in the Access table.

4. Notice that all fields contain text except for the Zip and Telephone fields.
   The Import Wizard will assign the Text data type to all text fields and the Number data type to the numeric fields. The Address field contains a mixture of numbers and text, so it will be assigned the Text data type.

5. Close the Pinnacle Employee Data worksheet and exit Excel.

Initiate the Import Wizard

6. Start Access and open the Pinnacle Pet Care database.

7. Choose **File→Get External Data→Import** from the menu bar.
   The Import box will be displayed.

8. Choose Microsoft Excel from the *Files of type* list as the bottom of the dialog box.

9. Choose the location where your Pinnacle Employee Data file is stored (most likely your exercise diskette) from the *Look in* list at the top of the dialog box.

10. Choose the Pinnacle Employee Data worksheet and click the **Import** button.
    The first Import Spreadsheet Wizard screen will appear.

(Continued on the next page)

Use the Import Spreadsheet Wizard

11. Click the **Next** button on the first Wizard screen to choose the *Show Worksheets* option.
The Wizard lets you import entire worksheets or named ranges within worksheets.

12. Check the *First Row Contains Column Headings* option in the second Wizard screen.
The Wizard will display the first worksheet row with a gray background. These headings will become the field names in the table.

13. Click **Next** to display the third Wizard screen.

14. Click **Next** again to instruct the Wizard to store the data in a new table.
The Existing Table option lets you append the data to the end of an existing table.

15. Follow these steps to examine the Field Options screen; however, don't change any of the options.

Ⓐ *Notice that the current field name and its data type are displayed here. You can enter a different field name if desired; however, you can't change the data type from within the Wizard.*

Ⓑ *This option lets you index fields. Indexing helps Access search large databases efficiently.*

Ⓒ *You can choose to not import a field by checking this box.*

Ⓓ *Click on another field and the Field Options for that field will be displayed. Feel free to click on the various fields, but don't change any of the options.*

16. Click **Next** without changing any of the field options to display the next Wizard screen.
The Wizard will propose a primary key field named ID. This primary key will use an AutoNumber data type.

17. Click **Next** to accept the proposed primary key.

18. Type the name **Employees** in the last Wizard screen and click the **Finish** button.

19. Click **OK** on the message box that appears to complete the import.

Examine the Imported Table

20. Double-click the Employees table in the Tables section of the database window to open it in datasheet view.
All 14 records from the Excel worksheet should be present.

21. Click the Design view button on the left end of the toolbar.

22. Change the name of the ID field to **Employee ID**.

23. Take a moment to examine the other fields and their data types.

24. Close the table when you have finished and save the changes.
You will continue to work with the table in the next exercise.

Input Masks

Access lets you define input masks to help you enter formatted data. An input mask consists of a series of characters that define how the data is to be formatted. Input masks can be used for a variety of formatting tasks. For example, you can use an input mask to force all characters entered to be uppercase or to automatically insert parenthesis and dashes in phone numbers. The input mask character string is entered in the Input Mask field property in table design view. Once an input mask is set up in a table, the mask formats display data in queries, forms, and reports.

The Input Mask Wizard

Setting up an input mask can be a tedious process. Fortunately, Access provides an Input Mask Wizard to help you set up common input mask formats. The following illustration discusses the process of setting up an input mask using the Input Mask Wizard.

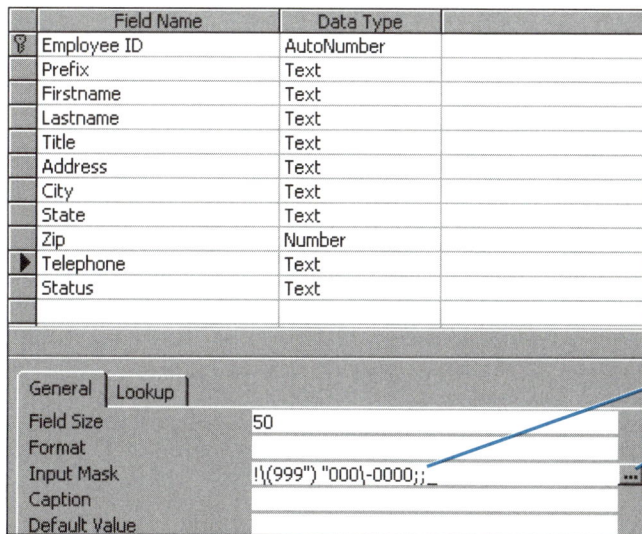

*A Build button appears when you click in the **Input Mask** field property box. The Build button initiates the **Input Mask Wizard**. This input mask character string formats telephone numbers with parenthesis and dashes. In this example, the **Telephone** field data type has been changed to Text because the Input Mask Wizard can only be used with fields that have a Text or Date data type.*

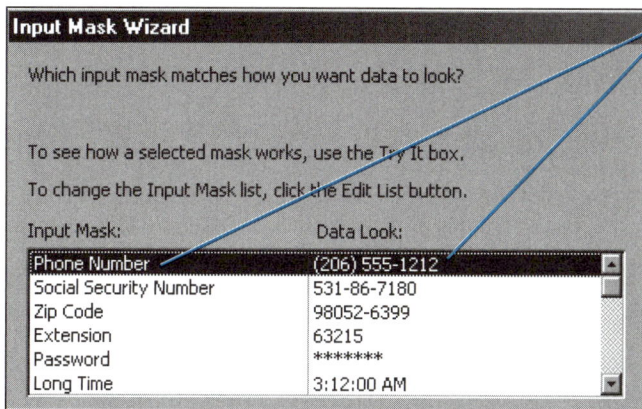

The Input Mask Wizard lets you choose common mask formats.

Installing the Input Mask Wizard

The Input Mask Wizard may not be installed on your system as part of the typical Microsoft Office installation. If this is true, then you will need to install the Wizard using the Office installation CD ROM.

Hands-On 7.2 Use the Input Mask Wizard

In this exercise, you will apply input masks to the Zip and Telephone fields. Currently, these fields have a Number data type. The Import Wizard set the data type to Number. In Steps 5 and 6, you will change the data types to Text. This is necessary because the Input Mask Wizard can only be used with Date and Text data types. This will have no effect on your ability to use the data since you won't need to perform calculations on the Zip and Telephone fields.

Change the Data Types

1. Double-click the Employees table in the Tables section of the database window to open it in Datasheet view.

2. If necessary, maximize ☐ the table window.

3. Scroll to the right until the Zip and Telephone fields are visible.
   Notice how the fields contain unformatted numbers.

4. Click the Design view 🔲 Design button to switch to Design view.

5. Click in the Zip field and change the data type from Number to Text.

6. Change the data type of the Telephone field from Number to Text.

Apply the Zip Code Input Mask

7. Click in the Zip field and then click in the Input Mask box in the Field Properties section in the lower part of the window.
   The Build button will appear on the right side of the Input Mask box.

8. Click the Build 🔲 button and Access will prompt you to save the table.

9. Click the **Yes** button to save the table.

10. Choose the Zip Code format in the first Wizard screen and click the **Next** button.
    The second Wizard screen will display a sample and allow you to change the placeholder character.

11. Click **Next** to accept the defaults and display the next screen.
    The next screen will give you the option of saving the data with or without the symbol characters in the mask. Storing the symbol characters with the data can be useful if you want to export the characters along with the data to Excel or another program. For our purposes, however, we will not save the characters with the data.

12. Make sure the *Without the symbols* option is chosen and click **Next.**

13. Click the **Finish** button to complete the input mask.
    Access will display the input mask characters 00000/-9999;;_ in the Input Mask box. In a moment, you will view the formatted data.

Apply the Telephone Input Mask

14. Click in the Telephone field and then click in the Input Mask box.

15. Click the Build ![...] button and choose **Yes** to save the table.

16. Make sure the Phone Number mask is chosen in the first Wizard screen and click **Next.**

17. Click **Next** on the second Wizard screen to accept the proposed mask format.

18. Make sure the *Without the symbols* option is chosen in the third screen and click **Next.**

19. Click the **Finish** button to complete the input mask.
    Access will display the input mask characters !(999) 000-0000;;_ in the Input Mask box.

Enter Data Using the Masks

20. Click the Datasheet view ![icon] button on the Access toolbar and choose **Yes** to save the table.

21. Scroll to the right until the Zip and Telephone fields are visible.
    Notice how the input masks have formatted the previously unformatted data.

22. Enter the following data into a new record at the bottom of the datasheet. Access will automatically assign the employee ID. You will enter the zip, telephone, and status data in the next few steps.

Employee ID	Prefix	Firstname	Lastname	Title	Address	City	State
15	Dr.	Reggie	Williams	Veterinarian	1200 Palmer Court	El Sobrante	CA

23. Click in the Zip field, type **948032323**, and tap the (TAB) key.
    Notice how the input mask assists you with the data entry by positioning the hyphen between the first five and last four digits.

24. Type **5102234545** in the phone field and tap the (TAB) key.
    As you can see, the phone input mask is quite useful for entering telephone numbers.

25. Type **Salaried** in the Status field.

26. Leave the Employees table open as you will continue to use it in the next exercise.

Sorting Records

The Sort Ascending 🔼 and Sort Descending 🔽 buttons on the Access toolbar let you sort records in tables and forms. By default, Access sorts records based upon the primary key field. If a table does not have a primary key, then Access sequences the records in the order in which they were entered. You can use the Sort Ascending and Sort Descending buttons to change the sort order. Simply click in the desired table column or form field and click the desired button to sort the records. When you close a table that has been sorted, Access will ask if you want to save the changes. If you save the changes, the records will appear in the new sort order the next time the table is opened in Datasheet view. Access automatically saves the new sort order when a sorted form is closed.

Hands-On 7.3 Sort Records in Datasheet View

1. Make sure the Employees table is displayed in Datasheet view.
   The table should already be displayed in Datasheet view from the previous exercise.

2. Notice that the records are sorted based upon the Employee ID field.
   The Employee ID is the primary key field so Access uses that field as the default sort key.

3. Click in any cell in the Lastname column and then click the Sort Ascending 🔼 button.
   The records should now be sorted on the Lastname field.

4. Click in the Zip column and click the Sort Descending 🔽 button.
   The records should be sorted in descending order based upon the Zip field.

5. Click in the Employee ID column and click the Sort Ascending 🔼 button.

6. Close the table and save the changes.

The Lookup Wizard

The Lookup Wizard can be used to set up lookup columns in table Datasheet view. Lookup columns function like combo boxes on forms; however, lookup columns are used in table Datasheet view. Lookup columns let you enter data by choosing from a drop down list.

	Employee ID	Prefix	Firstname
	13	Mr.	Carlos
	14	Mr.	Richard
	15	Dr.	Reggie
🖉	17	Mrs. ▾	
✱	(AutoNumber)	Dr.	
		Mr.	
		Mrs.	
		Ms.	

*In this example, the Lookup Wizard was used to set up a lookup column within the **Prefix** field in the Employees table. In Datasheet view, a drop-down button appears, and a list of acceptable prefixes is displayed. The lookup column receives its values from a **Prefix** lookup table.*

Initiating the Lookup Wizard

The Lookup Wizard is initiated in table Design view by clicking in the Data Type box of the desired field and choosing Lookup Wizard from the Data Type list. The Lookup Wizard works like the Combo Box Wizard. Prior to initiating the Lookup Wizard, you should set up a lookup table if you want the lookup column to display values from a lookup table.

Hands-On 7.4 Use Lookup Lists

Set Up Lookup Tables

In this exercise, you will set up lookup columns for the Prefix and Status fields in the Employees tables. The lookup columns will receive their values from Prefix and Status lookup tables, which you will set up.

1. Double-click the *Create table in Design view* option in the Tables section of the database window.

2. Type the name **Prefix** in the first Field Name box and change the field size to **4** in the Field Properties section at the bottom of the dialog box.

3. Click in the Prefix field name box and click the Primary Key button on the Access toolbar.

4. Save the table with the name **Prefix**.

5. Click the Datasheet view button on the left end of the Access toolbar.

6. Enter into the table the four records shown to the right.

Prefix
Mr.
Mrs.
Ms.
Dr.

7. Close the table when you have finished.
   You just set up a Prefix lookup table. The values from this table will be displayed on the Prefix lookup list later in this exercise.

8. Follow these guidelines to set up another lookup table.

   ■ Create a new table with a single field named **Status**.

   ■ Set the field size of the Status field to **10**.

Status
Hourly
Partner
Salaried

   ■ Make the Status field a primary key.

   ■ Save the table with the name **Status**.

   ■ Enter into the table the data shown above, and then close the table.

(Continued on the next page)

Use the Lookup Wizard to Set Up a Prefix Lookup Column

9. Open the Employees table in Design view.

10. Follow these steps to initiate the Lookup Wizard.

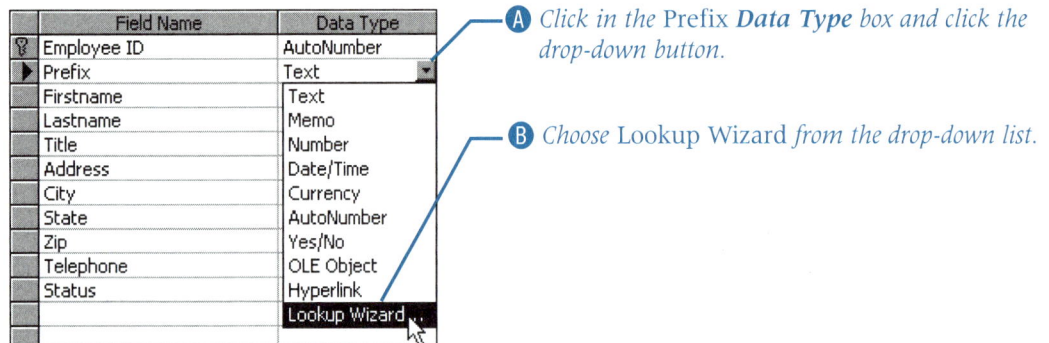

A *Click in the* Prefix **Data Type** *box and click the drop-down button.*

B *Choose* Lookup Wizard *from the drop-down list.*

The first Wizard screen will ask where the lookup column will get its values. Your lookup column will get its values from the Prefix field in the Prefix table.

11. Make sure the *I want the lookup column to look up the values in a table or query* option is chosen, and click **Next.**
    The next screen will ask which table or query should provide the values for the lookup column.

12. Choose the Prefix table and click **Next.**
    The next screen will ask which fields you want included in the lookup column.

13. Use the Add Field [>] button to add the Prefix field to the Selected Fields list.

14. Click **Next,** and then click **Next** again to bypass the screen that asks you to adjust the column width.

15. Make sure the name **Prefix** is entered in the label box of the final Wizard screen and click the **Finish** button.

16. Choose **Yes** when Access asks if you want to establish a relationship.

Use the Lookup Wizard to Set Up a Prefix Lookup Column

17. Click in the Data Type box for the Status field and choose *Lookup Wizard* from the drop-down list.

18. Make sure the I *want the lookup column to look up the values in a table or query* option is chosen in the first Wizard screen and click **Next.**

19. Choose the Status table in the second Wizard screen and click **Next.**

20. Use the Add Field [>] button to add the Status field to the Selected Fields list in the third screen and click **Next.**

21. Click **Next** again to bypass the column width screen.

22. Make sure the name **Status** is entered in the label box of the final Wizard screen and click the **Finish** button.

23. Choose **Yes** when Access asks if you want to establish a relationship.

Use the Lookup Columns to Enter Data

24. Click the Datasheet ▦ view button on the left end of the Access toolbar.

25. Follow these steps to begin entering data.

	15	Dr.		Reggie
✎	16	Mrs. ▾		
*	(AutoNumber)	Dr.		
		Mr.		
		Mrs.		
		Ms.		

Ⓐ *Click in the Prefix field for a new record, and a drop-down button will appear.*

Ⓑ *Click the drop-down button and choose* Mrs.

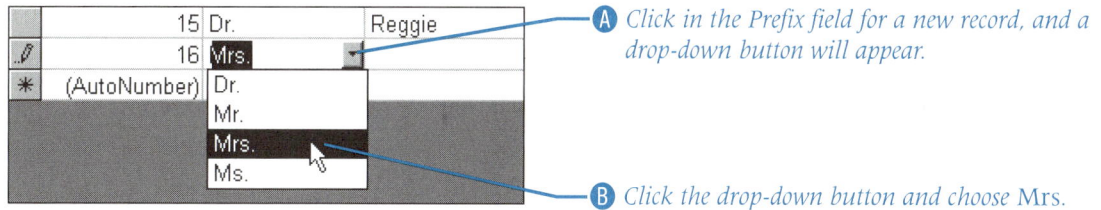

26. Complete the current record and add another record using the following data. Use the drop-down lists in the Prefix and Status columns to enter those data items.

Prefix	Firstname	Lastname	Title	Address	City	State	Zip	Telephone	Status
Mrs.	Samantha	Torres	Trainer	2450 Wilson Lane	El Sobrante	CA	94804-	(510) 222-3222	Salaried
Mr.	Carl	Adamson	Receptionist	2100 Valley View	El Sobrante	CA	98408-	(510) 222-4343	Hourly

27. Save 💾 the Employees table, and then close it.

Subdatasheets

Subdatasheets are a new feature in Access 2000. Subdatasheets allow you to display records that are related to records in an open table from within the open table. The following illustration shows the Pets table with a subdatasheet displayed. The subdatasheet displays related records from the Visits table.

A minus sign *appears once a subdatasheet has been expanded. Clicking the minus sign collapses the subdatasheet.*

	Pet ID	Pet Name	Pet Type	Breed	Gender	Color	Date of Birth	Last Visit
⊞	CT02	Max	Cat	Unknown	Male	White	1/7/86	9/7/99
⊟	CT16	Stripes	Cat	Tortoise shell	Male	Black and brown	10/8/90	7/15/99

	Visit ID	Visit Date	Pet ID	Visit Notes
▶	5	10/11/99	CT16	Stripes was suffering from a virus.
	7	10/12/99	CT16	Stripes viral infection seems to have been cured.
*	Number)		CT16	

	Pet ID	Pet Name	Pet Type	Breed	Gender	Color	Date of Birth	Last Visit
⊞	CT92	Tony	Cat	Unknown	Male	Brown with black stripes	4/3/97	7/7/99
⊞	DG12	Wolfy	Dog	German Shepherd	Male	Brown	6/6/91	7/15/99
⊞	DG13	Dillon	Dog	Mutt	Male	Black	10/5/94	7/7/99
⊞	DG14	Fetch	Dog	German Shepherd	Male	Black and brown	6/12/96	9/10/99
⊞	DG24	Ben	Dog	Terrier	Male	Black	6/1/92	10/8/99

When a one-to-many relationship has been established between two tables, plus signs appear next to records in the table on the one *side of the relationship. When you click a plus sign, the related records on the* many *side of the relationship are expanded and displayed in a subdatasheet. In this example, the visits for* Stripes, *the cat, are displayed.*

Hands-On 7.5 Use Subdatasheets

1. Double-click the Pets table in the Tables section of the database window.
   Notice the plus sign next to each record. The plus signs indicate that the table has a relationship with another table. In this case, the related table is the Visits table. The relationship is a one-to-many relationship established between the Pet ID fields in the tables. The relationship establishes that each pet can have many visits but each visit can be associated with just one pet. Clicking a plus sign will display all visit records for that pet.

2. Click any plus sign to view the subdatasheet.

3. Click the minus sign to collapse the subdatasheet.

4. Feel free to expand and collapse other subdatasheets as desired.

5. Close the Pets table when you have finished.

Customizing Reports

Report Design view is used to customize reports. You can set up a report from scratch using Report Design view, or you can use the Report Wizard to set up a report and then modify it in Design view. The second approach is often the most efficient, as the Wizard can set up basic report structures.

Hands-On 7.6 Use the Report Wizard to Set Up a Report

In this exercise, you will use the Report Wizard to set up a visit details report. In the next few topics, you will use Report Design view to customize the report.

1. Click the Reports button on the Objects bar in the database window.

2. Double-click the *Create report by using wizard* option.

3. Choose the *Query - Visit Details* query from the Tables/Queries list in the first wizard screen.

4. Add all fields to the Selected Fields list and click the **Next** button.

5. Click **Next** again to bypass the Grouping screen.
   In a later exercise, you will use Report Design view to establish grouping levels.

6. Click **Next** two more times to accept the default wizard options.

7. Choose the Corporate style in the next Wizard screen, and click the **Next** button.

8. Type the report name **Visit Details Report** in the final wizard screen and click the **Finish** button.
   Access will display a preview of the report.

9. Take a moment to examine the report.

   Notice that the report displays the visit details for each visit. The report is based upon the Query - Visit Details query. This query displays the Visit ID, Service/Product, Unit Price, and Quantity fields, and calculates the extended price.

10. Click the Design View ![icon] button on the left end of the Access toolbar.

    Access will display the report in Report Design view. You will use Report Design view to customize the report.

Report Sections

Reports are comprised of various sections. For example, the report you just displayed in Design view has Report Header, Page Header, Detail, Page Footer, and Report Footer sections. Each section is used for a particular purpose as described in the following table. The table also describes the Group Header and Group Footer sections, which you will add to the report in a moment.

Report Section	Purpose
Report Header	The Report Header prints at the top of the first page only. This section typically contains just the report title.
Page Header	The Page Header prints at the top of every page. This section typically contains descriptive headings for the fields displayed in the Detail section. In your report, the Visit ID, Service/Product, Unit Price, Quantity, and Extended Price labels in the Page Header section will print at the top of every page.
Detail	The Detail section typically contains text box controls that display data from the table or query that the report is based upon. Your report has Visit ID, Service/Product, Unit Price, Quantity, and Extended Price controls in the Detail section. When the report is displayed in Print Preview mode, the Query - Visit Details query which the report is based upon is run, and the records are displayed in the Detail section of the report. The report will use as many pages as necessary to display all records generated by the query.
Page Footer	The Page Footer prints at the bottom of every page. The Page Footer typically contains page numbers, the date and/or time, and other elements.
Report Footer	The Report Footer prints below the last detail record on the last report page. The Report Footer may not be used at all or it may contain calculated controls that produce totals of all details records on the report.
Group Header	Reports can group records on one or more fields. For example, in your report you will add a grouping level that groups the records on the Visit ID field. This way, all of the detail records for a particular visit will be grouped together. The Group Header section can be used to print a descriptive heading for each group.
Group Footer	The Group Footer section is typically used to calculate totals for each group of records. For example, you will insert a calculated control in the Group Footer section to calculate a total for each group of visit detail records. This will produce a total for each Visit ID.

Report Groups

The Sorting and Grouping ![icon] button on the Report Design view toolbar displays the Sorting and Grouping box. The Sorting and Grouping box is used to establish report groups. You can group records on one or more fields. The Sorting and Grouping box lets you display a group header and a group footer for your groups. As mentioned in the preceding table, the group header is used to display descriptive headings for groups while the group footer typically contains calculated controls. The calculated controls in the footer are typically used to sum one or more fields in each group. The following illustration describes the Sorting and Grouping box.

*The **Sorting and Grouping** box lets you choose one or more fields from the table or query on which the report is based.* ———

*The **Group Properties** for the current field are displayed here. You can set the **Group Header** and/or **Group Footer** properties to* Yes *to display a group header and/or footer in the report.* ———

Hands-On 7.7 Establish a Group

The Visit Details report should be displayed in Design view from the previous exercise.

1. If necessary, click the Sorting and Grouping ![icon] button on the Access toolbar or choose **View→Sorting and Grouping** to display the Sorting and Grouping box.

2. Click in the first *Field/Expression* box, click the drop-down button, and choose **Visit ID.**

3. Click in the *Group Footer* box near the bottom of the dialog box and set the Group Footer property to **Yes.**
   A Visit ID Footer section will be added to the report. You will work with this section in the next exercise. You won't display a Group Header section for this report.

Using Controls in Reports

You can use the Toolbox in Report Design view to add controls to reports. Controls can be placed in any report section. You can format controls using the Properties box or with formatting buttons on the Access toolbar.

The Text Box ![abl] button can be used to add calculated controls to report sections. Calculated controls in reports use the same rules and syntax as calculated controls in forms. Calculated controls added to a group footer section perform calculations on the records in that group. Calculated controls added to the Report Footer section are used to calculate grand totals for the report. These concepts are discussed in the following illustration.

*Set the Group Footer property to Yes to add the **Visit ID Footer** section to the report.*

The Text Box ![abl] button adds this calculated control. Since the calculated control appears in the Visit ID Footer section (the group footer for the Visit ID field), it will sum the extended prices for each Visit ID group. This will produce a total for each Visit ID.

*Placing calculated controls in the **Report Footer** section calculates the sum and average of all extended prices in the report.*

Add a Calculated Control to the Group Footer

1. If necessary, click the Properties ⬚ button on the Access toolbar to display the Properties box.

2. Click the Text Box ⬚ button on the toolbox.

3. Follow these steps to add a calculated control to the Visit ID Footer section.

Ⓐ *Click in the **Visit ID Footer** section to position the Text Box control.*

Ⓑ *Click the Data tab on the Properties box, and type the expression* **=Sum([Extended Price])** *in the Control Source box. Make sure you enter the expression exactly as shown.*

Ⓒ *Click the label to the left of the control, select the label text, and type* **Visit Total**, *as shown here.*

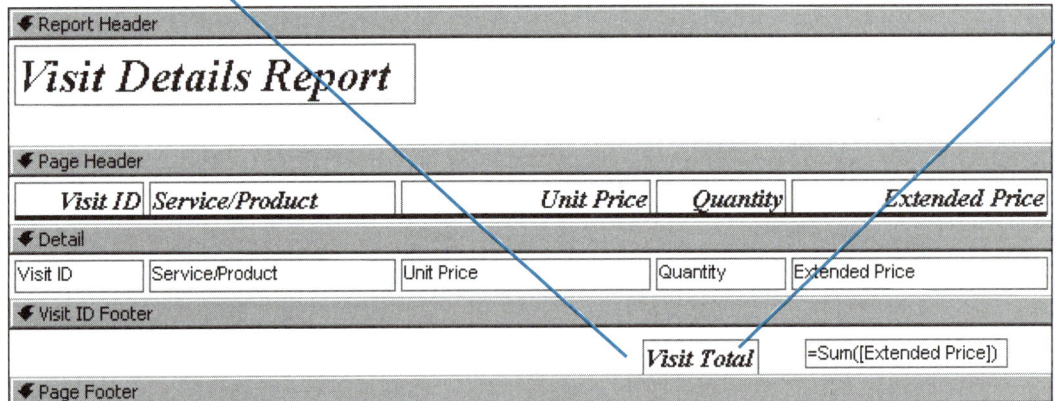

◆ Report Header	
Visit Details Report	
◆ Page Header	
Visit ID | Service/Product | Unit Price | Quantity | Extended Price	
◆ Detail	
Visit ID | Service/Product | Unit Price | Quantity | Extended Price	
◆ Visit ID Footer	
Visit Total | =Sum([Extended Price])	
◆ Page Footer	

4. Click the View ⬚ button on the left end of the Access toolbar to display the report. *The calculated control should calculate a total for each group.*

5. Follow these steps to examine the report.

Ⓐ *This report header prints only at the top of the report.*

Ⓑ *The page header prints at the top of every page.*

Visit Details Report

Visit ID	Service/Product	Unit Price	Quantity	Extended Price
1	Flea Shampoo	$12.50	2	$25.00
1	Flea Bath	$35.00	1	$35.00
		Visit Total		60
2	Advanced Obedience Training	$85.00	1	$85.00
2	Leather Collar	$23.89	1	$23.89
2	Deluxe Chain	$16.50	1	$16.50
		Visit Total		125.39

Ⓒ *The records are grouped on the Visit ID field.*

Ⓓ *The Visit ID Footer calculates the total for each group. At this point, the calculated control is not formatting the totals with the Currency format, nor are the totals aligned with the Extended Price controls.*

Format the Controls

6. Click the Design View ⊠ button on the left end of the Access toolbar to switch back to Report Design view.

7. Follow these steps to align the controls and to set the format property of the calculated control.

Ⓐ *Click the **Visit ID** label in the **Page Header** section, press* (SHIFT), *and then click the* Visit ID *control in the **Detail** section.*

Ⓑ *Click the Center ▤ button on the Access toolbar to center-align the objects.*

Ⓒ *Click the* Extended Price *control, press* (SHIFT), *and then click the calculated control.*

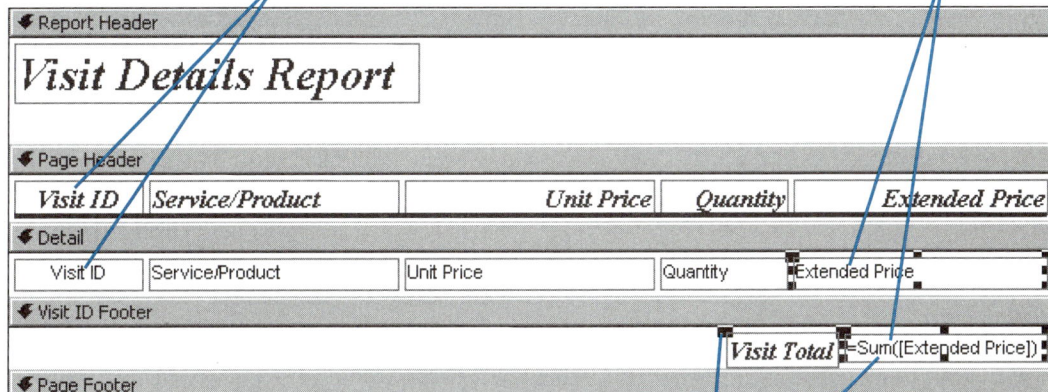

```
◆ Report Header

  Visit Details Report

◆ Page Header

  Visit ID    Service/Product         Unit Price    Quantity         Extended Price
◆ Detail
     Visit ID    Service/Product       Unit Price        Quantity       Extended Price
◆ Visit ID Footer
                                                      Visit Total   =Sum([Extended Price])
◆ Page Footer
```

Ⓓ *Choose **Format→Align→Right** to align the objects on the right.*

Ⓔ *Click the **Visit Total** label, and then drag it to the right by dragging the large black box at the top-left corner of the label.*

Ⓕ *Click the calculated control, and set the Format property on the Format tab of the Properties box to* Currency.

8. Click the View ⊡ button to display the report.
The Visit Totals should now have a Currency format and be right aligned with the visit detail records.

9. Use the record navigation bar at the bottom-left corner of the window to display the second page of the report.
The report should end with the Visit Total for Visit ID 11. In the next few steps, you will add calculated controls to the Report Footer section. These controls will display the total and average of all visits below the Visit ID 11 total.

10. Click the Design View ⊠ button to switch back to Report Design view.

(Continued on the next page)

Add Calculated Controls in the Report Footer

11. Click the Text Box [abl] button on the toolbox.

12. Follow these steps to add calculated controls to the Report Footer section.

A *Click in the Report Footer section to add a Text Box control.*

B *Click the Data tab on the Properties box, and type the expression* **=Sum([Extended Price])** *in the Control Source box.*

Detail				
Visit ID	Service/Product	Unit Price	Quantity	Extended Price

Visit ID Footer

Visit Total =Sum([Extended Price])

Page Footer

=Now() ="Page " & [Page] & " of " & [Pages]

Report Footer

Grand Total =Sum([Extended Price])

Average =Avg([Extended Price])

C *Click the label to the left of the control, select the label text, and type* **Grand Total**.

D *Add the* **Average** *calculated control, and modify the label text as shown here. Enter the expression* **=Avg([Extended Price])** *in the Control Source property box.*

At this point, you won't be able to see the entire expressions within the text box controls. The controls have been widened in this illustration to enable you to see the complete expressions.

13. Click the View [🔍] button to display the report.

14. Use the record navigation bar at the bottom of the report to navigate to the second page. *You should see a grand total and average calculation displayed below the last Visit ID total. The grand total should equal 915.39 and the average should equal 45.7695. In the next few steps, you will format the controls.*

15. Click the Design View [📐] button to switch back to Design view.

Format the Grand Total and Average Labels

16. Click the *Grand Total* label, press (SHIFT), and click the Average label to select both labels.

17. Use the Font Size button on the Access toolbar to set the font size to **12.**

18. Click on an empty part of the form to deselect the labels.

19. Click the *Grand Total* label and then widen the label slightly by dragging the right middle sizing handle to the right. Make the label just wide enough until all of the label text is visible.

20. Now widen the Average label slightly until it is completely visible.

Format the Calculated Controls

21. Click the *Grand Total* calculated control, press (SHIFT), and then click the *Average* calculated control to select both controls.

22. Use the Font Size button on the Access toolbar to set the font size to **11.**

23. Click the Bold [B] and Italics [I] buttons on the Access toolbar.

24. Use the Font Color [A▾] button on the Access toolbar to apply the same font color that is used for the label to the left of the controls.

25. Click the Format tab in the Properties box, click in the Format box, and set the Format property to Currency.

Your controls will be too narrow to completely display the expressions within the controls. This is OK; however, because the control only needs to be wide enough to display the calculated numbers when the report is previewed or printed.

26. Follow these steps to align the controls and labels.

Ⓐ *Select the calculated controls and the control in the Page Footer section, and use the* **Format→Align→Right** *command to align the controls.*

Ⓑ *Move the* **Grand Total** *and* **Average** *labels close to the calculated controls, and align them as shown.*

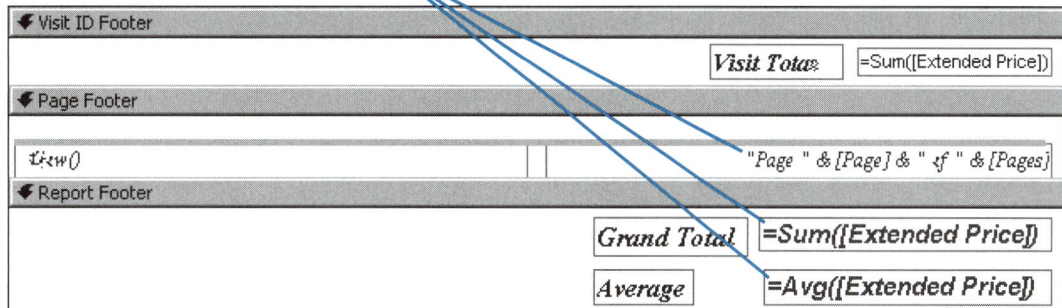

Ⓒ *Arrange the controls until they match the following example. Keep in mind that your calculated controls will be too narrow to completely display the expressions.*

27. Click the View button to display the report.

28. Use the record navigation bar at the bottom of the report to navigate to the second page.
The Grand Total and Average labels and controls should now be properly formatted and aligned.

29. Feel free to make additional adjustments to your report. You will need to switch to Design view to make any changes.

30. When you have finished, close the report, save the changes, and close the database.

Saving Objects as Web Pages

Access 2000 lets you save tables, queries, forms, and reports as web pages. You can easily publish any of these objects to the World Wide Web using the procedure outlined in the following Quick Reference table. There is no Hands-On exercise to accompany this topic. If you wish to publish one of these objects, you will need access to a web server. Additional information on this topic can be found in Access's online Help.

TO SAVE AN OBJECT AS A WEB PAGE

- Choose the desired object in the Access database window.
- Choose **File→Export** and choose **HTML Documents** from the Save as type list in the Export dialog box.
- Choose a location to save to and specify a filename.
- Check the **Save Formatted** box and click the **Save** button.
- Decide whether you want to use an HTML template (see online Help for more information on this feature) and click **OK**.

Concepts Review

True/False Questions

1. Imported data can be placed in a new table or appended to an existing table. TRUE FALSE

2. Input masks are used by the Import Wizard to determine the data types of the external data. TRUE FALSE

3. Input masks are defined in the Import Wizard box. TRUE FALSE

4. Records can be sorted while working in table Datasheet view. TRUE FALSE

5. Lookup columns are used in forms. TRUE FALSE

6. Subdatasheets are used primarily for running queries from table Datasheet view. TRUE FALSE

7. Reports can have a maximum of three different sections. TRUE FALSE

8. The primary purpose of groups is to sort the records in a report. TRUE FALSE

Multiple Choice Questions

1. Which command initiates the Import Wizard?
   a. File→Import Data
   b. File→Get Exernal Data
   c. Insert→File→External
   d. Insert→External Data

2. From which view is the Lookup Wizard initiated?
   a. Table Datasheet view
   b. Table Design view
   c. Form view
   d. Form Design view

3. What happens when a table is open in Datasheet view and one of the plus signs located to the left of the first field is clicked?
   a. A query is run.
   b. The table is displayed in Design view.
   c. A new record is added to the end of the table.
   d. A subdatasheet is displayed.

4. Where is the Page Header printed on reports?
   a. At the top of every page
   b. At the top of the first page only
   c. At the bottom of the report
   d. Next to the Page Footer

Skill Builders

Skill Builder 7.1 Sort a Table and Use the Lookup Wizard

In this exercise, you will sort the Trips table in the Tropical Getaways database. You will also use the Lookup Wizard to establish a lookup column in the table.

Set Up a Lookup Column

1. Open the Tropical Getaways database.

2. Click the Tables button on the Objects bar, then double-click the Package Category table to open it in Datasheet view.
   Notice that this table contains just Trip/Package categories. This lookup table is used as the data source for a combo box on the Custom Packages form. You will also use it as a lookup table for the Category field in the Trips table.

3. Close the table, then double-click the Trips table to open it in Datasheet view.
   Notice the Category field contains the same categories that are in the Package Category lookup table.

4. Click the Design view button ![icon] to switch to Design view.

5. Click in the Data Type box of the Category field.

6. Click the drop-down button that appears and choose **Lookup Wizard.**

7. Click **Next** to bypass the first screen.

8. Choose the *Package Category* table in the second screen and click **Next.**

9. Choose the *Package Category* field in the third screen and add it to the Selected Fields list.

10. Click **Next**, then click **Next** again to bypass the column width screen.

11. Click **Finish** on the final screen to choose the proposed name Category.

12. Click **Yes** when the Wizard asks if you want to establish the relationship.

Examine the Lookup Column in Datasheet View

13. Click the Datasheet view ![icon] button on the Access toolbar to view the table in Datasheet view.

14. Click in any cell in the **Category** column and a drop-down button will appear.

15. Click the drop-down button and notice that the lookup table data appears on the lookup list.

16. Tap (ESC) to close the lookup list without choosing from it.
    If desired, you could now use the list when entering data.

Sort the Table

17. Click in the **Customer ID** column.

18. Click the Sort Ascending ![icon] button to sort the records on the **Customer ID** column.

19. Close the table and save the changes.

Skill Builder 7.2 Use the Report Wizard

In this exercise, you will use the Report Wizard to set up a report. In the remaining Skill Builders, you will customize the report.

1. Click the **Reports** button on the Objects bar.

2. Double-click the *Create report by using wizard* option.

3. Choose the *Query - Package Details* query in the first Wizard screen, add all fields to the Selected Fields list, and click the **Next** button.

4. Click **Next** three times to bypass the next three screens.

5. Choose the Soft Gray report style in the next screen and click **Next.**

6. Enter the report name **Package Details Report** in the last Wizard screen and click the **Finish** button.
   The report will display all of the package details records along with the extended prices. The extended prices are calculated in the Query - Package Details query.

7. Click the Design view button and continue with the next exercise.

Skill Builder 7.3 Add Calculated Controls to the Report

Set Up a Group

1. If necessary, click the Sorting and Grouping [icon] button to display the Sorting and Grouping box.

2. Choose Package ID in the Field/Expression box to create a Package ID group.

3. Set the Group Footer property for the Package ID field to **Yes.**
   A Package ID Footer section should appear on the report.

Add a Subtotal Control

4. Click the Text Box [icon] button on the toolbox.

5. Click in the Package ID Footer section to position the control.

6. Set the Control Source property on the Data tab of the Properties box to **=Sum([Extended Price]).**
   Make sure you enter the expression exactly as shown.

7. Click the **Other** tab in the Properties box and set the Name property to **Subtotal**.
   You will reference this name in the Sales Tax and Total controls.

8. Change the label text to the left of the control to **Subtotal**.

(Continued on the next page)

Add Sales Tax and Total Controls

9. Follow these steps to add a Sales Tax control.

Report Header

Package Details Repor

Page Header

Package ID	Item		Unit Price	Quantity	Extended Price

Detail

Package ID	Item		Unit Price	Quantity	Extended Price

Package ID Footer

Subtotal =Sum([Extended Price])

Sales Tax =[Subtotal]*0.075

Page Footer

=Now() ="Page " & [Page] & " of " & [Pages]

Report Footer

Ⓐ *Drag the* **Page Footer** *bar down to increase the height of the* **Package ID Footer** *section. Make sure there is enough room for two additional controls below the Subtotal control.*

Ⓑ *Click the Text Box* `ab|` *button, and click below the* Subtotal *control to position the new control.*

Ⓒ *Set the Control Source property on the Data tab to* `=[Subtotal]*0.075`*; set the Name property on the Other tab to* **Sales Tax***, and change the label text to* **Sales Tax***.*

10. Add another text box control below the Sales Tax control.

11. Set the Control Source property of the new control to `=[Subtotal]+[Sales Tax]`.

12. Set the Name property of the new control to **Total**.

13. Change the label text to the left of the control to **Total**.

14. Click the View ![icon] button on the left end of the toolbar to view the report.
The subtotal, sales tax, and total controls should display calculations for each group of Packaged IDs. The calculations for Package ID 1 should be Subtotal = 4645, Sales Tax = 348.375, and Total = 4993.375.

15. Click the Design view ![icon] button to switch to Design view.

16. If your controls did not calculate correctly, then check the expressions you entered and the names you assigned in the Name property, and correct any mistakes. Continue to debug your report until the controls calculate correctly.

17. Save the changes to the report and continue with the next exercise.

Skill Builder 7.4 Format the Report

1. Select all three calculated controls and set the Format property on the Format tab of the Properties box to Currency.

2. Right-align the controls with the Extended Price control in the Detail section.

3. Move the Subtotal, Sales Tax, and Total labels closer to the controls and then left-align the labels.

4. Apply **Bold** formatting to the Total control.

5. Center ▦ the Package ID controls in the Page Header and Detail sections.

6. Click the View 🔍 button to view the completed report. The report should closely match the following example. The example shows only the first Package ID records.

Package Details Report

Package ID	Item	Unit Price	Quantity	Extended Price
1	Hotel rooms	$75.00	28	$2,100.00
1	Rental car	$35.00	7	$245.00
1	Disneyland package	$125.00	4	$500.00
1	Airfare	$450.00	4	$1,800.00
			Subtotal	$4,645.00
			Sales Tax	$348.38
			Total	$4,993.38

7. If necessary, maximize ☐ the report and use the record navigation bar to view the various pages. Your report should have two or three pages.

8. Save the changes when you have finished.

9. Close the Tropical Getaways database.

Assessments

Assessment 7.1 Set Up a Lookup Column and Customized Report

1. Open the Classic Cars database.

2. Use the Lookup Wizard to convert the Sponsor field in the Events table to a lookup column. Use the Sponsors lookup table as the data source for the lookup column.

3. View the modified Events table in Datasheet view to verify that the lookup column functions properly, but don't modify the data in the table.

4. Use the Report Wizard and these guidelines to set up a new report.

   ■ Use the *Query - Event Details* query as the basis for the report.

   ■ Use all fields from the query in the report.

   ■ Do not use the Report Wizard to set up grouping levels or sorting.

   ■ Bypass the fourth wizard screen and choose the Compact report style in the fifth screen.

   ■ Assign the name **Event Details Report** to the report in the last wizard screen.

5. Follow these guidelines to modify the report in Design view.

   ■ Establish a grouping level for the Event ID field.

   ■ Display a group footer for the Event ID group.

   ■ Add a calculated control to the Event ID Footer section that sums the detail records in each group.

   ■ Change the label text to the left of the calculated control to **Event Total**.

6. Follow these guidelines to format the report.

   ■ Format the calculated control with a Currency format.

   ■ Right-align the calculated control with the Total control in the Detail section.

   ■ Apply bold formatting to the calculated control.

   ■ Move the Event Total label close to the calculated control.

   ■ Center-align the Event ID label in the Page Header section and the Event ID control in the Detail section.

7. Your completed report should closely match the following example.

Event Details Report

Event ID	Item	Daily Cost	Number of Days	Total
1	Utilities	$125.00	2	$250.00
1	Security	$180.00	2	$360.00
1	Location fee	$500.00	2	$1,000.00
			Event Total	**$1,610.00**
2	Location fee	$850.00	4	$3,400.00
2	Set up fees	$3,000.00	1	$3,000.00
2	Utilities	$350.00	4	$1,400.00
			Event Total	**$7,800.00**

8. Follow these guidelines to add a calculated control that calculates the total of all detail records on the report.

- The control should appear at the end of the report.

- Format the control with the Currency format.

- Change the label text to the left of the calculated control to Grand Total.

- Apply any text formats that you desire.

9. Save the changes and close the report.

10. Close the Classic Cars database.

LESSON 8

Switchboards, Macros, and Command Buttons

Making databases user friendly is one of the main goals of database designers. User friendliness begins with an easy-to-use switchboard form that provides quick access to the most frequently used database objects. In this lesson, you will set up a switchboard form that provides one-click access to forms and reports. The switchboard will also automatically open when the database is started. Access lets you create macros that automate processes. Macros can be assigned to events such as the opening of a form or the clicking of an object. You will use macros to simplify data entry, open forms, and navigate to records.

In This Lesson

Case Study

Al Smith realizes that the staff at Pinnacle Pet Care is constantly changing. New employees are being hired and current employees occasionally leave. In addition, Al frequently needs to employ temporary personnel. For this reason, he wants to make the database as easy to use as possible. Al sets up a switchboard form that provides easy access to common forms and reports. In addition, he simplifies the entry of dates by using macros. He sets up the database so that when a user clicks a date field, the current date is automatically entered in the field. The switchboard form that Al sets up is shown below.

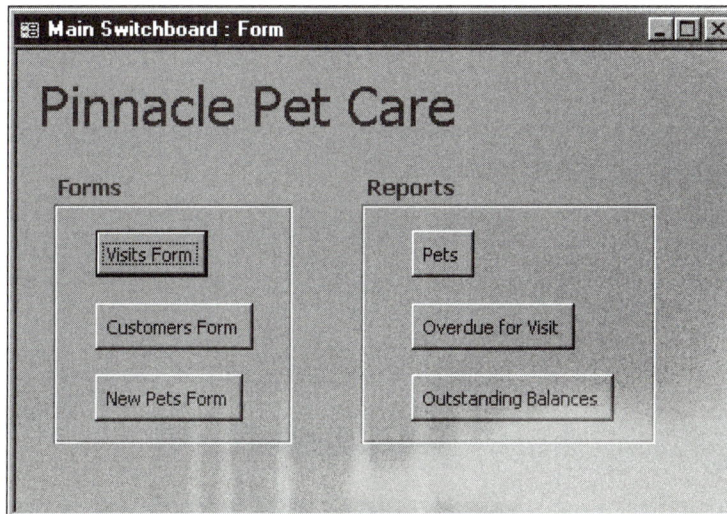

Switchboards

Database systems are often used by data entry personnel with little computer experience. For this reason, database designers must make databases easy to use. For example, many databases have a main switchboard that functions as a launch pad to various parts of the database. Switchboards are forms that contain command buttons that initiate events. You can easily create a switchboard by setting up a form and adding command buttons to them. Most switchboards also contain text boxes, rectangles, and other objects to enhance the appearance of the switchboard. The illustration on the preceding page shows the switchboard that you will set up in this lesson.

Hands-On 8.1 Set Up a Switchboard

1. Start Access and open the Pinnacle Pet Care database.

2. Click the Forms button on the Objects bar and double-click the *Create form in Design view* option.
   Access will set up a new form in the Design view window. This form is not attached to an underlying table or query, so it is ideal for a switchboard. Switchboards contain command buttons, hyperlinks, and other unbound objects that are not dependent upon an underlying table or query.

3. Follow these steps to begin setting up the form.

Ⓐ *Click the Label* **Aa** *button (not the Text Box button) on the toolbox, and click at the top-left corner of the form to position a new label.*

Ⓑ *Type the phrase* **Pinnacle Pet Care** *in the new label box.*

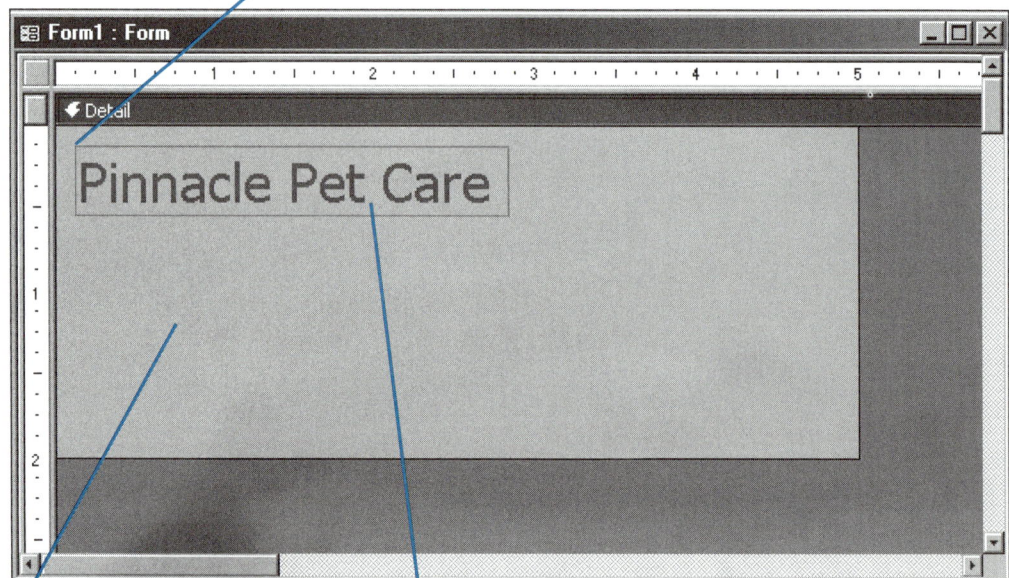

Ⓒ *Click on an empty part of the form to deselect the label.*

Ⓓ *Click the label to select it, increase the font size to 24, and apply the color of your choice. You will need to increase the size of the label box until the label text is visible, as shown here.*

4. Save 🖫 the form with the name **Main Switchboard**, and then close it.
   You will continue to modify the form as you progress through this lesson.

Macros

Macros are automated procedures that contain one or more Access commands. Macros are used to automate database activities and routine tasks.

Attaching Macros and Specifying Events

Database objects, such as forms, reports, and command buttons, have a variety of events associated with them. For example, events occur when buttons are clicked and when forms and reports are opened and closed. In Access, you can attach macros to forms, reports, command buttons, and other objects. Furthermore, you can specify the event(s) that must occur to initiate the macro. For example, you can instruct Access to run a particular macro when a command button is clicked.

The Macro Window

The [New] button appears on the toolbar in the Macro section of the database window. This button displays an empty Macro window where you can choose the commands or "actions" you wish to include in your macro. You can also specify arguments for each action. The following illustration shows the macro that you will create in the next exercise. The macro will open the Visits form and display a new record in it. In a later exercise, you will attach this macro to a command button on the Main Switchboard. The command button will run the macro when it is clicked.

*Macro actions are entered into the **Action** column. This macro has two actions. Actions are executed sequentially when the macro is run.*

*The **Action Arguments** section lets you specify arguments for each action. The arguments shown here are for the OpenForm action, which is selected in the **Action** column. Notice that the argument specifies Visits as the **Form Name**. This instructs the macro to open the Visits form when the OpenForm action is executed.*

1. Click the Macros button on the Objects bar in the database window.

2. Click the ⧉ New button to display the Macro window.

3. Follow these steps to choose the Open Form action and to specify the argument.

Ⓐ *Click the drop-down button in the **Action** box, scroll down through the list, and choose* OpenForm.

Ⓑ *Click in the **Form Name** box, click the drop-down button that appears, and choose* Visits. *Leave the other arguments set as shown here.*

Action	Comment
OpenForm	

Action Arguments

Form Name	Visits
View	Form
Filter Name	
Where Condition	
Data Mode	
Window Mode	Normal

Opens a form in Form view, Design view, Print Preview, or Datasheet view. Press F1 for help on this action.

4. Follow these steps to choose the GoToRecord action and to specify the argument.

Ⓐ *Click in the second **Action** box and choose* GoToRecord.

Ⓑ *Click in the **Record** box, and choose the* New *argument. This argument will display a new record after the form is opened.*

Action	Comment
OpenForm	
GoToRecord	

Action Arguments

Object Type	
Object Name	
Record	New
Offset	

Makes the specified record the current record in a table, form, or query result set. Press F1 for help on this action.

OpenForm and GoToRecord are the only actions that your macro will have. In the next few steps, you will save and close the Macro box. Macros are saved with a descriptive name like any other object.

5. Click the Close ☒ button at the top-right corner of the macro window.

6. Click **Yes** when Access asks is you want to save the macro.

7. Type the name **Open Visits Form** in the Save As box and click **OK**.
   The Open Visits Form macro will appear in the database window.

Testing and Editing Macros

You should run a macro after creating it to make sure it is functioning properly. You can run a macro by choosing it in the Macros section of the database window and clicking the Run button. You can also edit a macro by choosing it in the Macros section and clicking the Design button. Access also has a macro debugging mode known as Single Step mode. Single Step mode executes a macro one step at a time so that you can determine where problems are occurring.

Hands-On 8.3 Test the Macro

1. Make sure the Open Visits Form macro is chosen, and click the ⌜ **! Run** ⌝ button.
   The Visits form should open, and the record navigation bar should indicate that record 12 is displayed. The GoToRecord command instructed Access to display a new empty record.

2. Close the Visits form without entering any data.

3. If your macro did not perform as expected, then choose it in the database window and click the Design button. Follow the instructions in the preceding exercise until the macro is correct. You can rerun the macro after it has been edited.

Command Buttons

The Command Button ⬚ button on the Form Design toolbox initiates the Command Button Wizard, which guides you through the setup of command buttons. You can use command buttons to open forms and reports, run macros, and perform other tasks. Command buttons are usually placed on switchboards or in the header or footer sections of forms.

Hands-On 8.4 Set Command Buttons and Macros

In this exercise, you will create several macros and command buttons.

Set Up the Visits Form Command Button

1. Click the Forms button on the Objects bar in the database window.

2. Choose the Main Switchboard form and click the 🗹 Design button.

3. If necessary, use the **View→Toolbox** command to display the toolbox.

4. Click the Command Button ⬚ on the toolbox.

5. Follow this step to specify the location of the command button.

   Ⓐ *Click below the* Pinnacle Pet Care *label to make the first Wizard screen appear.*

Detail
Pinnacle Pet Care

6. Follow these steps to explore the category and action options and to choose the Run Macro action.

   Ⓐ *Click the various categories, and notice the available actions that appear in the right column. You can assign any of these actions to a command button.*

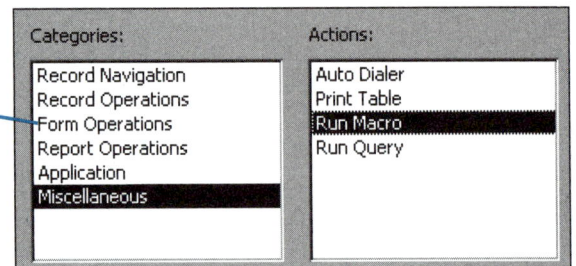

Categories:	Actions:
Record Navigation	Auto Dialer
Record Operations	Print Table
Form Operations	Run Macro
Report Operations	Run Query
Application	
Miscellaneous	

   Ⓑ *Choose the* Miscellaneous *category and the* Run Macro *action, as shown here.*

7. Click the **Next** button.
   The Wizard will display a list of macros that have been created in the database. At this point, the Open Visits Form macro will be the only macro listed.

8. Click the **Next** button to choose the Open Visits Form macro.
   The third Wizard screen gives you the option of displaying a picture/icon on the button or using descriptive text on the button.

9. Follow this step to specify descriptive text.

   Ⓐ *Click the **Text** button and type* **Visits Form** *in the box. The phrase* Visits Form *will appear on the command button when the button is created.*

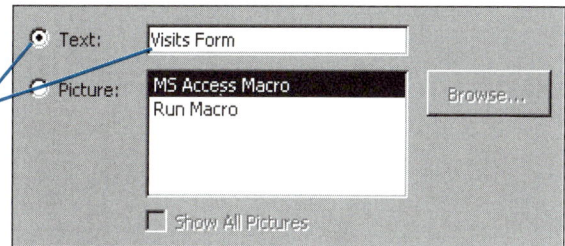

10. Click **Next**, type the name **Visits Form** in the last Wizard screen, and click the **Finish** button.
    The button should appear below the Pinnacle Pet Care label.

11. Click the Form view 🔲 button on the Access toolbar and the appearance of your switchboard should be similar to the following example.

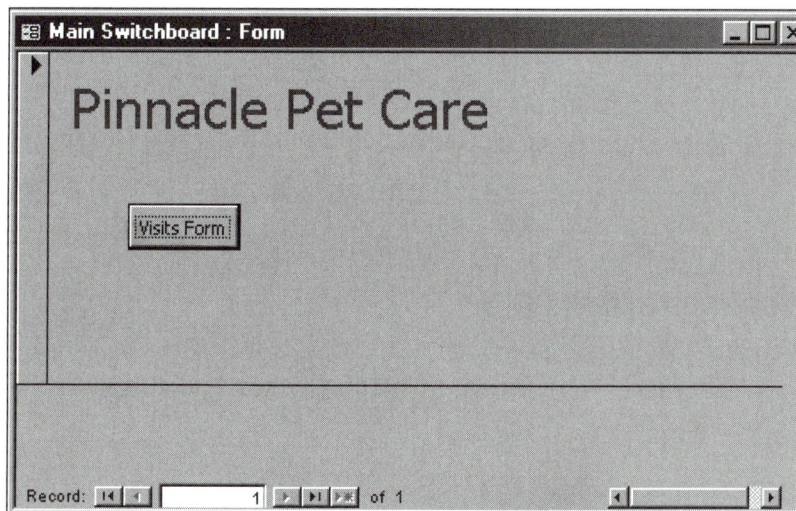

(Continued on the next page)

12. Click the Visits Form button and notice the new record displayed.
Clicking the Visits Form button runs the Open Visits Form macro. The macro opens the Visits form and displays the new record.

13. Close the Visits form.

14. Close the Main Switchboard form, and save the changes.

Set Up a Macro to Open the Customers Form

15. Click the Macros button on the Objects bar.

16. Click the [New] button.

17. Set up the OpenForm and GoToRecord actions as shown below. Make sure you set the Form Name argument to **Customers** for the OpenForm action. Also, change the Record argument for the GoToRecord action to **New**.

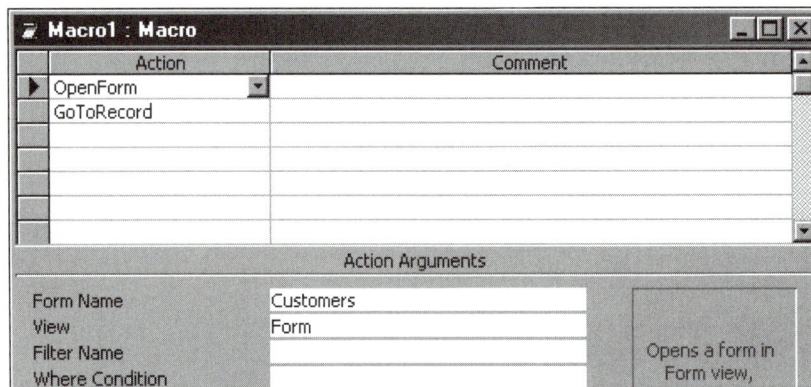

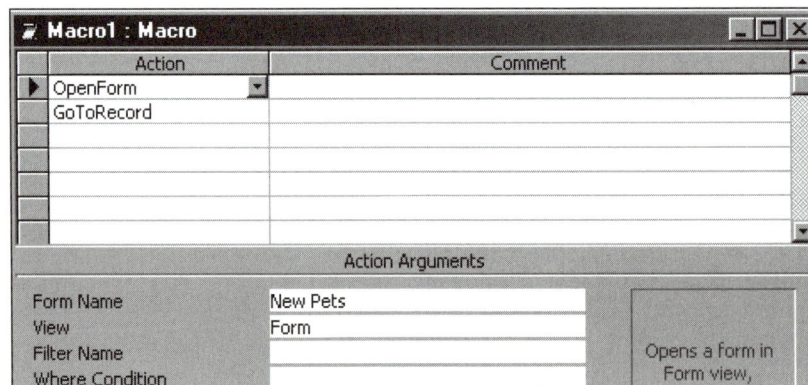

Macro1 : Macro		
Action	**Comment**	
OpenForm		
GoToRecord		
Action Arguments		
Form Name	Customers	
View	Form	Opens a form in
Filter Name		Form view,
Where Condition		

18. **Close** the macro when you have finished and give it the name **Open Customers Form**.

19. Test the macro by choosing it in the Macros window and clicking the [! Run] button.

20. **Close** the Customers form without entering data.

Set Up a Macro to Open the New Pets Form

21. Set up another new macro, as shown below. Make sure you set the Form Name argument to **New Pets** for the OpenForm action. Also, change the Record argument for the GoToRecord action to **New**.

Macro1 : Macro		
Action	**Comment**	
OpenForm		
GoToRecord		
Action Arguments		
Form Name	New Pets	
View	Form	Opens a form in
Filter Name		Form view,
Where Condition		

22. When you have finished, close the macro and save it as **Open New Pets Form**.

23. Test the macro to make sure it functions correctly.

Assign the New Macros to Command Buttons

24. Click the Forms button on the Objects bar, and open the Main Switchboard in Design view.

25. Click the Command Button ⬜ on the toolbox, and click below the Visits Form button to position the new button on the Main Switchboard form.

26. Choose the Miscellaneous category in the first screen and choose the **Run Macro** action.

27. Click **Next** and choose Open Customers Form in the second Wizard screen.

28. Click **Next**, choose the Text option, and type **Customers Form** in the third Wizard screen.

29. Click **Next**, type **Customers Form** in the last screen, and click the **Finish** button.
In the next step, you will place another command button on the Main Switchboard form. If you need more room on the Main Switchboard, then drag its bottom and/or right edge to increase the size.

30. Create another command button that runs the Open New Pets Form macro. Use the phrase **New Pets Form** on the face of the button as shown on the following page. Assign the name **New Pets Form** to the button in the last Wizard screen.

31. Switch to Form view ⬛ to view the Main Switchboard form.
Your switchboard should have three command buttons. Don't be concerned if your buttons are not aligned. You will align the buttons and enhance the appearance of the form in a moment.

32. Test your new command buttons by clicking them.
The Customers form and New Pets form should open when the buttons are clicked.

33. Close the Customers and New Pets forms.

Set Up Command Buttons To Open Reports

In the next few steps, you will create three new command buttons. The command buttons will display reports in Print Preview mode. You will use the Command Button Wizard's built-in actions for previewing reports. These built-in actions eliminate the need for macros to perform certain actions, such as previewing reports.

34. Make sure the Main Switchboard form is active and switch to Design view ⬛.

(Continued on the next page)

35. Use the Command Button Wizard ▣ and these guidelines to add the three command buttons shown below to the switchboard.

- ▪ Position the command buttons as shown. You will need to choose the Report Operations category and the Preview Report action in the first Wizard screen.

- ▪ Assign the Pets, Overdue for Visit, and Outstanding Balances reports to the buttons as shown below. Also, assign any name you desire to the buttons in the last Wizard screen.

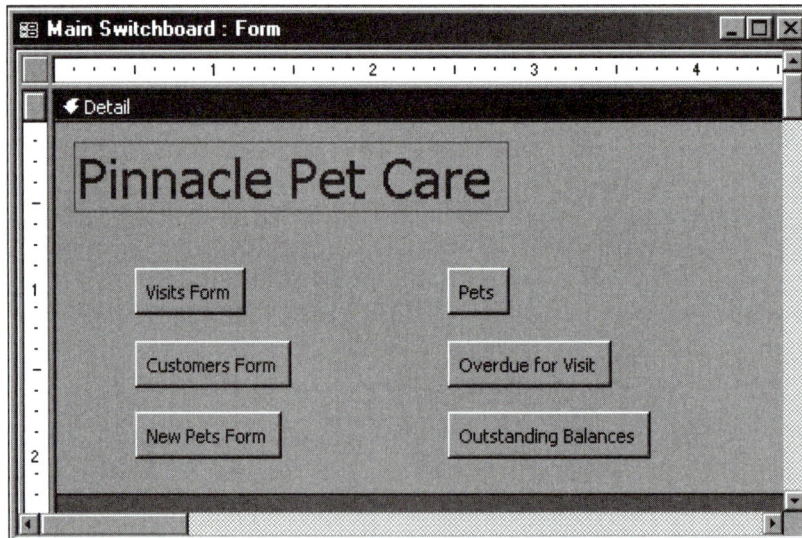

36. When you have finished, switch to Form view ▦ and test the buttons. The buttons should display the indicated reports. The Overdue for Visit report will require you to enter a date in a pop-up box. Use the date 9/1/99. This report requests you to enter a date because it is based upon a query with a pop-up box criterion.

Removing Objects from Switchboard Forms

Switchboard forms are used as launch pads for opening forms, reports, and other objects. For this reason, the controls on switchboards are typically limited to command buttons and controls that enhance the appearance of the switchboard. Scroll bars, record navigation bars, the record selection bar, and dividing lines are unnecessary on switchboards and are often removed. You can remove any of these objects by first selecting the form in Design view with the **Edit→Select** Form command. Then, you can remove objects by setting properties on the Format tab of the Properties box as described below.

Object to Remove	Property Setting
Scroll bars	Set the Scroll Bars property to *Neither*
Record navigation bar	Set the Navigation Buttons property to *No*
Record selection bar	Set the Record Selectors property to *No*
Dividing lines	Set the Dividing Lines property to *No*

Hands-On 8.5 Remove Objects from the Switchboard

In this exercise, you will remove the scroll bars, navigation bar, record selector bar, and dividing lines from the Switchboard. You will also add rectangles and labels, and enhance the appearance of the switchboard.

1. Use the Design view [icon] button to display the switchboard in Design view.

2. Choose **Edit→Select Form** from the menu bar.

3. If necessary, use the Properties [icon] button to display the Properties box.

4. Click the **Format** tab.

5. Set the Scroll Bars property to **Neither**, the Record Selectors property to **No**, the Navigation Buttons property to **No**, and the Dividing Lines property to **No**.

6. Switch to Form view [icon] and the objects should be removed from the form.

7. Switch back to Design view [icon].

(Continued on the next page)

8. Follow these guidelines to enhance the appearance of the form until it has the appearance shown below.

- ■ Use the **Format→Align** commands to align the buttons as shown. You will need to select the appropriate buttons prior to using the alignment commands.

- ■ Use the Rectangle ▣ tool to add rectangles to the form as shown below.

- ■ Use the Label 𝐴𝑎 button to add the Forms and Reports labels. Increase the size of the text to 10 and use the same color that you used for the Pinnacle Pet Care label.

- ■ Adjust the size of the form until it has the approximate dimensions shown below, reducing the light gray area on the form and the overall size of the form in Design view.

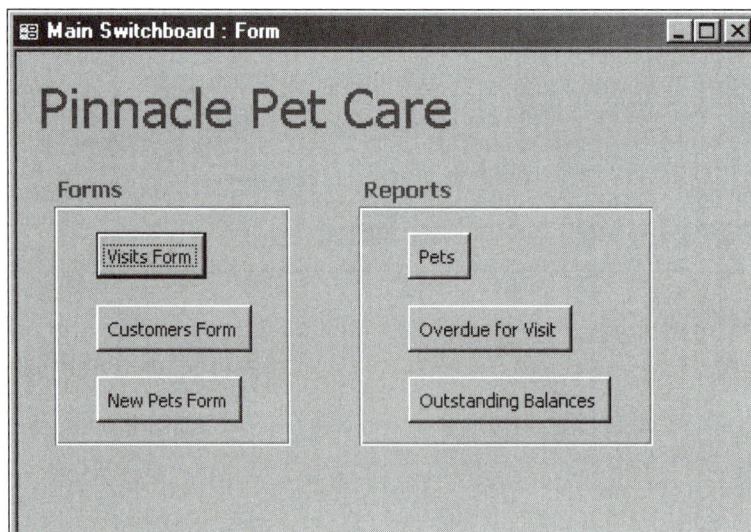

9. Switch to Form view ▦ and your form should have the appearance shown above.

10. Close the Main Switchboard form when you have finished and save the changes.

Startup Options for Databases

Access lets you specify Startup options for databases. The startup options let you specify a form to open whenever a database is started. A main switchboard form is usually specified as the startup form. This way, the switchboard automatically appears when the database is opened. The Startup options dialog box is displayed from the main database window with the **Tools→Startup** command.

1. Choose **Tools**→**Startup** from the menu bar.

2. Follow these steps to specify the Main Switchboard as the startup form.

Ⓐ *Choose* Main Switchboard *from the drop-down list in this box. This instructs Access to display the Main Switchboard form when this database is started.*

Ⓑ *Take a moment to check out the other options (but do not change them). You can get information on an option by clicking this Help button and then clicking the option.*

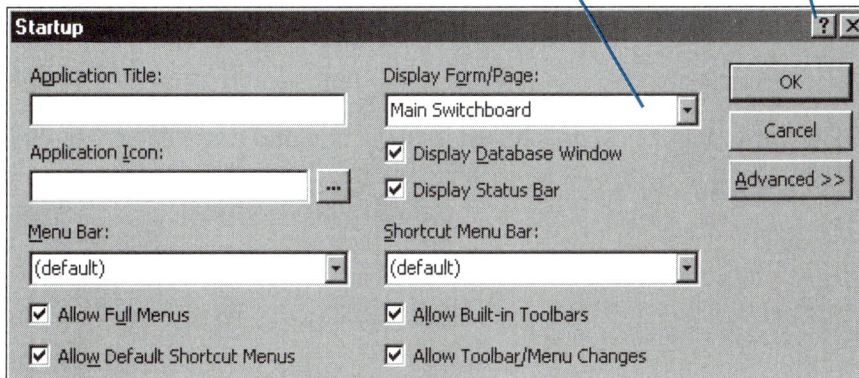

Startup

Application Title:	Display Form/Page:	OK
	Main Switchboard	Cancel
Application Icon:	☑ Display Database Window	Advanced >>
	☑ Display Status Bar	
Menu Bar:	Shortcut Menu Bar:	
(default)	(default)	
☑ Allow Full Menus	☑ Allow Built-in Toolbars	
☑ Allow Default Shortcut Menus	☑ Allow Toolbar/Menu Changes	

3. Click **OK** to set the Display Form option.

4. Close the Pinnacle Pet Care database.

5. Now open the Pinnacle Pet Care database and the Main Switchboard form should be displayed. *The Main Switchboard will appear whenever this database is started.*

The SetValue Action

The SetValue Action is a frequently used action in macros. The SetValue action can be used to copy data from a field in one table or form to a field in another table or form. This action can also be used to set the value of a date field to the current date. This is accomplished by setting the value of the date field to Now( ). Now( ) is a built-in Access function that assigns the current date to a field.

The Expression Builder

The Build [...] button appears in many property and argument boxes. In many cases, the Build button displays the Expression Builder box. The Expression Builder lets you build expressions for use in macros, forms, and other objects. You build expressions by navigating through a series of folders that represent the objects you wish to reference in the expression. You will use the Expression Builder in the next exercise to set up the SetValue action in a macro.

Events

Events can be used to initiate macros. For example, in the next exercise, you will set the "On Click" event for the Visit Date control in the Visits form. Whenever the Visit Date control is clicked, the event will initiate a macro that contains a SetValue action. The SetValue action will set the value to the current date using the Now( ) function. This process will allow you to enter the current date by simply clicking the control.

Hands-On 8.7 Set Up a Macro and Specify An Event

1. Click the Macros button on the Objects bar and then click the ⏱ New button.

2. Follow these steps to choose the Set Value action and initiate the Expression Builder.

   A *Choose* SetValue *from the drop-down list in the Action box.*

   B *Notice that the arguments for the* SetValue *action are* **Item** *and* **Expression***. Item is the control that will have its value set. Expression is the expression, or value, that will be used to set the Item control.*

   C *Click in the Item box, and then click the* **Build** *button.*

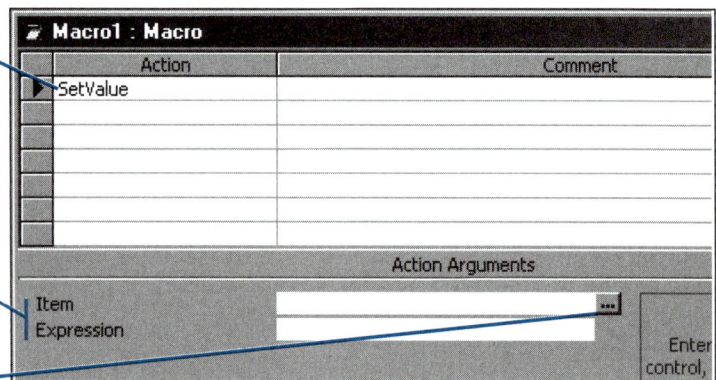

3. Follow these steps to build an expression. The expression that you build will specify the Visit Date control on the Visits form.

   A *Double-click the* Forms *folder.*

   B *Double-click the* All Forms *folder.*

   C *Double-click the* Visits *folder.*

   D *Double-click the* Visit Date *control.*

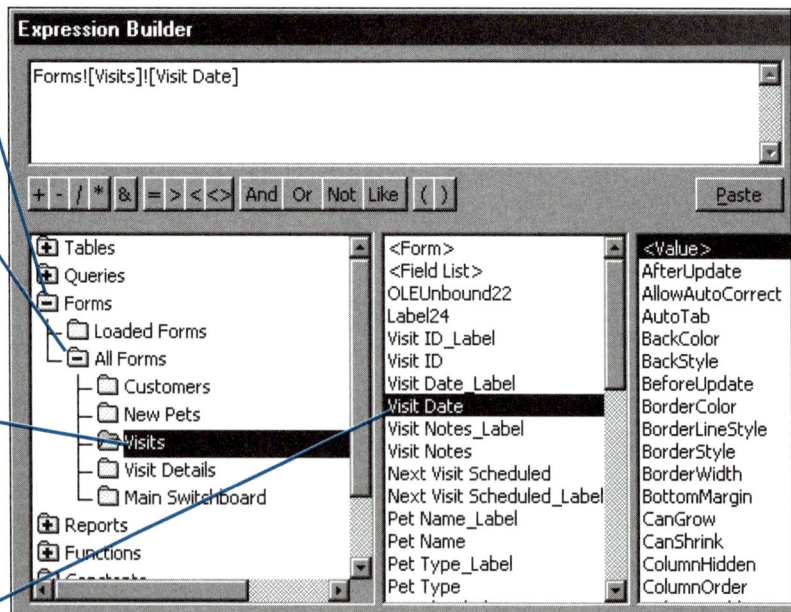

   Notice that the expression Forms![Visits]![Visit Date] appears at the top of the Expression Builder. Keep in mind that this exercise is not designed to make you an expert on using the Expression Builder. The purpose of this exercise is to introduce the capabilities of the Expression Builder. A complete discussion of the Expression Builder (and expressions for that matter) is beyond the scope of this course.

4. Click **OK**, and the expression should appear in the Item box.

5. Follow this step to specify the Expression argument.

Ⓐ *Click in the Expression box, and type the expression* **Now()**. *You could have used the Expression Builder to build this expression, but the expression is relatively simple, so it is easier just to type it. At this point, your dialog box should match the example shown here.*

Macro1 : Macro		
Action		**Comment**
▶ SetValue ▾		
	Action Arguments	

Item   [Forms]![Visits]![Visit Date]
Expression   Now()

6. Click the Close ✕ button on the Macro window.

7. Click the **Yes** button and save the macro with the name **Set Visit Date**.

Attach the Macro To the Visit Date Control

8. Open the Visits form in Design view.

9. Click the Visit Date control near the top of the form and it will become selected.

10. Make sure the Properties box is displayed, then follow these steps to attach the Set Visit Date macro to the On Click event.

Ⓐ *Click the* **Event** *tab. Notice the variety of events. Access can execute a macro when the* **Visit Date** *control experiences any of these events.*

Ⓑ *Click in the* **On Click** *box, and choose* Set Visit Date *from the drop-down menu.*

Text Box: Visit Date				✕
Format	Data	Event	Other	All

Before Update . . . .
After Update . . . .
On Change . . . .
On Enter . . . .
On Exit . . . .
On Got Focus . . . .
On Lost Focus . . . .
On Click . . . .   Set Visit Date ▾ ...
On Dbl Click . . . .

This event setting will run the Set Visit Date macro whenever the Visit Date control is clicked on the Visits form. The macro will then set the date to the current date.

11. Close the Visits form and save the changes.

(Continued on the next page)

Use the Macro to Enter Data Into a New Record

12. Click the Visits Form button on the Main Switchboard.
The Visits form will open and a new record will be displayed.

13. Click the Visit Date control and Access will set the date to the current date.

14. Choose Pet ID **DG24** from the Pet ID drop-down list.
Access will display all of the pet information for "Ben the dog."

15. Enter data into the remaining fields as shown below. Your Visit Date should be set to the current date (not the date shown below).

16. Close the Visits form when you have finished.

17. Close the Pinnacle Pet Care database and continue with the end-of-lesson questions and exercises.

Concepts Review

True/False Questions

1. Switchboard forms must be based upon a table or query. **TRUE   FALSE**

2. Macros are limited to just one action per macro. **TRUE   FALSE**

3. Events can be used to initiate macros. **TRUE   FALSE**

4. Macros are created in the Macros window. **TRUE   FALSE**

5. Command buttons can only be used to initiate macros. **TRUE   FALSE**

6. Scroll bars cannot be removed from switchboard forms. **TRUE   FALSE**

7. Dividing lines can be removed from forms by setting the Dividing Lines property to No. **TRUE   FALSE**

8. The SetValue action can be used to set the values of controls on forms. **TRUE   FALSE**

Multiple Choice Questions

1. Which macro action is used to open a form?
   a. DisplayForm
   b. OpenForm
   c. GoToForm
   d. None of these

2. Which macro action is used to go to a specific record?
   a. GoToRecord
   b. GoToNext
   c. GoToNew
   d. None of these

3. Which command is used to display the Startup options box?
   a. Tools→Startup
   b. Edit→Startup
   c. Format→Startup
   d. None of these

4. Which command is used to select an entire form?
   a. Format→Form→Select
   b. File→Select Form
   c. Edit→Select Form
   d. None of these

Skill Builders

Skill Builder 8.1 Create a Switchboard

In this exercise, you will create a switchboard for the Tropical Getaways database.

1. Open the Tropical Getaways database.

2. Click the Forms button on the Objects bar and double-click the *Create form in Design view* option.

3. Add a label with the text **Tropical Getaways** at the top left of the form.

4. Increase the size of the label text to **18**, apply the color of your choice, and increase the size of the label box until all label text is visible.

5. Use the **Edit→Select Form** command to select the entire form.

6. If necessary, display the Properties box and click the Format tab.

7. Set the Scroll Bars property to **Neither**.

8. Set the Record Selectors, Navigation Buttons, and Dividing Lines properties to **No**. *These settings will remove the indicated objects from the form when it is displayed in Form view.*

9. Close the form and save it as **Main Switchboard**.

Skill Builder 8.2 Set Up Macros

In this exercise, you will set up several macros. One of the macros will set the value of the Order Date control on the Custom Packages form while the other macros will open forms.

1. Click the Macros button on the Objects bar and click the ⌁ New button.

2. Set up the OpenForm and GoToRecord actions as shown below. Make sure you set the Form Name argument to **Customers** for the OpenForm action. Also, change the Record argument for the GoToRecord action to **New**.

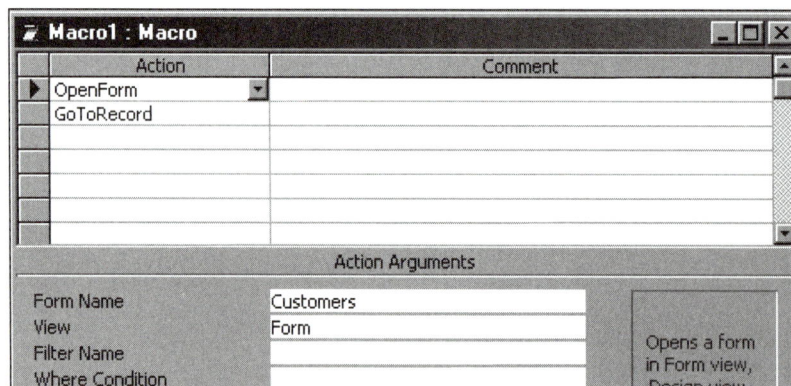

3. Close the macro when you have finished and save it as **Open Customers Form**.

4. Test the macro by choosing it in the Macros window and clicking the [! Run] button.

5. Close the Customers form without entering data.

6. Set up another new macro as shown below. Make sure you set the Form Name argument to **New Trips** for the OpenForm action. Also, change the Record argument for the GoToRecord action to **New**.

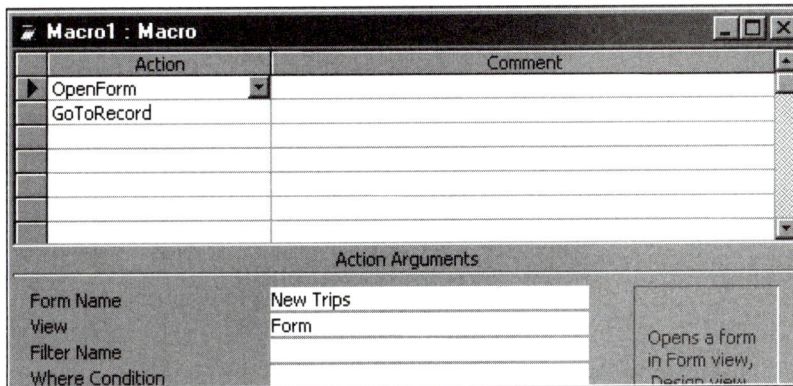

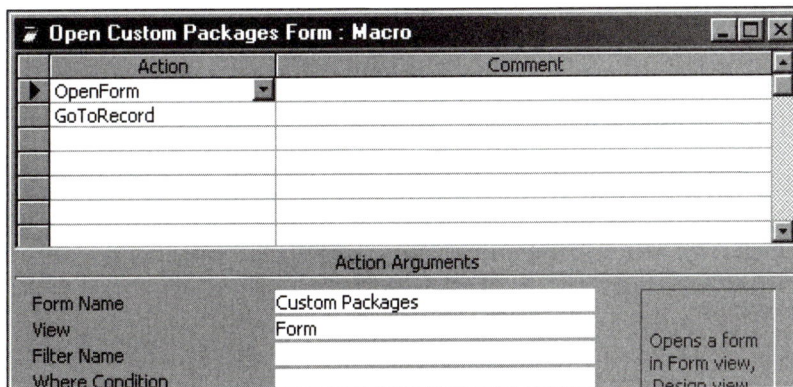

Macro1 : Macro	
Action	**Comment**
OpenForm	
GoToRecord	

Action Arguments	
Form Name	New Trips
View	Form
Filter Name	
Where Condition	

Opens a form in Form view, Design view

7. Close the macro when you have finished and save it as **Open New Trips Form**.

8. Test the macro to make sure it functions correctly.

9. Close the New Trips form.

10. Set up another new macro as shown below. Make sure you set the Form Name argument to **Custom Packages** for the OpenForm action. Also, change the Record argument for the GoToRecord action to **New**.

Open Custom Packages Form : Macro	
Action	**Comment**
OpenForm	
GoToRecord	

Action Arguments	
Form Name	Custom Packages
View	Form
Filter Name	
Where Condition	

Opens a form in Form view, Design view

(Continued on the next page)

11. Close the macro when you have finished and save it as **Open Custom Packages Form**.

12. Test the macro to make sure it functions correctly.

13. Close the Custom Packages form.

14. Set up another new macro.

15. Follow these steps to choose the Set Value action and initiate the Expression Builder.

Ⓐ *Choose* SetValue *from the drop-down list in the* **Action** *box.*

Ⓑ *Click in the* **Item** *box, and then click the* Build *button.*

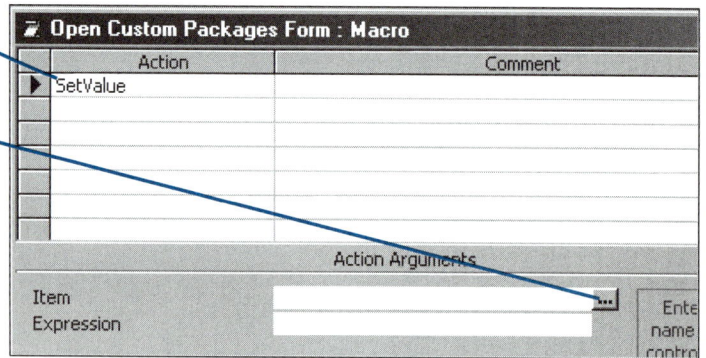

16. Follow these steps to build an expression. The expression that you build will specify the Order Date field on the Custom Packages form. In a later exercise, you will use this macro to enter the current date into the Order Date field.

Ⓐ Double-click *the* Forms *folder.*

Ⓑ Double-click *the* All Forms *folder.*

Ⓒ Double-click *the* Custom Packages *folder.*

Ⓓ Double-click *the* Order Date *control.*

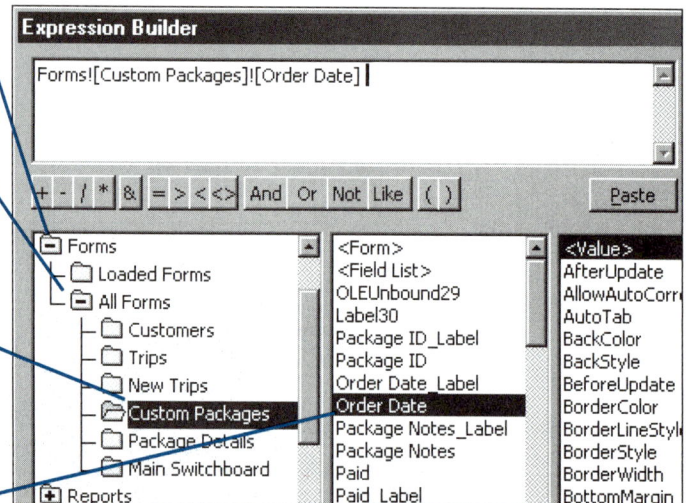

The expression Forms![Custom Packages]![Order Date] should appear at the top of the Expression Builder.

17. Click **OK** and the expression should appear in the Item box.

18. Enter the expression **Now()** in the Expression box as shown below.

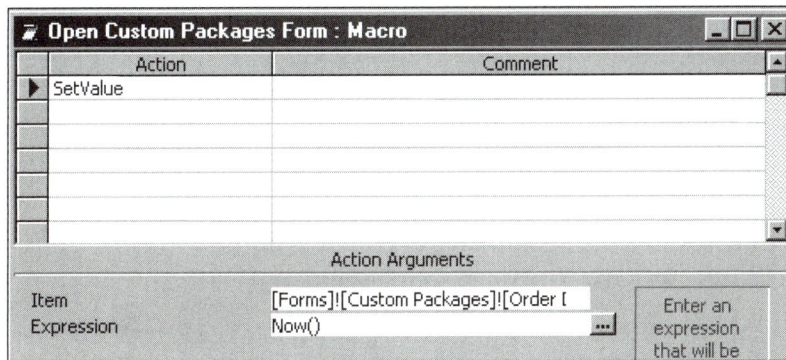

19. Close the Macro window, choose **Yes** when Access asks you to save the macro, and assign the macro the name **Set Order Date**.

Skill Builder 8.3 Set Up Command Buttons

In this exercise, you will add command buttons to the Main Switchboard. Some of the buttons will initiate macros while others will open reports in Print Preview mode.

1. Open the Main Switchboard form in Design view.

2. Follow these guidelines to add command buttons, labels, and rectangles to the form as shown below.

   ■ Create the command buttons in the positions shown below.

   ■ Assign macros to the command buttons shown in the Forms rectangle. In the previous exercise, you created a macro for each button.

   ■ Assign reports to the command buttons shown in the Reports rectangle. You can choose the indicated reports in the Command Button Wizard. Make sure you choose the *Print Preview* option in the Wizard so that the reports open in Print Preview mode.

   ■ Add the labels and rectangles to the form as shown. Also, adjust the size of the form and align the command buttons as shown.

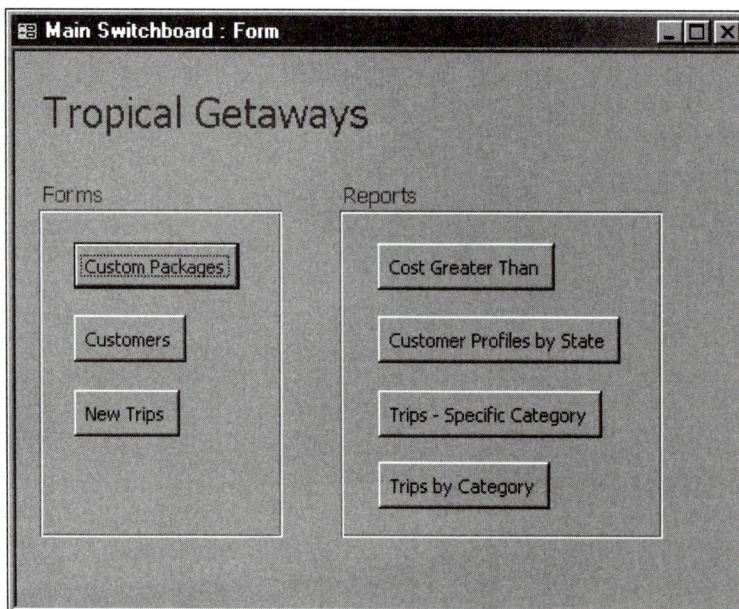

3. When you have finished, switch to Form view [icon] and test the buttons. The buttons should open the indicated forms and display the indicated reports in Print Preview. The Cost Greater Than report will require you to enter a number in a pop up box. Use the number **3,000**. Only trips with a cost greater than 3,000 will appear in the report. Also, the Trips - Specific Category report will prompt you to enter a category. Enter the **Adventure** category when prompted to do so.

4. When you have finished, close the Main Switchboard form and save the changes.

Skill Builder 8.4 Specify a Startup Form

In this exercise, you will specify the Main Switchboard as the startup form for the database. The Main Switchboard will be displayed as soon as the database is started.

1. Choose **Tools→Startup** from the menu bar.

2. Set the Display Form option to Main Switchboard and click **OK**.

3. Close the Tropical Getaways database.

4. Now open the Tropical Getaways database, and the Main Switchboard form should be displayed.

Skill Builder 8.5 Assign a Macro to an Event

In this exercise, you will assign the Set Order Date macro to the On Click event for the Order Date control in the Custom Packages form. The macro will set the Order Date field to the current date whenever the Order Date control is clicked.

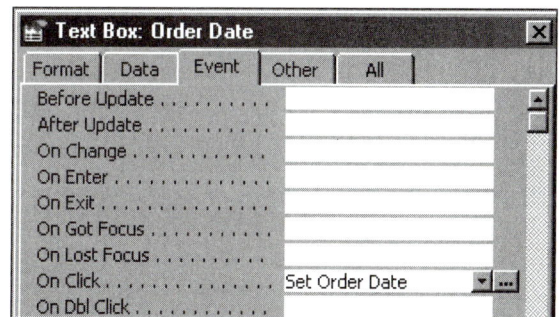

1. Open the Custom Packages form in Design view.

2. Click the Order Date control near the top of the form and it will become selected.

3. Make sure the Properties box is displayed and set the On Click event to Set Order Date, as shown to the right.

4. Close the Custom Packages form, and save the changes.

Skill Builder 8.6 Enter Data

In this exercise, you will enter a new record into the Custom Packages form. You will set the Order Date field to the current date by simply clicking the Order Date control.

1. Click the **Custom Packages** button on the Main Switchboard.

2. Click the Order Date control and Access will set the date to the current date.

3. Choose *Customer ID 3* from the Customer ID drop-down list.
   Access will display all of the customer information for Ted Wilkins.

4. Enter data into the remaining fields as shown below. Your Order Date should be set to the current date (not the date shown below).

⊞ Custom Packages				_□×

Tropical Getaways – Custom Packages

Package ID	11	Order Date	10/25/99	Package Notes	
Customer ID	3 ▾				
Firstname	Ted				
Lastname	Wilkins		Package Category	Adventure ▾	
Address	900 C Street		Destination	Amazon Jungle 1 ▾	
City	Fort Worth		Paid	☑	
State	TX				
Zip	76104				
Profile	Adventure				

Package Details

	Package ID	Item	Unit Price	Quantity	Extended Price
	11	Airfare	$875.00	1	$875.00
▶	11	All inclusive jungle package	$3,200.00	1	$3,200.00
*	11		$0.00	0	

Record: |◀ ◀ 2 ▶ ▶| ▶* of 2

Subtotal	$4,075.00
Sales Tax	$305.63
Total	**$4,380.63**

Record: |◀ ◀ 11 ▶ ▶| ▶* of 11

5. Close the Custom Packages form when you have finished.

6. Close the Tropical Getaways database and continue with the Assessment project.

Assessments

1. Open the Classic Cars database.

2. Follow these guidelines to create the main switchboard form shown below.

   ■ Create three macros that open the Events, Collectors, and New Cars forms, and then display new records in the forms.

   ■ Create command buttons as shown below The buttons in the Forms rectangle should initiate macros while the buttons in the Reports rectangle should display the indicated reports in Print Preview mode.

   ■ Add labels and rectangles to the form as shown below.

   ■ Remove the scroll bars, record navigation bar, record selector bar, and dividing lines from the form.

   ■ Assign the name **Main Switchboard** to the form.

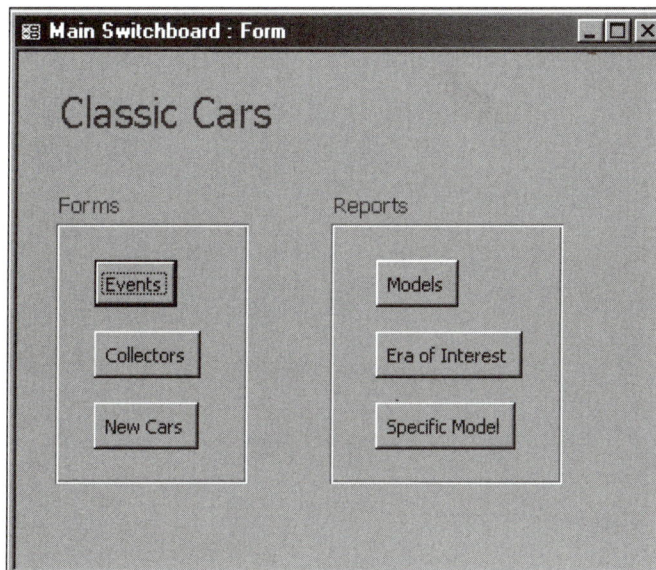

(Continued on the next page)

3. Set the startup options so that the Main Switchboard is automatically displayed when the Classic Cars database is opened.

4. Create a macro that automatically sets the Event Date control in the Events form to the current date. Assign the name **Set Event Date** to the macro.

5. Set the On Click property of the Event Date control in the Events form to initiate the Set Event Date macro when the Event Date control is clicked.

6. Close all open forms and save the changes.

7. Close the Classic Cars database.

8. Open the Classic Cars database and the Main Switchboard should automatically appear.

9. Click the **Events** button on the Main Switchboard.
   The Events form should open and a new record should be displayed.

10. Enter the following data into the new record. You should be able to set the Event Date field to the current date by clicking the Event Date control. However, the date will be different than the date shown below. Also, the collector's first name and last name can be displayed by choosing the indicated Collector ID in the Collector ID control.

Events

Classic Cars - Scheduled Events

Event ID	7		Event Title	West Palm Auto Show
Collector ID	3		Event Date	1/3/99
Firstname	Ed		Sponsor	American Collect
Lastname	Larkson		Location	Palm Beach Florida
			Entrance Fee	$80.00
			Mailing Sent	☐

Notes: Attendance is estimated at 12,500 this year.

Event Details

	Event ID	Item	Daily Cost	Number of Days	Total
▶	7	Location	$1,250.00	3	$3,750.00
	7	Utilities	$235.00	3	$705.00
	7	Security	$350.00	3	$1,050.00
*	7		$0.00	0	

Record: 1 of 3

Grand Total $5,505.00

Record: 7 of 7

11. Close the Classic Cars database when you have finished.

Integration with Word and Excel

Access databases are the information banks for many organizations. Customer mailing lists, order data, and other types of information often reside in Access databases. Access' Office Links tools make it easy to export data to Word and Excel. Word is often used to conduct mail merges using Access address data, while Excel is often used to analyze financial data. In this lesson, you will set up a mail merge between a Word form letter and an Access query. You will also use Excel to analyze financial data exported from Access. Finally, you will learn important techniques for maintaining databases.

In This Lesson

Case Study

The staff at Pinnacle Pet Care needs to conduct period mailings to Pinnacle customers. Al Smith wants to be able to easily choose customers from the Access database for inclusion in these mailings. He also wants to take advantage of the powerful word processing features available in Microsoft Word. Al sets up the Pinnacle Pet Care database so that his staff can choose customers to be included in a mailing by simply checking a Mailing List box on the Customers form. This same check box allows the staff to effortlessly generate mailing labels from within Access.

Firstname	Lastname	Address	City	State	Zip
Mark	Roth	760 Maple Avenue	Fremont	CA	94538-
Jason	Jones	2233 Crystal Street	San Mateo	CA	94403-
Jacob	Samuels	2300 North Pratt Street	Atlanta	GA	30309-

An Access query is merged with a Word form letter to create personalized letters.

December 16, 1999

Mr. «Firstname» «Lastname»
«Address»
«City», «State» «Zip»

Dear Mr. «Lastname»:

We are pleased to inform you that our annual Pinnacle Pet Care Dog Show on March 15 at our facilities. You are cordially invited to enroll your dog in You also may bring as many guests as you like.

A letter is produced for each record selected by the query.

December 16, 1999

Mr. Mark Roth
760 Maple Avenue
Fremont, CA 94538

Dear Mr. Roth:

We are pleased to inform you that on March 15 at our facilities. You You also may bring as many guest

December 16, 1999

Mr. Jason Jones
2233 Crystal Street
San Mateo, CA 94403

Dear Mr. Jones:

We are pleased to inform you th on March 15 at our facilities. Y You also may bring as many gu

December 16, 1999

Mr. Jacob Samuels
2300 North Pratt Street
Atlanta, GA 30309

Dear Mr. Samuels:

We are pleased to inform you that our on March 15 at our facilities. You are You also may bring as many guests as

Using Access and Word to Conduct Mailings

Many businesses use Access databases as the bank for customer and order information. A properly designed Access database should make it easy for individuals or businesses to send form letters, generate mailing labels, and perform other types of mailing functions. A typical mailing requires mailing labels and personalized letters. You can easily set up mailing labels using the Mailing Label Wizard in Access. Access is also tightly integrated with Microsoft Word. You can use Word to set up a form letter and then merge the form letter with a table or query in your Access database. The resulting letters will be personalized with the name and address information of your customers. The following illustrations discuss the process that is used to conduct mailings using Access and Word.

Step 1—A table containing the desired customer information is chosen in the Access database. In this example, a Mailing List field with a Yes/No data type has been added to the table. The user can choose records to include in the mailing by checking the Mailing List box for the desired records.

Firstname	Lastname	Address	City	State	Zip	Phone	Last Visit	Current Balance	Mailing List
Mark	Roth	760 Maple Avenue	Fremont	CA	94538-	(510) 234-9090	7/7/99	$235.00	☑
Tony	Simpson	312 York Lane	Richmond	CA	94804-	(510) 238-2233	9/7/99	$185.00	☐
Jason	Jones	2233 Crystal Street	San Mateo	CA	94403-	(415) 312-2312	7/15/99	$48.00	☑
Jacob	Samuels	2300 North Pratt Str	Atlanta	GA	30309-	(404) 367-8002	10/8/97	$250.50	☑

Step 2—A query based on the table is created. The query contains criteria that choose the desired records for the mailing. In this example, the query chooses only those records where the Mailing List field is set to **Yes** (checked).

Field:	Firstname	Lastname	Address	City	State	Zip	Mailing List
Table:	Customers	Customers	Customers	Customers	Customers	Customers	Customers
Sort:							
Show:	☑	☑	☑	☑	☑	☑	☐
Criteria:							Yes

Step 3—The Merge It With MS Word Office Links button is used to establish a Dynamic Data Exchange (DDE) link between the query and a Word document. Field codes and text are inserted into the Word mail merge document, as shown to the right. The document is then merged with the query to produce personalized letters.

December 16, 1999

Mr. «Firstname» «Lastname»
«Address»
«City», «State» «Zip»

Dear Mr. «Lastname»:

We are pleased to inform you that our annual Pinr on March 15 at our facilities. You are cordially inv You also may bring as many guests as you like.

Step 4—The query is also used as the basis for a mailing label report. Mailing labels are generated only for those records that meet the criteria specified in the query.

Mr. Jacob Samuels 2300 North Pratt Street Atlanta, GA 30309	Mr. Jason Jones 2233 Crystal Street San Mateo, CA 94403	Mr. Mark Roth 760 Maple Avenue Fremont, CA 94538

Setting up a Mailing List Query

There are times that you will need to randomly select records from Access tables. For example, you may want to send a mailing to a group of customers that can't be categorized in any particular manner. In this situation, you must have some way of identifying the customers that you wish to include in the mailing. You can accomplish this by adding a **Yes/No** field to the table from which you wish to randomly choose records. The Yes/No box can be checked for those records that you wish to choose. A query can then be used to choose only those records where the Yes/No field is set to yes (checked). Reports, and other objects that are based on the query, will only include the records that have the Yes/No field set to yes.

Hands-On 9.1 Modify a Table and Set Up a Query

In this exercise, you will add a Yes/No field to the Customers table. The field will be used to mark records for inclusion in mailings. You will also base a new query upon the table.

Add a Mailing List Check Box to the Customers Table

1. Start Access and open the Pinnacle Pet Care database.

2. Close the Main Switchboard form and click the **Tables** button on the Objects bar.

3. Choose the **Customers** table and click the [Design] button.

4. Follow these steps to add a Mailing List field to the table.

Field Name	Data Type
Customer ID	AutoNumber
Firstname	Text
Lastname	Text
Address	Text
City	Text
State	Text
Zip	Text
Phone	Text
Last Visit	Date/Time
Current Balance	Currency
Mailing List	Yes/No

Ⓐ *Click in a new **Field Name** box, and type the name* **Mailing List**.

Ⓑ *Set the data type to Yes/No.*

(Continued on the next page)

5. Click the Datasheet view ▦ button on the left end of the Access toolbar.

6. Click the **Yes** button when Access asks if you want to save the table.

7. Check the Mailing List boxes for all records except the Tony Simpson record.
   Only the first, third, and fourth records should have their Mailing List boxes checked.

8. **Close** the table when you have finished.

Set Up a Mailing List Query

9. Click the **Queries** button on the Objects bar.

10. Double-click the **Create query in Design** view option.

11. Add the Customers table to the design grid and close the Show Table box.

12. Follow these steps to set up the query.

Ⓐ *Add the field names shown here to the design grid.* Ⓑ *Type the word* **Yes** *in the* **Criteria** *box of the Mailing List field.*

Field:	Firstname	Lastname	Address	City	State	Zip	Mailing List
Table:	Customers	Customers	Customers	Customers	Customers	Customers	Customers
Sort:							
Show:	☑	☑	☑	☑	☑	☑	☐
Criteria:							Yes

Ⓒ *Remove the check from the Mailing List* **Show** *box.*

13. Run ▣! the query, and the following recordset should be generated.
    Notice that the Mailing List criterion was used to select the records. However, the Mailing List field is not displayed in the recordset because you unchecked the Show box.

	Firstname	Lastname	Address	City	State	Zip
	Mark	Roth	760 Maple Avenue	Fremont	CA	94538-
	Jason	Jones	2233 Crystal Street	San Mateo	CA	94403-
	Jacob	Samuels	2300 North Pratt Street	Atlanta	GA	30309-

14. **Close** the query, and save it as **Mailing List**.

Integrating Access with Word

The true power of Office 2000 is found in the integration of various programs. Access provides the database, storage, and querying capabilities in Office 2000. Word is most useful for creating letters, memos, and other word processing documents. However, Word also has a mail merge feature that lets you generate personalized letters using the address information from a data source. An Access table or query can be used as the data source for a mail merge. The DDE (Dynamic Data Exchange) capabilities of Office 2000 make this possible. The next exercise will guide you through the process of merging a Word form letter with an Access query. However, you may want to use Labyrinth Publications *Word 2000 Expert Course* book for a complete discussion of mail merge.

The Merge It With MS Word Office Link

The Merge It With MS Word [icon] Office Link button is available whenever a table or query is highlighted in the Access database window. This button starts a Mail Merge Wizard that guides you through the process of merging a table or query with a Word form letter. Once you have specified the table or query and the Word form letter, the Wizard displays the form letter and Word's Mail Merge toolbar. The Mail Merge toolbar contains various buttons used to conduct mail merges. The Insert Merge Field button displays the complete field list from the Access table or query. You can add merge fields to the form letter by choosing them from the list.

Hands-On 9.2 Set Up a Word Mail Merge Document

In this exercise, you will set up a Word mail merge document that is linked to the Mailing List query in the Pinnacle Pet Care database.

1. If necessary, click the **Queries** button on the Objects bar.

2. Follow these steps to choose the Mailing List query and start the Mail Merge Wizard.

Ⓐ *Choose the* Mailing List *query.*

Ⓑ *Click the* OfficeLinks *drop-down button, and choose* Merge it with MS Word.

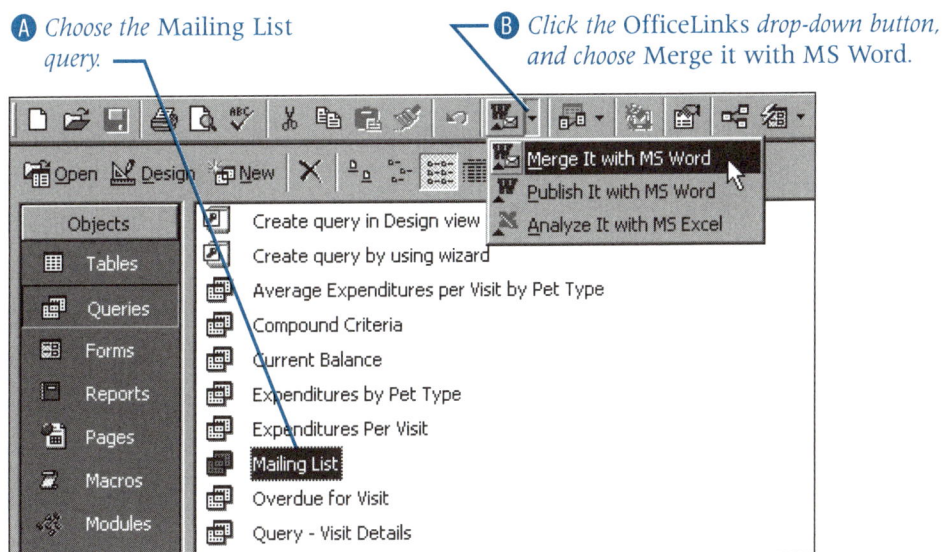

3. Choose the *Create a new document and then link the data to it* option in the first Wizard screen and click **OK**.
   Access will start Word and establish a Dynamic Data Exchange (DDE) link between the new Word document and the Mailing List query in Access. You will learn more about this link in a moment.

4. Maximize [icon] the Word window and tap (ENTER) six times.
   This will position the insertion point approximately 2" down from the top of the page. Most business letters begin at this point.

(Continued on the next page)

5. Choose **Insert→Date and Time** from the menu bar.

6. Choose the third date format in the Date and Time box, and make sure the *Update Automatically* box near the bottom of the dialog box is checked .
   Checking the Update Automatically box instructs Access to insert the date as a field. This way, the current date will be inserted in the document whenever the document is opened.

7. Click **OK** to insert the date and then tap (ENTER) four times.

8. Type **Mr.**, and tap the (SPACE BAR) once.
   Formal business letters require that the individual's name be preceded by a prefix such as Mr., Ms., or Mrs. All of the customers in your database are men, so typing the prefix Mr. is sufficient. If your customer table had a combination of male and female names, then you would need to include a Prefix field in the table with the appropriate prefix for each customer. The Prefix field could then be used in the mail merge document to insert the appropriate prefix.

9. Follow these steps to insert the first merge field.

   Ⓐ *Click the* **Insert Merge Field** *button on the Mail Merge toolbar.*

   Ⓑ *Choose* Firstname *from the field list. Notice that these field names are the same ones that you inserted in the Mailing List query.*

   Ⓒ *A* Firstname *field code should be inserted in the document. When you merge the letter with the query, the first names from the query will be inserted into the letters at this location.*

   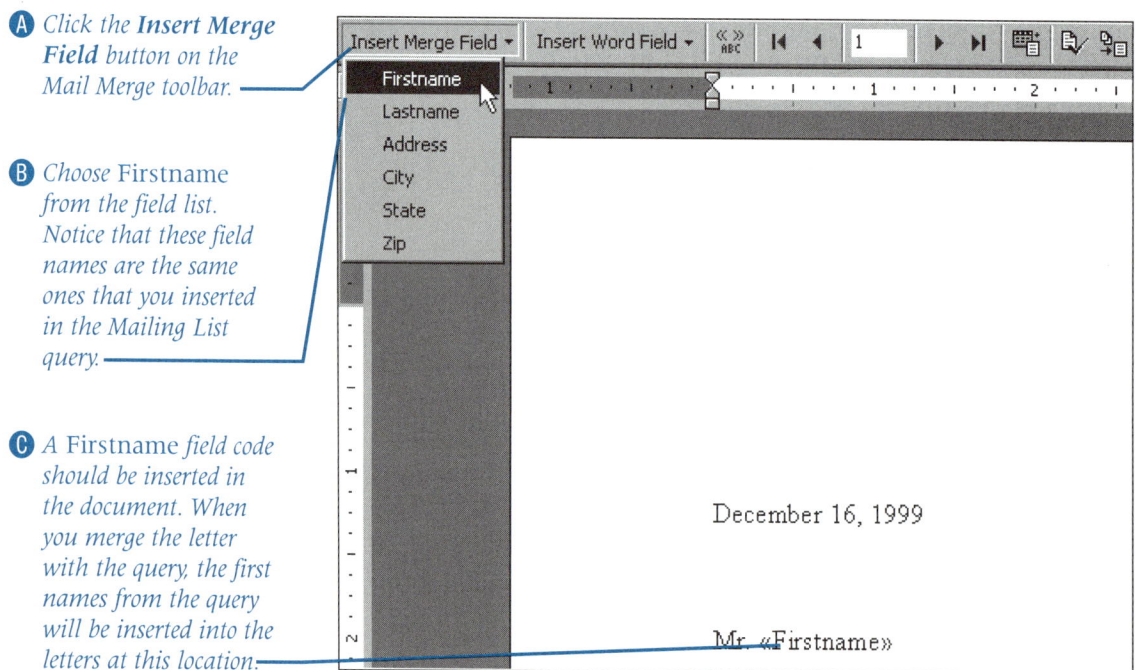

   December 16, 1999

   Mr. «Firstname»

10. The first name and last name should have a space between them, so tap the (SPACE BAR) once.
    During the merge, Word will insert the data exactly as it appears in the query. For this reason, you should place spaces, commas, and other punctuation marks at the appropriate locations in the letter.

11. Click the **Insert Merge Field** button, and choose the Lastname field.

12. Tap (ENTER) to move the insertion point to the next line.

13. Repeat Steps 11 and 12 to insert the Address field, and then tap (ENTER).

14. Insert the City field, type a comma, and tap the (SPACE BAR).

15. Insert the State field, and tap the (SPACE BAR).

16. Insert the Zip field, and tap (ENTER) twice.

17. Type **Dear Mr.**, and tap the (SPACE BAR).

18. Insert the Lastname field, type a colon, and tap (ENTER) twice.

    You have now set up the merge fields for a Word form letter. The form letter is linked to the Mailing List query through a Dynamic Data Exchange (DDE) link. The DDE link will run the Mailing List query whenever the form letter is opened in Word. This way, the form letter will always have "fresh" data from the Access database. The query data will be used to create personalized letters during the merge.

19. Now complete the letter by typing the body as shown below.

December 16, 1999

Mr. «Firstname» «Lastname»
«Address»
«City», «State» «Zip»

Dear Mr. «Lastname»:

We are pleased to inform you that our annual Pinnacle Pet Care Dog Show will be held on March 15 at our facilities. You are cordially invited to enroll your dog in the show. You also may bring as many guests as you like.

Please respond by February 28, so that we may reserve a spot for your pet.

Sincerely,

Cindy Marshall
Training Manager

---

20. Click the Save ⊞ button and save the letter to your exercise diskette with the name **Mailing List Form Letter**.

If you are setting up a form letter for an organization, you should consider saving it as a Word template. This way, you can use the template over and over as the basis for new form letters. Each form letter created from the template will be linked to the Access Mailing List query.

(Continued on the next page)

21. Conduct the merge by clicking the Merge to New Document ▦ button, on the Mail Merge toolbar.

22. Browse through the merged letters and note the three personalized letters.
A letter was generated for each record selected by the Mailing List query.

23. Close the merged letters without saving them.
Merged letters and other merge documents are rarely saved since they can be easily regenerated by conducting the merge again. Merged documents may also require large amounts of disk space because they often contain many pages.

24. Close Word and, if necessary, save the changes to the Mailing List Form Letter document.

Setting up Mailing Labels in Access

The ▦ New button in the Reports section of the database window provides access to several report wizards and AutoReport tools. The Label Wizard can be used to set up mailing labels. The Label Wizard creates a report that is based upon a table or query. The report is formatted to print on the mailing label paper stock that you specify.

Hands-On 9.3 Set Up Mailing Labels For the Mailing List Query

In this exercise, you will set up mailing labels that are based upon the Mailing List query. A mailing label will be generated for each record in the Customers table that has the Mailing List box checked.

1. Click the **Reports** button on the Objects bar in the Access database window.

2. Click the ▦ New button to display the New Report box.

3. Choose the Label Wizard, choose Mailing List from the table/query list, and click **OK**.

4. Follow these steps to choose a label format.

Ⓐ *Choose* Avery *from the manufacturer's list.*

Ⓑ *Choose* English *as the* **Unit of Measure***, and make sure the* **Label Type** *is set to* Sheet feed*.*

Ⓒ *Choose the* 5160 *label type, and click the* **Next** *button.*

Product number:	Dimensions:	Number across:
5095	2 1/2" x 3 3/8"	2
5096	2 3/4" x 2 3/4"	3
5097	1 1/2" x 4"	2
5160	1" x 2 5/8"	3
5161	1" x 4"	2

Unit of Measure: ● English ○ Metric

Label Type: ● Sheet feed ○ Continuous

Filter by manufacturer: Avery

Customize...   ☐ Show custom label sizes

5. Click **Next** again to bypass the font and color options screen.
   The next Wizard screen lets you arrange the fields on the labels.

6. Follow these steps to arrange the fields.

   Ⓐ *Type* **Mr.** *in the Prototype label box, and tap* SPACE BAR.

   Ⓑ *Make sure the* Firstname *field is chosen on the* **Available fields** *list, and click the* **Add Field** *button.*

   Ⓒ *Tap* SPACE BAR, *choose the* Lastname *field from the* **Available fields** *list, and click the* **Add Field** *button.*

   Ⓓ *Tap* ENTER, *and add the* Address *field.*

   Ⓔ *Tap* ENTER, *and add the* City *field.*

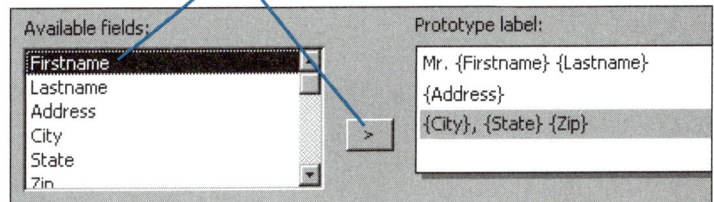

   Available fields:
   Firstname
   Lastname
   Address
   City
   State
   Zip

   >

   Prototype label:
   Mr. {Firstname} {Lastname}
   {Address}
   {City}, {State} {Zip}

   Ⓕ *Type a comma, tap* SPACE BAR, *and add the* State *field.*

   Ⓖ *Tap* SPACE BAR, *and add the* Zip *field. Your completed label should match the example shown here.*

7. Click **Next** and the wizard will ask on which field you wish to sort.

8. Choose the Zip field and click the Add Field [>] button.

9. Click **Next** and type the name **Mailing Labels** in the last Wizard screen.

10. Make sure the *See the labels as they will look printed* option is chosen, and click the **Finish** button.
    Access will create the report, and the labels shown below should appear.

    Mr. Jacob Samuels
    2300 North Pratt Street
    Atlanta, GA 30309

    Mr. Jason Jones
    2233 Crystal Street
    San Mateo, CA 94403

    Mr. Mark Roth
    760 Maple Avenue
    Fremont, CA 94538

11. Click the Design [icon] view button to display the report in Design view.
    This report is quite intricate and would require a substantial amount of effort if you were to set it up from scratch. Notice that the report includes the Trim function. The Trim function removes all blank spaces from a text string except for the spaces between words. This function can be quite useful when producing labels and other types of reports.

12. Close the report, and the Mailing Labels report should appear in the Reports section.
    From this point forward, you can generate mailing labels by opening this report. Whenever this report is opened, a label will be generated for each record that has the Mailing List box checked in the Customers table. Once again, the report is based upon the Mailing List query, which selects only those records in the Customers table where the Mailing List box is checked. Also, keep in mind that it is usually easier to recreate a mailing label report using the Wizard rather than attempting to modify a report that did not turn out the way you intended.

Managing Mailing Lists

The Mailing List query that forms the basis of your mail merge system is flexible because it allows you to mark any record from the Customers table for inclusion in a mailing. You can also easily modify the query to select certain records. For example, you may want the query to choose only customers where the state is equal to CA (California), as discussed in the following illustration.

Field:	Firstname	Lastname	Address	City	State	Zip	Mailing List
Table:	Customers	Customers	Customers	Customers	Customers	Customers	Customers
Sort:							
Show:	☑	☑	☑	☑	☑	☑	☐
Criteria:					"CA"		

The criterion CA has been added to the State field, and the Yes criterion has been removed from the Mailing List field. The query's recordset now will display only records where the state is CA. The CA records will be used the next time the Word form letter or the mailing labels report is opened.

Update Queries and Filters

Another important aspect of managing mailing lists is being able to easily remove checks from the Mailing List box if that box is used to randomly choose records for inclusion in the mailing. You could simply navigate through the records in the Customers table and uncheck the Mailing List boxes. However, this could become tedious if your Customers table has a large number of records. A better technique is to use filters or an update query.

Filters—The Filter by Selection 🔲 button can be used to manage a mailing list. For example, in the Pinnacle Pet Care database, you could add a Mailing List checkbox to the Customers form. Then, you could check the Mailing List box of any record, click the Filter by Selection button, and navigate through the filtered records, unchecking all of the Mailing List boxes.

Update Queries—Update queries let you update any field in a table to the value you specify. You could use an update query in the Pinnacle Pet Care database to effortlessly set all of the Mailing List fields in the table to No (unchecked). The following illustration discusses the process of setting up an update query.

A new query is set up with just the one field that you want to update. In this example, the Mailing List field is added from the Customers table.

Field:	Mailing List
Table:	Customers
Update To:	No
Criteria:	Yes

The Query→Update Query command is chosen from the menu bar to add an Update To row to the query.

The value you wish to Update To (No, in this example), and the Criteria (Yes, in this example) are specified. In this example, when the query is run, all records where the Mailing List field is set to Yes (checked) are updated to No (unchecked).

Hands-On 9.4 Manage the Mailing List

In this exercise, you will experiment with various techniques for managing your mailing list.

Set Up a Check Box On the Customers Form

1. Click the **Forms** button on the Objects bar in the database window.

2. Choose the *Customers* form and click the [Design] button.

3. Make sure the Properties box and the toolbox are displayed.

4. Click the Check Box [☑] button on the toolbox.

5. Follow these steps to add a Mailing List check box to the form.

Ⓐ *Click here to position the checkbox.*

Ⓑ *Click the Data tab in the Properties box, and set the Control Source property to Mailing List. This will bind the check box to the Mailing List field in the Customers table.*

Ⓒ *Change the label text to* **Mailing List***.*

✦ Detail	
Customer ID	Customer ID
Firstname	Firstname
Lastname	Lastname
Address	Address
City	City
State	State
Zip	Zip
Phone	Phone
Last Visit	Last Visit
Current Balance	Current Balance
	GoTo New Pets Form
	☑ Mailing List

Navigate Through Records

6. Click the Form view [📧] button on the Access toolbar.

7. Navigate through the records, and notice that the Mailing List box displays check marks for the three records that have the Mailing List field checked.

    You can use this check box to choose records for a mailing. You can also remove records from a mailing by unchecking the box. If you want to include a particular individual in a mailing, you can use the Edit→Find command to search the lastname field (or some other field) for the desired name. Then, the Mailing List box can be checked or unchecked.

(Continued on the next page)

Filter By Selection

8. If necessary, navigate to the first record.
   The Record Navigation bar at the bottom of the form should indicated that you are on record 1 of 4.

9. Click the Mailing List field to remove the check.

10. Now click the Mailing List field again to recheck the box.
    In the next step, you will filter by selection. You unchecked and then checked the box to first make Mailing List the active field and then to check the field. This way, when you filter by selection, the filter will display only those records where the Mailing List field is checked.

11. Click the Filter By Selection ![button] button on the Access toolbar.
    The Record Navigation bar should now indicate that you are viewing 1 of 3 filtered records. Only records where the Mailing List field is checked are displayed.

12. Navigate through the records.
    If you had a database with thousands of records and wanted to uncheck a few boxes, this would certainly speed up the process.

13. Click the Remove Filter ![button] button on the Access toolbar.

14. Close the Customers form and save the changes.

Set Up An Update Query

15. Click the Queries button on the Objects bar in the database window.

16. Double-click the *Create query in Design* view option.

17. Add the **Customers** table, and close the Add Table box.

18. Scroll to the bottom of the field names on the Customers list, and double-click Mailing List to add that field to the design grid.

19. Choose **Query→Update Query** to add the Update To row to the design grid.

20. Click in the Update To box in the design grid and type **No**.

21. Click in the Criteria box and type **Yes**.

22. Click the Run ![button] button, and choose **Yes** when Access informs you that you are about to update three records.

23. Close the query and save it as **Update Mailing List**.

Add a Command Button to the Customers Form

24. Click the **Forms** tab on the Objects bar and then double-click the Customers form to open it in Form view.

25. Navigate through the records, and the Mailing List box will be unchecked for each record.
    The update query reset all Mailing List fields to No (unchecked).

26. Click the Design view ![button] button to display the Customers form in Design view.

27. If necessary, display the toolbox, and then click the Command Button ![button].

28. Click in the blank area of the form below the Current Balance label and to the left of the Mailing List check box.

29. Choose the Miscellaneous category and the Run Query action in the first wizard screen.

30. Click the **Next** button, choose the **Update Mailing List** query in the second wizard screen, and click **Next** again.

31. Choose the Text option in the third screen, and type **Uncheck Boxes**.

32. Click **Next**, type **Update Mailing List** in the last screen, and click the **Finish** button.

Use the Command Button

33. Click the Form view [icon] button to switch to Form view.

34. Navigate through the records and check any two records.

35. Navigate backwards or forwards to one of the records that is unchecked.
    Access doesn't save the changes made to a record until you navigate to another record or close the form.

36. Click the **Uncheck Boxes** button and choose **Yes** when Access indicates that you are about to run an update query.

37. Choose **Yes** again when access indicates that you are about to update two records.

18. Navigate through the records, and notice that the Mailing List box is unchecked for all records.

39. Close the Customers form, and save the changes.
    As you can see, you have now developed a flexible and powerful system for conducting and managing large mailings.

Exporting Data to Excel

The Analyze It With MS Excel [icon] Office Links button exports to Excel the table or query selected in the database window. The table or query field names become a heading row in the Excel worksheet. If you export a table, all rows from the table are output to Excel. If you export a query, the query is run, and the entire recordset is exported to Excel.

Using Copy and Paste

You can also open a table or run a query in Access, select and copy the desired data, and then paste the data into an Excel worksheet. This can be useful if don't want to export the entire table or query recordset. However, if you do want to export the entire table or recordset, then the Office Links button is probably your best choice; it will format the worksheet for you.

Subtotaling and Pivot Tables in Excel

Excel has a variety of powerful tools for analyzing data. Subtotals and Pivot Tables are two of these tools. Many organizations have order information, and other types of numeric data, stored in Access database systems. This data can easily be analyzed by exporting it to Excel and using subtotals, Pivot Tables, and other analytic tools. In the following exercise, you will receive a brief introduction to Excel's subtotaling feature. For complete coverage of all of Excel's tools, see Labyrinth Publications *Excel 2000 Expert Course* text.

Export the Data

1. Click the **Queries** button on the Objects bar in the database window.

2. Choose the Query - Visit Details query, and click the Office Links [icon] drop-down button on the Access toolbar.

3. Choose the Analyze It With MS Excel [icon] button. Choose Yes if Access asks you to replace the file.

   Access will run the query, start Excel, and output the recordset.

Subtotal the Data

The first step in the subtotaling process is to sort the data on the field that you wish to subtotal. In the following steps, you will sort on the Service/Product field and then subtotal on that field.

4. Click in any cell in the Service/Product column.

5. Click the Sort Ascending [icon] button on Excel's toolbar.

6. Choose **Data→Subtotals** from Excel's menu bar.

7. Follow these steps to set up the subtotals.

   Ⓐ *Choose* Service/Product *from this list.*

   Ⓑ *Make sure the* Sum *function is chosen.*

   Ⓒ *Make sure the* Extended Price *box is checked. This will create an Extended Price subtotal for each group of Service/Products.*

   Ⓓ *Click* **OK***, and Excel will produce the subtotals.*

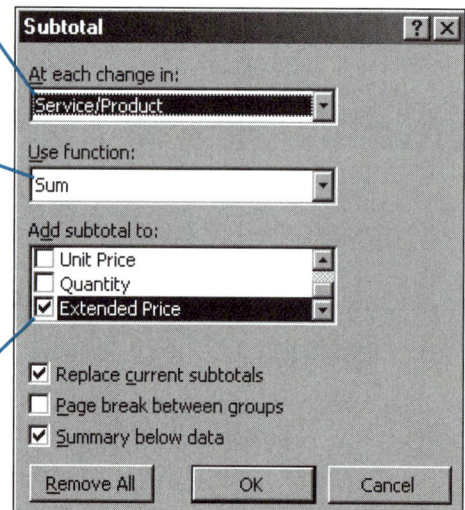

Take a moment to examine the worksheet and notice that a subtotal has been produced for each Service/Product.

8. Feel free to experiment with subtotals. You can remove subtotals by displaying the Subtotals box with the **Data→Subtotals** command and then clicking the **Remove All** button.

9. Exit from Excel when you have finished, but do not save the worksheet.

Database Maintenance

Access databases are often the information banks for entire organizations. For this reason, it is important that databases be properly maintained. The following topics discuss the most useful techniques for maintaining databases.

Backing Up and Restoring a Database

You should always make a copy of your database before making significant changes to its structure. Some procedures, such as modifying the design of tables or deleting tables, can result in lost data. It is also recommended that, periodically, you make a backup copy of your database—in case it gets damaged.

Access assigns a .mdb extension to database files. For example, your Pinnacle Pet Care database has the name *Pinnacle Pet Care.mdb*. You can backup a database by making a copy of the mdb file. It is recommended that the copy be placed on a different computer system or in an off site location. If your database gets damaged, you can replace it with the back-up copy.

You can also make copies of objects, such as tables, forms, and reports, using the Copy and Paste buttons in the database window. You may want to do this prior to making design changes to objects. If the design changes don't work out as planned, you can delete an object and replace it with the backup copy.

Compacting and Repairing a Database

Databases may become fragmented as you delete unwanted records and objects. This can reduce the performance of large databases that have many transactions. Compacting defragments a database, improves the performance, and reduces the size of the mdb file. The compacting operation also repairs any internal problems encountered with the database.

Quick Reference

COMPACT AND REPAIR A DATABASE

- Start Access, but do not open the database. A database cannot be open when running the compact utility.

- Choose **Tools→Database Utilities→Compact and Repair Database** from the menu bar.

- Navigate to the mdb file that you wish to compact.

- Click the **Compact** button.

- Enter a name for the compacted database. You can enter the same name as the database you are compacting. If you use the same name, Access will replace your database with the compacted version. Otherwise, a new compacted copy of the database will be created with the name you specify.

Hands-On 9.6 Compact and Repair a Database

In this exercise, you will compact and repair the Pinnacle Pet Care database.

1. Close the Pinnacle Pet Care database, but leave the Access window open.
   The Access program window should be visible.

2. Choose **Tools→Database Utilities→Compact and Repair Database** from the menu bar.

3. Navigate to the location of your Pinnacle Pet Care database file.

4. Choose the Pinnacle Pet Care.mdb file and click the **Compact** button.
   Access will display the Look in list again, prompting you to enter a name for the compacted database file it is about to create.

5. Choose your Pinnacle Pet Care.mdb file from the list, and click the **Save** button.

6. Choose **Yes** when Access informs you that your original database will be replaced.
   Access will compact the database and replace your original database with the compacted version.

7. Choose **File** from the menu bar, and then choose the Pinnacle Pet Care file from the frequently used files list at the bottom of the menu.

8. Feel free to browse the objects in your compacted database.
   You won't notice any changes in the database. If you had compacted a large, heavily-used database, then you would probably notice an increase in performance if you were to access data.

9. Close the database, and continue with the end-of-lesson questions and exercises.

Concepts Review

True/False Questions

1. Word Mail Merge form letters can be linked to Access queries.   TRUE   FALSE

2. The OfficeLinks ▣ button is used to initiate the Mail Merge Wizard.   TRUE   FALSE

3. DDE is an acronym for Dynamic Data Exchange.   TRUE   FALSE

4. Form letters can contain merge fields originated in an Access query.   TRUE   FALSE

5. The Mailing Label Wizard can be used to set up form letters in Word.   TRUE   FALSE

6. The Mailing Label Wizard lets you choose from a variety of label formats.   TRUE   FALSE

7. The Analyze It With MS Excel ▣ Office Links button exports data to Excel and automatically subtotals the data.   TRUE   FALSE

8. Backing up a database defragments the mdb file and reduces its size.   TRUE   FALSE

Multiple Choice Questions

1. Which button establishes a DDE link between an Access query and a Word form letter?
   a. ▣
   b. ▣
   c. ▣
   d. ▣

2. Which button is used to export data to Excel?
   a. ▣
   b. ▣
   c. ▣
   d. ▣

3. Which section of the database window should be active if you want to establish a DDE link between an Access object and a Word document?
   a. Tables
   b. Forms
   c. Queries
   d. Either a or c

4. Which of these will potentially reduce the size of an mdb file?
   a. Backing up
   b. Compacting
   c. Restoring
   d. All of these

Skill Builders

Skill Builder 9.1 Modify a Table and Set Up a Query

In this exercise, you will add a Mailing List field to the Customers table in the Tropical Getaways database. You will also create a query that selects records from the Customers table only if the Mailing List field is checked.

Modify the Customers Table

1. Open the Tropical Getaways database and close the Main Switchboard form.

2. Click the Tables button on the Objects bar.

3. Choose the **Customers** table and click the [Design] button.

Field Name	Data Type
Customer ID	AutoNumber
Firstname	Text
Lastname	Text
Address	Text
City	Text
State	Text
Zip	Text
Profile	Text
Mailing List	Yes/No

4. Add a Mailing List field to the table, and set the Data Type to **Yes/No**, as shown to the right.

5. Click the Datasheet view [icon] button on the left end of the Access toolbar.

6. Click the **Yes** button when Access asks if you want to save the table.

7. Check the Mailing List boxes for all records where the state is equal to **TX** as shown below.

Firstname	Lastname	Address	City	State	Zip	Profile	Mailing List
Debbie	Thomas	450 Crestwood Lane	Austin	TX	78752	Adventure	☑
Wilma	Boyd	855 State Street	Richmond	NY	12954	Leisure	☐
Ted	Wilkins	900 C Street	Fort Worth	TX	76104	Adventure	☑
Alice	Simpson	2450 Ridge Road	Fort Worth	TX	76105	Family	☑
Victor	Thomas	2311 Wilmont Street	Danvers	MA	01923	Adventure	☐
Lisa	Simms	100 Westside Drive	Batavia	NY	14020	Leisure	☐
Ted	Carter	250 Smith Street	Charlton	MA	01507	Family	☐

8. Close the table.

Set Up a Mailing List Query

9. Click the Queries button on the Objects bar.

10. Double-click the *Create query in Design view* option.

11. Add the Customers table to the design grid, and close the Show Table box.

12. Set up the query as shown below. Make sure to uncheck the Show box for the Mailing List field. Also, enter the word **Yes** in the Criteria box of the Mailing List field.

Field:	Firstname	Lastname	Address	City	State	Zip	Mailing List
Table:	Customers	Customers	Customers	Customers	Customers	Customers	Customers
Sort:							
Show:	☑	☑	☑	☑	☑	☑	☐
Criteria:							Yes

13. Run ⚠ the query to produce the following recordset.

Firstname	Lastname	Address	City	State	Zip
Debbie	Thomas	450 Crestwood Lane	Austin	TX	78752
Ted	Wilkins	900 C Street	Fort Worth	TX	76104
Alice	Simpson	2450 Ridge Road	Fort Worth	TX	76105

14. Close the query and save it as **Mailing List**.

Skill Builder 9.2 Conduct a Mail Merge

In this exercise, you will set up a Word form letter. You will also merge the form letter with the Mailing List query.

Set Up the Mail Merge and Form Letter

TIP!

Your Customers table does not currently include a prefix field for prefixes such as Mr., Mrs., and Ms. If desired, you can add a Prefix field to your table, include the Prefix field in the query you will set up, and use the Prefix field in your form letter as you did in the Pinnacle Pet Care database.

1. If necessary, click the **Queries** button on the Objects bar.

2. Choose the **Mailing List** query, and click the OfficeLinks [icon] drop-down button.

3. Choose the *Merge It With MS Word* option.

4. Choose the *Create a new document* option in the first Wizard screen and click **OK**.

5. Maximize the Word program window.

6. Tap (ENTER) six times, and choose **Insert→Date and Time** from the Word menu bar.

7. Choose the third date format in the **Date and Time** box, and make sure the **Update Automatically** box is checked.

8. Click **OK** to insert the date and then tap (ENTER) four times.

9. Click the **Insert Merge Field** button and choose **Firstname**.

10. Tap the (SPACE BAR) once, and insert the Lastname field.

(Continued on the next page)

11. Insert merge fields and type text until your form letter matches the following example. Make sure to use the proper spaces and punctuation between merge fields.

December 16, 2000

«Firstname» «Lastname»
«Address»
«City», «State» «Zip»

Dear «Firstname»:

We are celebrating the opening of our new Dallas office with a special promotion. Texas residents will receive a 25% discount on any Tropical Getaways vacation package purchased during the next 60 days.

For more information, contact Linda Jones in our Dallas office. As always, we thank you for your support.

Sincerely,

Jack Carter
Promotions Director

---

12. Save the document to your exercise diskette as **Tropical Getaways Form Letter**.

Conduct the Merge

13. Click the Merge to New Document ▣ button on the Mail Merge toolbar.
A personalized letter should be addressed to each Texas resident.

14. Close the merged letters without saving them.

15. If you noticed a problem in your merged letters, make any necessary correction(s), and redo the merge.

16. When you have finished, close Word and save any changes that you have made to the form letter.

Skill Builder 9.3 Set Up Mailing Labels

In this exercise, you will set up mailing labels for the Mailing List query.

1. Click the **Reports** button on the Objects bar.

2. Click the ⟨New⟩ button to display the New Report box.

3. Choose the **Label Wizard**, choose **Mailing List** from the table/query list, and click **OK**.

4. Choose Avery from the Manufacturer's list in the second screen.

5. Choose English as the Units of Measure, and make sure the Label Type is set the Sheet feed.

6. Choose the 5160 product number, and click **Next**.

7. Click **Next** again to bypass the font and color options screen.

8. Add fields and insert spaces and punctuation marks in the Prototype field box until your prototype label matches the example shown to the right.

   Prototype label:
   {Firstname} {Lastname}
   {Address}
   {City}, {State} {Zip}

9. Click **Next**, and the wizard will ask which field you wish to sort on.

10. Choose the **Zip** field and click the Add Field ⟨ > ⟩ button.

11. Click **Next** and type the name `Mailing Labels` in the last Wizard screen.

12. Make sure the *See the labels as they will look printed* option is chosen, and click the **Finish** button.
    Access will create the report, and the labels shown below should appear.

Ted Wilkins	Alice Simpson	Debbie Thomas
900 C Street	2450 Ridge Road	450 Crestwood Lane
Fort Worth, TX 76104	Fort Worth, TX 76105	Austin, TX 78752

13. Click the Close ☒ button at the top right corner of the report.

14. Close the Tropical Getaways database and continue with the Assessment project.

Assessments

Assessment 9.1 Set Up a Mail Merge

1. Open the Classic Cars database, and Close the Main Switchboard form.

2. Add a field named Mailing List to the Collectors table. Set the data type of the Mailing List field to **Yes/No**.

3. Switch to Datasheet view and save the changes to the table.

4. Check the Mailing List box for all records where the Era of Interest is 1950s or 1960s.

5. Close the Collectors table.

6. Create a query that produces the following recordset. Notice that the query chooses records from the Collectors table where the Mailing List field is set to Yes.

Firstname	Lastname	Address	City	State	Zip
Cindy	Johnson	4220 Edward Street	Northlake	IL	60164
Tammy	Olson	1200 Big Pine Drive	Moses Lake	WA	98837
Bob	Barker	6340 Palm Drive	Rockridge	FL	32955

7. Close the query, and save it as **Mailing List**.

8. Use the OfficeLinks [button icon] button to establish a DDE link between the Mailing List query and a new Word document.

9. Using Word, set up the form letter that appears on the facing page. Use Word's **Insert→Date and Time** command to insert the date as a field that is automatically updated.

10. Save the form letter to your exercise diskette as **Classic Cars Form Letter**.

11. Merge [button icon] the form letter with the Mailing List query.

12. Close the merged letters without saving them.

13. Close the form letter and save any changes.

14. Use the Access Label Wizard and these guidelines to produce the mailing labels shown below.

   - Base the labels report upon the **Mailing Labels** query.

   - Use the Avery **5160** label style and **English** units of measure.

   - Sort the labels by zip code.

   - Assign the name **Mailing Labels** to the report.

Bob Barker 6340 Palm Drive Rockridge, FL 32955	Cindy Johnson 4220 Edward Street Northlake, IL 60164	Tammy Olson 1200 Big Pine Drive Moses Lake, WA 98837

15. Close the Classic Cars database and exit from Access.

December 16, 1999

«Firstname» «Lastname»
«Address»
«City», «State» «Zip»

Dear «Firstname»:

The Classic Cars Promotion Department is creating a pictorial for the 1950s and 1960s. We need color photographs of 1950s and 1960s automobiles. Members who are interested in participating may send photographs and supporting data to Jason Jackson in the Promotion Department.

Please submit your photographs promptly as our printing deadline is approaching.

Sincerely,

Wanda Allison
Chairperson

Index

sizing
    forms, 139–142
    subforms, 182–184
sorting
    query results, 67–68
    records, 220
Sorting and Grouping button, 226
SQL data, 214
square brackets ([ ])
    in calculated fields, 76
    in expressions, 189
    in query pop-up box, 111
starting Access, 4
startup options for databases, 252–253
statistical functions within queries, 79–81
subdatasheets, 223–224
subforms, 175–186
    calculated controls, 187–193
    data entry with, 185–186
    queries for, 177–178
    setting up, 176, 179–182
    sizing, 182–184
    subtotals in, 188–193
    synchronizing main form and subform, 179
    See also forms
Subform Wizard, 179–182
subtotals in subforms, 188–193
SUM (summation) function, 79, 189
switchboards, 242
    removing objects from, 251–252
    as the startup form, 253
synchronizing main form and subform, 179
syntax
    for calculated fields, 76
    for expressions, 188–190
    for pop-up box criteria, 111

T

tables
    changing the structure of, 17–19
    column width adjustments, 25
    creating in Design view, 9–12, 134
    field names, 8
    field properties, 8
    fields in, 7
    importing data to, 214
    margins, 26
    navigating in, 20
    page orientation, 26
    primary key for, 12–13
    printing, 23–24
    records in, 7
    relationships between, 92–95
    saving, 13
    structure of, 7–8

Table Wizard, 26–31
telephone number input mask, 219
temporary table (recordset), 61
testing macros, 245
text fields, 8
text format properties, setting, 194–195
time. See Date/Time
toolbox for forms controls, 143
Totals row, 79

U

unbound controls, 139
update queries, 278, 280
user input, prompting for in queries, 110–111

V

VAR (variance) function, 79
views, switching between, 17

W

Web pages, saving objects as, 231
wizards
    Combo Box Wizard, 148
    Command Button Wizard, 250
    Form Wizard, 96–97
    Input Mask Wizard, 217–219
    Lookup Wizard, 220–223
    Query Wizard, 62
    Report Wizard, 47, 48–50, 224–231
    Subform Wizard, 179–182
    Table Wizard, 26–31
Word
    mailing tasks with, 270–276
    mail merge document setup, 273–276

Y

Yes/No data type, 134

Z

zip code input mask, 218–219